D0073162

526070

FREE TRADE AND COMPETITION IN THE EEC:
Law, Policy and Practice

To what extent are Member States of the EEC bound to operate under principles of free trade and undistorted competition? How much of a free market really is the EEC in so far as the States themselves are concerned?

This book examines these issues and attempts to establish the conditions under which a State may operate in the market through the medium of the undertakings which it controls and the Member State's responsibility for these undertakings.

It looks at the extent to which Member States may intervene and regulate this market through general measures and tamper with free market forces without infringing the principle of free competition and whether state liability can be established. In the context of the above, the book also assesses the separate liability of both public and private undertakings which operate under the direction of the State or in a so heavily regulated environment that a certain anti-competitive behaviour is made possible or virtually imposed by the State.

The book concludes that the system as it operates is not as successful as it might be as the Treaty leaves a lot of room for conflicting interpretation influenced by political considerations. In the light of the above the view adopted is that the matter should be solved at the Community level by the Council of Ministers and the Commission elaborating guidelines in order to avoid national policies jeopardising Common Market objectives. On the judicial level the book recommends the use of a rule of reason within the context of the articles of competition.

FREE TRADE AND COMPETITION IN THE EEC
Law, Policy and Practice

HELEN PAPACONSTANTINOU

ROUTLEDGE
London and New York

First Published 1988
by Routledge
11 New Fetter Lane, London EC4P 4EE
29 West 35th Street, New York, NY 10001

© 1988 H. Papaconstantinou

Printed and bound in Great Britain by
Biddles Ltd, Guildford and King's Lynn

British Library Cataloguing in Publication Data

Papaconstantinou, Helen
  Free trade and competition in the E.E.C. :
  law, policy and practice.
  1. European Community countries. Economic
  policies. Implications of European
  Community law.
  I. Title
  341′.7′5′0614
  ISBN 0-415-00110-2

Library of Congress Cataloging-in-Publication Data
ISBN 0-415-00110-2

CONTENTS

Contents

Contents

Contents

LIST OF ABBREVIATIONS

INSTITUTIONS AND ORGANIZATIONS

A.G.	Advocate General at the Court of Justice of the European Communities
BGH	Bundesgerichtshof
CECA	Communauté Européenne du Charbon et de l'Acier
CE	Communautés européennes
CEE	Communauté économique européenne
CEEP	Centre Européen de l'Entreprise Publique
Community	European Economic Community
Court of Justice	Court of Justice of the European Communities
EAEC	European Atomic Energy Community (Euratom)
EC	European Communities
ECJ	European Court of Justice (Court of Justice of the European Communities)
ECSC	European Coal and Steel Community
EEC	European Economic Community
EFTA	European Free Trade Association
EP	European Parliament
Euratom	European Atomic Energy Community (EAEC)
EWG	Europäische Wirtschaftsgemeinschaft
FIDE	Fédération International de Droit Européen
GATT	General Agreement on Tariffs and Trade
IBA	International Bar Association
M.E.P.	Member of European Parliament
Treaty	Treaty of Rome instituting the EEC

ULB	Université Libre de Bruxelles
UN	United Nations
UNICE	Union des Industries de la CE

PUBLICATIONS

Ann. Fac. Droit Liège	Annales de la Faculté de Droit de Liège
BGHZ	Bundesgerichtshof, Zivilsachen
C.M.L. Rev.	Common Market Law Review
ECLR	European Competition Law Review
ECR	European Court Reports (Recueil de la Jurisprudence)
E.L. Rev.	European Law Review
EuR	Europarecht
J.O.	Journal Officiel des CE (Official Journal of the EC (C - Information and Notice; L - Legislation)
N.J.W.	Neue Juristische Wochenschrift
O.J.	Official Journal of the EC (Journal officiel)
Recueil (Rec.)	Recueil de la Cour de Justice de CE
R.M.C.	Revue du Marché Commun
Rev. Trim. Dr. Eur.	Revue Trimestrielle de Droit Européen
Riv. Dir. Ind.	Rivista di Diritto Industriale
WuW	Wirtschaft und Wettbewerb
WuW/BGH	Wirtschaft und Wettbewerb/Bundesgerichtshof
WuW/EBGH	Wirtschaft und Wettbewerb/Entscheidungen des Bundesgerichtshof

Chapter One

INTRODUCTION

State intervention in the economy has become a common feature of contemporary societies independently of their political system. The creation of the welfare state, the development of international trade which led to great interdependence as well as competition between States, and, more recently, the economic crisis have made a certain degree of economic regulation and coordination inevitable. Even the most fervent supporters of a laissez-faire, free market ideology may find it necessary - at least in exceptional circumstances - to save failing industries, encourage and support new investment, adopt incentives for the development of backward regions and take measures for the protection of the environment.

1. FORMS OF STATE INTERVENTION IN THE ECONOMY

State intervention in the economy may actually take two forms: on the one hand the State may coordinate and regulate the economic process by issuing guidelines and setting the rules within which the market must operate without actively participating in it.

On the other hand the State may directly participate in the economy through the establishment of public undertakings or the taking of control of private ones. State participation is not, as such, inconsistent with the Treaty. Article 222 actually provides that the establishment of the Common Market cannot affect the system of property of each Member State.

However, notwithstanding the fact that neither form of

1

state intervention is, as such, inconsistent with the Treaty it is not left totally uncontrolled by it, but must, instead, be exercised within its framework and in the light of the Treaty objectives. As may be derived from articles 2 and 3 of the Treaty the fundamental objectives of the Treaty are the creation of a Common Market where goods, services, persons and capital circulate freely and competition remains undistorted. In view of the fact that any kind of state intervention in the economy is likely, somehow, to affect the market mechanism the purpose of this book will be to examine the extent to which the State may intervene in the market without violating the Treaty rules. In doing so it is important to note that the Treaty contains no specific provision addressed to Member States prohibiting them, in general, from adopting measures which may have as their object or effect to distort competition. Instead, it contains provisions preventing only specific anticompetitive activities of the State. Thus, articles 92-94 only allow the Commission to prohibit certain categories of state aids and article 90 only prohibits state measures with respect to undertakings which Member States control.

The above, however, must not be interpreted to mean that the State is only bound by the principle of free competition when it actually participates in the market as entrepreneur through the medium of undertakings which it controls or when it grants subsidies favouring certain undertakings or the production of certain goods. In addition to the fact that the frontier between state regulation and participation may be blurred, since extensive regulation of a certain sector may amount to virtual nationalization thereof, to exempt the State's regulatory activities from the competition rules would frustrate the Treaty objectives. Although it is true that the establishment of liability under the competition rules for the State's regulatory activities requires a broad teleological interpretation of the Treaty which may involve conflicting ideological aspects, in this thesis we shall try to delimit the extent to which the Member States may intervene in the market without tampering with the principle of free competition and without frustrating the Treaty objectives and the establishment of the Common Market.

In doing so it must be kept in mind that a certain degree of economic regulation and coordination is also required by the Treaty of Rome particularly if one of the basic objectives of the Community, the approximation of the economic policies of the Member States, is to be achieved. This is further made specific in Title II of the Treaty, titled Economic Policy, and in particular article 103 which provides that Member States shall regard their conjunctural policies as a matter of common concern and article 105 which imposes an obligation on Member States to take common action in order to ensure a high level of employment and a stable level of prices. The implementation of such common Community action necessarily requires the adoption of state regulations and measures.

In the light of the above the purpose of this book shall be: first, to establish the conditions under which a State may operate in the market through the medium of the undertakings which it controls and the Member State's responsibility for the behaviour of the latter. This involves an analysis of article 90 para 1 which actually extends state responsibility beyond the competition rules by making Member States liable in the case of public undertakings for state measures which are contrary to any of the rules of the Treaty. Article 90 para 2, which exempts certain undertakings entrusted with the operation of services of general economic interest from the rules of competition, and article 90 para 3, which grants the Commission special power to issue directives or decisions to Member States contravening article 90, shall also be examined in this connection.

Second, we shall establish the extent to which Member States may intervene and regulate the market through general measures and tamper with the free market forces without infringing the principle of free competition. In the absence of a specific provision addressed to Member States, we shall examine whether state liability can be established under the combined effects of the general principles and the particular rules of competition applicable to undertakings. In this connection account must be taken of the fact that to absolve Member States from liability for distorting competition would greatly frustrate the Treaty objectives.

Third, in the above context and in order to give a complete picture of the effects of state intervention in the market under the Treaty we shall also examine the separate liability of both private and public undertakings which operate either under the direction of the State or in a so heavily regulated environment that a certain anticompetitive behaviour is made possible or virtually imposed by the State.

2. IS NATIONALIZATION CONSISTENT WITH THE TREATY?

One drastic form of state intervention in the economy is the nationalization or socialization of a certain industry or sector of the economy. For the purposes of this book and in order to examine the effects that the above form of state intervention may have upon the Community system it is not necessary to distinguish between the two or try to establish that nationalization is only one aspect of socialization. Whether a certain activity is reserved for the State or a public body does not matter: what is important is that this activity is excluded from private initiative. (1)

Nationalizations, as such, are not prohibited by the Treaty. According to article 222 of the Treaty of Rome 'This Treaty shall in no way prejudice the rules in Member States governing the system of property ownership'. (2) The same principle has been adopted in the Treaty for the establishment of the European Coal and Steel Community which also provides that 'the establishment of the Community shall in no way prejudice the system of property of the undertakings to which this Treaty applies' (Article 83 of ECSC Treaty) as well as in article 91 of the Euratom Treaty according to which 'The system of ownership applicable to all objects, materials and assets which are not vested in the Community under this chapter shall be determined by the law of each Member State'.

The above articles were not included in the Treaties only in order to satisfy the different ideologies of the contracting States and to guarantee the acceptance of the Communities by most of the political parties. The economic structure of the Member States was not necessarily the result of a conscious ideological development. The creation of the public sector was due to circumstances and needs particular in each Member State and very different from any political doctrine favouring it. (3) It was therefore also the difference between the economic structures of the original Member States and the existence of a more or less extended public sector in all of them that made the adoption of those provisions necessary.

The view that private initiative may be curtailed for the general interest and that certain activities may be exercised by the State is also to be found in the liberal-democratic constitutions of the Member States. Thus, article 15 of the Grundgesetz provides that land and buildings, natural resources and means of production may, for the purpose of their socialization, be transferred to joint ownership or any other form of social organization by law providing the way and level of compensation. The German Supreme Court has itself stated that the Constitution does not imply a constitutional preference for a certain economic system. The French Constitution has reserved for the legislature 'the nationalization of undertakings' and the 'fundamental principles of the system of property' (article 34). The Italian Constitution while mentioning in article 42 that 'property may be either public or private and that the economic goods belong either to the State or to legal or natural persons' allows, through article 43, the acquisition by the State of certain undertakings or categories of undertakings.

The above national clauses, which are given by way of example, therefore allow the legislator to reserve for the public authorities the exploitation of a certain sector of the economy. At the same time, in the Italian and German Constitutions the extent of those sectors is limited by those same clauses.

As early as 1962 the EEC Commission in its answer to a parliamentary question of Philipp, M.E.P. stated that the nationalization of electric energy in Italy was not contrary to the Treaty. (4) That approach, which was further strengthened by the decision of the European Court of Justice in Costa v ENEL, (5) has been reaffirmed thereafter. Therefore, the arguments put forward by Stendardi (6) and based on the Italian text, that article 222 concerns only the preexisting system of property and that new nationalizations are not permitted, find no support in the jurisprudence and the caselaw of the ECJ.

Stendardi's view, although extreme, did not stand all alone at the time of the establishment of the Common Market. In the beginning, notwithstanding the existence of article 222, many writers put forward the view that public undertakings were not consistent with the fundamental principles of the Treaty. As Colliard noted (7), the expression 'Common Market' naturally evokes a market economy and one could be led to think that the economic system of the EEC is that of a market economy. Furthermore, the relevant provisions are rare and incidental (articles 222, 37 and 90), imprecise (they contain numerous terms which are not defined, the reason being the variety which existed in Member States) and of exceptional character. Such a view may also be supported by the fact that nationalizations are mostly associated with a political ideology which disapproves of such free market system. Nevertheless, despite the above, the author himself concluded that, as caselaw and practice have shown, public undertakings are there to stay and also destined to play an important role in the formulation of economic policy. (8) However, public undertakings must operate within the Community system and obey its principles, among which are those of free and fair competition and non-discrimination.

Taking, therefore, the existence of a public sector within the Community for granted the next step is to determine which are the limitations to nationalization or other forms of state intervention set either by the general or particular provisions of the Treaty or, possibly, by its general scheme.

First, even if nationalization, as such, is not contrary to the Treaty, the particular measures taken may be illegal if they are contrary to the basic principles of free competition (article 3f) and non-discrimination (article 7). As the Heads of the Delegations had already made clear in their report of 1956 which formed the basis of the EEC Treaty, among the basic conditions for the creation of a Common Market and a necessary element for the institution of a system of free competition was the establishment of rules and procedures to redress the effects of state intervention and monopolies. (9)

Article 3(f) is made specific in Chapter I of Title I of Part III of the Treaty (articles 85-94) which contains the rules on competition. These articles act as an important obstacle to state intervention since, not only do they subject both private and public undertakings to the obligations to observe the rules of free competition (articles 85-96) but, in addition, through article 90, impose an obligation upon the States to obey the rules of the Treaty by safeguarding that public undertakings or undertakings with special or exclusive rights do the same. If such equality between private and public undertakings did not exist Member States would be able to jeopardise the objectives of the Treaty by nationalizing a certain industry or group of industries and thus taking it out of the realm of competition.

At the same time, however, in the eyes of the

Commission article 90 does not limit the principle contained in article 222. As the Commission stated in its 6th Report on Competition Policy, Member States remain completely free to determine the extent, composition and internal organization of their public sector and to introduce whatever reforms they believe necessary in their rules governing property ownership. (10)

In the light of the above we must therefore consider whether there are any other limitations to the continuous expansion of the public sector which are inherent in the Treaty or whether the Common Market, as conceived by its founders, could also function within a socialistic and state-controlled framework.

Except for article 37 which has been interpreted as requiring the abolition of state or state-controlled trading monopolies and prohibiting the creation of new ones (11) no other form of state monopoly (such as service or production monopoly) has been, as yet, held inconsistent with the Treaty. The standstill clauses prohibiting the introduction of any new restriction on the right of establishment, the freedom to provide services and the movement of capital (articles 53, 62, 71 of the Treaty of Rome) are not considered as posing any obstacle to nationalization in so far as the prohibition to exercise nationalized activities is equally applicable to nationals and foreigners.

Although the above view has received the support of the ECJ (12) it must be observed that the mere fact that a law or prohibition applies to both nationals and inhabitants of the Member States does not ensure compliance with the Treaty if this law or prohibition is in fact discriminatory in the sense of article 7. In this context an analogy may be drawn from the decisions of the ECJ regarding the application of article 95. (13) In those cases the Court held incompatible with the Treaty a certain tax which, although imposed on both imported and domestic products of the same category, had the effect of protecting other domestic products which were also potentially in competition with those subject to the tax. Similar considerations may also be of relevance in the case of nationalization.

Furthermore, on a more theoretical level, the theory that the nationalization of an entire sector is contrary to the spirit of the Treaty, even if article 37 para 2 is not affected, is not without value. The Treaty is to a great extent based on a system of liberal economy restricted only in certain particular sectors, those of agriculture and transport. Even if a Common Market with totally nationalized sectors is not incompatible with the wording of the Treaty such a Common Market might be inconsistent with the spirit of the Treaty and the general principles to be derived therefrom. (14)

First, complete nationalization of the economies of the Member States would render the principle of free competition inoperative. The fact that the principle of competition is an economic necessity realized also by communist countries should not give rise to the implication that the Community system, as established by the Treaty, could function if the economies of the Member States were fully nationalized. (15) The competition between the national public undertakings would not be sufficient for the attainment of the Community objectives. The reason why the system has been functioning properly until now is, that, despite the existence of a public sector, private industries continue to be the rule and there is room for private initiative and profit in all Member States. Notwithstanding the Sacchi decision of the ECJ it is hard to see how the freedoms of establishment, provision of services and movement of capital could be ensured if all the economic activities of the Member States were carried out by the State itself. Even the distinction between the free movement of goods and the other three freedoms made by the ECJ in Sacchi is hard to justify if looked upon from that angle. The Common Market would be thus reduced to a simple customs union. While realizing the difficulty of drawing a line we shall, nevertheless, attempt to draw certain general guidelines in the chapters which follow.

Second, it must be observed that, notwithstanding the existence of article 222, the right of property forms an integral part of the general principles of law guaranteed in the Community legal order. As the ECJ has observed on more than one occasion (16) the right of property and the freedom to pursue trade or professional activities are fundamental rights which the Court must safeguard by drawing inspirations from the constitutions of the Member States and the First Protocol to the European Convention for the Protection of Human Rights to which Member States are signatories. Even if the constitutional rules and practices of the Member States permit the legislature to control the use of private property in accordance with the general interest this must be done on the condition that the substance of these fundamental rights is left untouched. (17)

While admitting that the constitutions of the Member States do permit the nationalization of private undertakings by the State for reasons of public interest provided just and adequate compensation is granted, nevertheless the above observations indicate that there is a limit to the extent to which the State may restrict the use of private property short of nationalizing it. In defining this limit account must be taken of the principle of proportionality which is also one of the general principles of law recognized by the Community legal order (18) and which requires the restriction to the exercise of the right of property to correspond to the objectives pursued. In this respect these objectives must be consistent with the Community interest which must always prevail.

NOTES

1.   Ferrari-Bravo, 'Les articles 90 et 37 dans leur relations avec un regime de concurrence non falsifiée', Semaine de Bruges (1968) at p. 411.

2.   This definition has finally been preferred to the ones originally suggested, that 'The Treaty shall in no way prejudice the rules in Member States governing the system of property or the means of production' (proposed by the Groupe de Redaction on 5.12.56) or '... governing the system of property of the undertakings subject to the provisions of the Treaty'. The term 'undertakings' was eliminated in the final draft. Neri-Sperl, 'Traité instituant la CEE' at p. 410.

3.   Delion, 'Entreprises publiques et CEE', (1966) R.M.C. at p. 68. See also Delion, ibid, for an examination of the creation and extension of the public sector in each Member State.

4.   J.O. No 121 of 20.11.62, p. 2716.

5.   Case 6/64, Costa v ENEL, (1964) ECR 585.

6.   Stendardi, 'Il regime di proprietà nei Paesi Membri delle Communita Europee' in Il diritto degli scambi internationali, 1963, p. 276 et seq.

7.   Colliard, 'L'entreprise publique et l'évolution du Marché Commun', Revue Trimestrielle de Droit Européen, Iere année, No I, Jan-Avril 1965, p. I.

8.   Ibid.

9.   Spaak Report of the Heads of the Delegations to the Ministers of Foreign Affairs at p. 15.

10.   6th Commission Report on Competition Policy,

(1976), at p. 143.
11.   Case 59/75, Manghera, (1976) ECR 91.
12.   Costa v ENEL, (1964) ECR at p. 597, cited supra.
In Case 155/73, Sacchi, (1974) ECR 409, the Court held that
the establishment of a service monopoly is not contrary to
the Treaty and that 'nothing in the Treaty prevents Member
States for considerations of public interest, of a non-
economic nature, from removing T.V. transmissions from
competition by conferring to one or more establishments the
exclusive right to conduct them'.
13.   Case 168/78, Commission v France, (1980) ECR
347, Case 169/78 Commission v Italy, (1980) ECR 385, Case
171/78, Commission v Denmark (1980) ECR 447. See also
Case 277/83, Commission v Italy, (Marsala), (1985) Rec
2053.
14.   See Deringer, 'Les articles 90 et 37 dans leur
relations avec un regime de concurrence non falsifiée',
Semaine de Bruges, 1968 at p. 407-8.
15.   According to Delion and Knapp it is not a question
of quantity of socialism but of quality. What is important is
to avoid 'dirigisme administratif'. Opposite view by Deringer
according to whom quantity may get transformed into
quality, Bruges (1968), op. cit. at p. 439-41.
16.   See for example Case 4/73, Nold, (1974) ECR 491
and Case 44/79, Hauer, (1979) ECR 3727.
17.   Hauer, (1979) ECR at p.3747, cited supra.
18.   Hauer at p. 3747, cited supra.

Chapter Two

GENERAL RESPONSIBILITY OF MEMBER STATES UNDER THE TREATY

The task of the Community established by the Treaty of Rome has been set out in article 2 of the Treaty and is the establishment of a Common Market and the approximation of the economic policies of the Member States. Article 3 goes on to provide that 'for the purposes set out in Article 2, the activities of the Community shall include, as provided in this Treaty and in accordance with the timetable set out therein', among others, (a) the elimination as between Member States, of customs duties and of quantitative restrictions on the import and export of goods, and of all other measures having equivalent effect and (f) the institution of a system ensuring that competition in the Common Market is not distorted.

The above two articles, placed in the Treaty under the title 'Principles', must be looked upon as a whole for the purpose of determining in an individual case whether a particular state, Community or private action promotes these aims. By virtue of signing the Treaty the signatories must be considered as being bound to observe its rules and promote its aims. Such obligation is inherent in the Treaty and independent of article 5 which only clarifies one aspect of this obligation by imposing a specific duty upon Member States. Under article 5 Member States have the duty to take all appropriate measures to ensure fulfilment of the obligations arising out of the Treaty or resulting from action taken by the institutions of the Community as well as to abstain from any measures which could jeopardise the attainment of the objectives of the Treaty.

Therefore, articles 2, 3, 4 and 5 must be seen as a consistent and interdependent whole while the view put forward by Advocate General Reischl in INNO (1) - that article 3(f) is directed to Community institutions, since it begins with the words 'the activities of the Community', and does not give rise to obligations for Member States - must be considered as unduly compartmentalizing this section of the Treaty. The fact that the Advocate General continued by saying that combination of the above with article 5 might mean that state measures are subject to certain restrictions, does not sufficiently bring into light the degree of state responsibility under the Treaty.

Article 5 performs a very useful function by enshrining and specifying the responsibility which Member States assumed by signing the Treaty to act in accordance with its rules and in pursuance of its objectives. Article 5, seen in the light of its position in the Treaty, is an all encompassing provision making the Member States addressees both of the general tasks of the Community contained in Part I of the Treaty and of the particular rules contained in subsequent chapters, as well as of any new obligations created by the Community institutions. We shall, therefore, proceed to examine its content and the extent of state responsibility under it.

On the one hand, the duty imposed by the first paragraph of article 5 is one to cooperate. This duty of the Member States has been reiterated by the ECJ in various actions brought by the Commission against them for failure to adopt the necessary measures in fulfilment of Community acts. (2) As the Court further observed in the case of SA Salumificio di Cornuda (3), reliance on the part of the State on its own delay in carrying out a decision of the Community would also constitute a breach of the first paragraph of article 5. Article 5 para I, therefore, imposes upon Member States a positive duty to facilitate the Community tasks and has been enforced by the Court in circumstances in which Member States have failed to do so.

On the other hand, the second paragraph of article 5 imposes on Member States the obligation to abstain from any measure which could jeopardise the attainment of the objectives of the Treaty. This section has raised a great deal of controversy because it does not simply impose a duty upon Member States to assist the Community organs in implementing a new policy already agreed upon by the Member States through their representation in the Council. In view of its standstill nature it also puts under constant review the legislative policy and governmental measures of

Member States in case such measures jeopardise the attainment of the objectives of the Treaty. Considering that the ideologies and, in particular, the views on the required degree of state intervention in the economy differ considerably among the Member States and the governments alternating in office and that the interpretation and understanding by the different governments of the objectives to be attained by the Community also differ accordingly, the application and interpretation of this section has caused an important debate.

This issue has mainly arisen before the ECJ in references for preliminary rulings.

Two questions were raised with respect to the second paragraph of article 5. The first concerns the definition of its content and, in particular, its application in circumstances in which a State takes measures jeopardising the objectives of the Treaty without concurrently giving rise to state liability under a specific provision thereof. This may be so either because there exists no specific provision, other than the general one of article 5 para 2, applicable to the particular case or because the relevant rule of the Treaty is not specifically addressed to Member States. The second question concerns the direct applicability of article 5 para 2 in national law, that is whether it creates rights and obligations for individuals which national courts must protect.

Both these issues have mainly arisen in the field of competition where the conditions of fair and equal competition were threatened by state intervention manifesting itself in state measures or direct state participation in the economic activity. The need for applying article 5 para 2 in this area is also derived from the fact that the Rules of Competition contained in Chapter I of Title I of Part III, do not sufficiently make clear the degree of state responsibility since they are not all addressed to Member States. Articles 85 and 86 which prohibit agreements, decisions or concerted practices between undertakings and the abuse of dominant position by one or more undertakings, make no mention of state liability in case the State has been responsible for such agreements or abuse or has brought about the same distortion of competition and effect on trade through other means. On the other hand, articles 90 and 92-94 which are addressed to Member States, only cover particular distortions of competition either through public undertakings and

13

undertakings with special or exclusive rights or through aids and do not, therefore, exhaust the cases of state responsibility.

The application of article 5 para 2 has not arisen in connection with other principles of the Treaty which Member States are equally obliged to observe, but often fail to do, such as the principle of the free movement of goods, mainly because the provisions of Part II of the Treaty and Title I in particular, are clearly addressed to Member States. Furthermore, the most important of these provisions (e.g. article 30) have been held to be directly applicable and have been given a very broad scope by the Court's caselaw. There is, thus, no need to resort to a more general provision such as article 5 para 2.

Article 5 para 2 has been held in Deutsche Grammophon and in subsequent cases to lay down a general duty for Member States the actual tenor of which depends in each individual case on the provisions of the Treaty and on the rules to be derived from its general scheme. (4) The above statement is sometimes interpreted to mean that, in fact, article 5 does nothing else than merely state a general principle which can only be applied as made specific in the particular provisions of the Treaty. In addition, it has been said to be vague and imprecise and to exclude the possibility of direct and autonomous application by national jurisdictions. (5)

Without denying the general terms in which article 5 para 2 is formulated such interpretation of article 5 para 2 cannot be accepted because it fails to take into account two factors. First, that the last part of the Court's statement provides that the actual tenor of the duty laid down by article 5 in each individual case depends not only on the provisions of the Treaty but also on the rules derived from its general scheme. Such rules may either be contained in Community acts adopted pursuant to the Treaty or be developed by the European Court in the process of interpreting the Treaty. Second, that article 5 para 2 is a reference rule which cannot be applied autonomously but the direct applicability of which depends on the particular provision or general principle to which it refers.

It is true that most of the provisions of the Treaty as well as of secondary Community law are applications of this general duty of Member States in areas specifically regulated by the Community. In these circumstances it is a well established legal rule that when a specific provision covers a particular situation it prevails over a general one and is to be applied. In addition to the provisions of Part II of the Treaty containing the foundations of the Community which impose specific obligations upon Member States, particular applications of this principle may be found in a series of decisions of the ECJ concerning state measures taken in connection with products subject to a common organization of the market. As the European Court has repeatedly held, once the Community has, pursuant to article 40, established a common organization of the market in a given sector, the assessment of national measures taken in this sector must be made exclusively within the context of the rules set by this common organization. (6)

In circumstances, therefore, in which the compatibility of national measures and the relevant state responsibility arise in a context where there exist specific Community rules and regulations it is obvious that both the definition of the content of article 5 and its direct applicability are not directly relevant since article 5 para 2 finds expression in the specific regulations under discussion.

The application of article 5 para 2 itself comes into play when there exist no specific, directly applicable Community rules addressed to Member States implementing it. Nevertheless, the state measures may be contrary to the general principles of the Treaty or to particular provisions thereof which may not, however, by themselves specifically give rise to the responsibility of Member States.

According to Advocate General Trabucchi in Geddo, article 5 para 2 can certainly have the effect of barring certain actions or of preventing certain uses of national law (as in Deutsche Grammophon) but only if national law and the use made thereof in practice clearly conflict with directly applicable provisions of Community law. On the other hand, the Advocate General observed that the general obligation contained in article 5 para 2 cannot confer the quality of direct applicability on a provision whose legislative content is insufficiently definite and clear. (7)

Without denying the truth of this statement, article 5 para 2 being a reference rule the direct applicability of which can only depend upon that of the general principle or particular rule which has been contravened by the State, it is not conclusive or illuminating as to the role of article 5 para 2 in subjecting Member States to the competition rules. One might deduce from the submissions of the Advocate General that he did not consider the general principles contained in article 3, including 3(f), as sufficiently definite and clear to confer upon article 5 para 2 direct applicability, this being an issue which shall be discussed in Chapter Four. However, the question remains open whether article 5 para 2 could be applied in combination with article 3(f) and the competition rules for the purpose of preventing Member States from taking general measures which have the effect of distorting competition.

State measures may do so either by enabling or encouraging agreements or concerted practices between undertakings under article 85 or the abuse of dominant position under article 86, or, even, by producing similar effects in the absence of an agreement, concerted practice or abuse. Since articles 85 and 86 are addressed to undertakings and cannot, by themselves, apply to state measures, the question arises whether state liability may be established under the combined effects of those articles with article 5 para 2 and the general principle of article 3(f) and under what conditions. Considering that the provisions of articles 85 and 86 are sufficiently definite and clear to confer rights to individuals, it will also be necessary to examine whether they continue to do so when applied, in combination with article 5 para 2, to state measures.

All these issues shall be discussed in detail in Chapter Four. In view of the existence of article 90 para 1, which is a particular application of article 5 para 2, the responsibility of Member States for measures taken in the case of public undertakings (8) and having the effect of distorting competition or contravening any other rule of the Treaty shall be dealt with in separate chapters.

NOTES

1.   A.G. Reischl in Case 13/77, INNO v ATAB, (1977) ECR 2115, 2166.

2.   See, for example, Case 137/80, Commission v Belgium, (1981) ECR 2393, Case 91/79, Commission v Italy, (1980) ECR 1099 and Case 68/79, Hans Just v Danish Ministry of Tax, (1980) ECR 501, where the ECJ held that the national courts are also subject to article 5 para 1.

3.   Case 130/78, Salumificio di Cornuda v Financial Administration of the State, (1979) ECR 867, 882.

4.   Case 78/70, Deutsche Grammophon, (1971) ECR 487, 499.

5.   A.G. Roemer in Case 9/70, Grad, (1970) ECR 825, 852. Also see Case 9/73, Schlüter, (1973) ECR 1135, 1161, A.G. Mayras in Case 192/73, Hag, (1974) ECR 731, 752, A.G. Trabucchi in Case 2/73, Geddo, (1973) ECR 865, 890 and A.G. Reischl in Sacchi, (1974) ECR at p. 435, cited supra.

6.   See, for example, Case 190/73, Van Haaster, (1974) ECR 1123, Case 31/74, Galli, (1975) ECR 47, Case 65/75, Tasca, (1976) ECR 291, Joined Cases 88-90/75, SADAM, (1976) ECR 323, Case 154/77, Dechmann, (1978) ECR 1573, Case 5/79, Hans Buys, (1979) ECR 3203.

7.   A.G. in Geddo, (1973) ECR at p. 890, cited supra. See also Schlüter, (1973) ECR 1135, cited supra.

8.   For ease of reference, the term 'public undertaking' shall often be employed throughout this text to denote any undertaking covered by article 90 para 1.

Chapter Three

STATE INTERVENTION AND COMPETITION: PUBLIC UNDERTAKINGS AND UNDERTAKINGS WITH SPECIAL OR EXCLUSIVE RIGHTS

1. RESPONSIBILITY OF MEMBER STATES: ARTICLE 90 PARA 1

In this section we shall attempt to define the responsibility of the Member States with regard to public undertakings and those that are granted special or exclusive rights by considering each of the terms of article 90 separately. In doing so regard must be given to its relation with article 5 para 2, its object and the functions it was intended to perform.

1.1 Relation and comparison of articles 5 para 2 and 90 para 1

As concluded from the previous chapter the general obligation of Member States to abstain from any measures which could jeopardise the attainment of the objectives of the Treaty - an obligation which is implied by the very adoption of the Treaty but is also enshrined in article 5 - finds expression in several other articles of the Treaty which specify and clarify it in the context of particular fields of state activity and, also, in secondary legislation. Such articles are, for example, articles 12, 31, 32, 53, 62, 71 which are situated in Part II of the Treaty, titled 'Foundations of the Community', and which impose upon Member States the obligation to refrain from introducing any new restrictions to the freedom of goods, services, persons and capital. Another such specific application of article 5 para 2 is article 90 para 1 which is found in Part III of the Treaty, titled 'Policy of the Community', under the rules relating to undertakings of the chapter on competition. This prohibits Member States, in connection with public undertakings and undertakings with special or exclusive rights, to enact or maintain any measure contrary to the rules of the Treaty and in particular to the provisions of articles 7 and 85-94.

The peculiarity of article 90 para 1, as opposed to the above mentioned articles contained in Part II which also enshrine the prohibition of article 5 para 2, is that the former is not restricted, as the latter are, to prohibiting state measures contravening a particular rule of the Treaty. Article 90 extends far beyond the competition rules among which it is situated and which are expressly referred to therein, to prohibiting state measures which may contravene any of the Treaty rules. From this aspect, therefore, it is a 'renvoi' (1) rule as wide as article 5 para 2, this having led commentators to argue that the first paragraph of article 90 is nothing more than a mere restatement of article 5 para 2 in the context of public undertakings and undertakings to which the State grants special or exclusive rights. (2) These commentators thus conclude that article 90 para 1 is not juridically necessary. (3)

The view that article 90 para 1 merely stresses the general prohibition of article 5 para 2 finds unanimous support among commentators (4) with the sole exception of Mestmacker (5) who bases his interpretation on a distinction between the objectives and the means of the Treaty.

According to Mestmacker while article 5 para 2 only prohibits measures which could endanger the realization of the objectives of the Treaty, these being expressed in article 2 thereof, article 90 para 1 safeguards that the means contained in article 3, including the establishment of a system where competition is not distorted, are used in order to attain the above mentioned objectives.

Such interpretation, in addition to drawing an artificial distinction between ends and means, gives rise to the wrong implication that, in the absence of article 90 para 1, a Member State would be authorized to take measures incompatible with free competition in pursuance of the objectives of article 2. This, however, would be contrary to the principle also expressed by the ECJ in its decision in the 'small revision' of the ECSC (6) that one should not neglect the 'means' provided by the Treaty in order to promote the general objectives through other means.

The above interpretation also unduly excludes the application of article 5 in areas in which article 90 could not apply due to the reason that it is restricted to public undertakings and undertakings with special or exclusive rights. Article 5 para 2 would, therefore, not prevent Member States from taking measures inducing private undertakings to adopt a behaviour contrary to 85 and 86 (7), which interpretation would also be inconsistent with the Treaty and the caselaw of the ECJ. (8) The application of article 5 para 2 in this regard shall be further explained in Chapter Four.

The view that article 90 para 1 is an application of the obligation of article 5 para 2 in the context of public undertakings and undertakings with special or exclusive rights has also been specifically endorsed by the ECJ in its decision in INNO v ATAB. After having recalled the general principle of article 5 para 2 and having observed that Member States 'may not enact measures enabling private undertakings to escape the constraints imposed by articles 85-94' the Court stated that 'in any case article 90 is only a particular application of certain general principles which bind Member States'. (9)

This statement, however, does not imply that article 90 para 1 is superfluous. To call article 90 para 1 superfluous would be equivalent to saying that several sections of the Treaty are superfluous since most of them only make specific the general tasks and objectives contained in Part I. Despite the fact that the equality of public and private undertakings may also be derived from the other articles of the Treaty all commentators agree that article 90 para 1 is still performing a useful and necessary function for the reasons which will be enumerated in the following section.

At the same time the warning has been issued that in comparison with article 5 para 2 the scope of article 90 para 1 should not be overestimated. (10) It has been argued that to extend the scope of article 90 beyond public undertakings and undertakings with special or exclusive rights may diminish the importance of article 5 and give the Commission great power to correct the economic policies of Member States, this being contrary to the rationale of the Treaty. (11) Therefore, sovereign acts of state such as laws establishing minimum prices, production quotas etc. should not be examined under article 90 but under the angle of articles 30 or 5. (12) At first glance, the above warning sounds out of place since the application of article 90 is, by its own wording, restricted to state measures taken in connection with the undertakings mentioned therein. Nevertheless, it must also be admitted that the range covered by article 90 may be greatly extended or restricted depending on the definition of the notions 'public undertaking' and 'special and exclusive rights' as well as that of 'measures'. In the subsequent sections we shall attempt to define those notions and delimit the application of article 90 para 1 as well as examine in a more general sense the restrictions that the Treaty puts to the intervention of the State in the market.

1.2 Functions and scope of article 90

For the purpose of determining the object and functions of article 90 account must be taken of all the relevant factors such as its wording, its position in the Treaty, its relation with article 5, the fact that it is the only provision of the Treaty in which there is specific reference to public undertakings, its particular reference to the remaining articles of the Treaty and not only to the competition rules and, of course, its relation with the Treaty objectives.

Article 90 is situated in Part III of the Treaty, titled 'Policy of the Community'. More particularly, it is the last of a series of articles under the section titled 'Rules applying to undertakings' of the chapter comprising the 'Rules on Competition'.

Notwithstanding its inclusion in the section containing the 'Rules applying to undertakings', article 90 paragraph 1 is not addressed to undertakings but to Member States and prohibits them, in the case of public undertakings and undertakings to which the State grants special or exclusive rights, from enacting or maintaining in force any measures contrary to the rules contained in the Treaty and in particular to the provisions of article 7 and articles 85-94. On the other hand, article 90 paragraph 2 provides for an exception from the Treaty rules of undertakings entrusted with the operation of services of general economic interest or having the character of a revenue producing monopoly. These are subject to the rules contained in the Treaty and in particular to the rules on competition, in so far as the application of such rules does not obstruct the performance, in law or in fact, of the particular tasks assigned to them. The development of trade must not be affected to such an extent as would be contrary to the interests of the Community. The third paragraph imposes an obligation upon the Commission to ensure the application of the provisions of this article and, where necessary, to address appropriate directives or decisions to Member States.

The fact that paragraphs 1 and 2 are addressed to different persons, concern different undertakings and are of heterogeneous content has led some commentators to argue that there is a lack of symmetry (1) and that paragraph 1, in particular, has been illogically placed in this section of the Treaty. (2) We cannot, however, agree with such a view. Notwithstanding the above mentioned apparent inconsistencies it may be counterargued that the underlying theme of articles 85-90 is not the person to whom those articles are addressed but the behaviour to be regulated which is that of undertakings. The fact that one proceeds against the State is secondary. (3)

It is also immaterial that actual behaviour on the part of the undertakings is not required for the purpose of establishing responsibility under this section (4) since some sort of potential anti-Treaty behaviour shall always be a prerequisite. In this respect it is also important to note that the application of article 90 extends beyond the other articles of the chapter on competition as the particular reference of both paragraphs 1 and 2 to the entire Treaty indicates.

The above debate is not without any justification. It has been stated that article 90 is one of the most confusing articles of the entire Treaty. (5) It appears that it was the object of painful negotiations and that its final draft was a real compromise. It is, therefore, not surprising that it is not so clear and that it is one of the most revolutionary articles of the Treaty. (6) As Baron Snoy et d'Oppuers, who participated in the negotiations, declared in public: 'We were asked not to be too clear because it would have been difficult to pass it through Parliaments' (7).

The disagreement which arose during the negotiations is explained by the diversity of the economic structures of the Member States. It appears that while, on the one hand, the Benelux countries wanted, through article 90 para 1, to avoid that their undertakings, mostly private, be forced to compete under unequal conditions with public undertakings in France and in Italy, (8) on the other the French and the Italians insisted on article 90 para 2, fearing that their public sectors would be hampered by the Treaty. (9)

On the basis of the above, different conceptions could be derived depending on whether the emphasis is placed on the first or the second paragraph of article 90. It would be possible to argue that while article 90 para 1 signifies the complete integration of the public sector in the Treaty, article 90 para 2 safeguards the national interests. (10) As our analysis will show, it would be wrong to draw any conclusions by taking such a formalistic approach. Instead, we must interpret article 90 in the light of the objectives of the Treaty and its role in their attainment.

Articles similar to 90 may also be found in other Treaties. Thus, article XVII of the GATT entitled 'State Trading Enterprises' makes the contracting parties responsible for the discriminatory behaviour in imports or exports of state enterprises and enterprises to which the State grants formally or in effect exclusive or special privileges. Article 14 of the EFTA Convention also imposes an obligation on Member States to ensure the progressive elimination in the practices of public undertakings of protectionist measures and trade discrimination which are inconsistent with the Convention. Article 66 para 7 of the ECSC Treaty makes clear that public undertakings are also subject to the rules of competition and may not abuse their dominant position.

The inclusion of such provisions in Treaties aiming at the liberalization of trade among States, indicates the awareness by the signatories of the danger that States may frustrate the Treaty objectives through the undertakings which they control. However, all these provisions regulate only particular aspects of the behaviour of public undertakings and are much narrower than article 90 which concerns the behaviour of the State as an entrepreneur (11) and covers the entire range of the State's activities as such. This is explained by the fact that the EEC Treaty is much wider than the GATT or the EFTA Convention, which only regulate certain aspects of interstate trade, or the ECSC which regulates a particular sector of the economy. Instead, the EEC Treaty aims at the creation of a real Common Market between the Member States and the integration of their economies in every respect. These objectives could not be attained if the entrepreneurial activities of the State were not also subject to the Treaty rules. (12) If public undertakings and the activities of the State through them were not covered by the Treaty, the Common Market and the competition rules could not operate since Member

States would be tempted to create new public undertakings for protective reasons incompatible with the Treaty objectives. (13)

In the light of the above we shall proceed to determine and examine the functions and objectives of article 90.

1. As has already been mentioned, article 90 para 1 is the only provision of the Treaty containing particular reference to public undertakings. It could also be added that article 90 para 1 together with article 37 are the only provisions of the Treaty actually concerning undertakings which are not private and do not have a private objective. (14) In the light of this rare mention of the public sector in the Treaty and irrespective of whether a similar view could be adopted even in the absence of article 90, this article further indicates that public undertakings are not a domain outside the scope of the Treaty but are subject to the same rules as private undertakings.

Equality is one of the functions of article 90 often emphasized by commentators. (15) Although almost nobody denies that such equality is guaranteed by the provisions on undertakings (articles 85 and 86) which apply indiscriminately to both public and private undertakings, (16) article 90 para 1, by imposing a further obligation on Member States, makes even clearer that the public sector is subject to the Treaty and in particular the competition rules. (17)

There exist authors, however, who refuse to see the principle of equality embodied in article 90 and deny that this is one of its functions. (18) They maintain that such a view has no legal basis, since article 90 is addressed to Member States and not to undertakings. They say that to consider equality as one of the functions of article 90 only gives indirect support to those who argue that public undertakings are not subject to articles 85 and 86 on the ground that their equality with private undertakings is achieved exclusively through article 90.

In reality, nobody disputes the fact that article 90 para 1 is addressed to Member States and that no action against the undertakings could be taken under it. However, as will be explained in Chapter Five, we believe that there are strong arguments in favour of the view that public undertakings are subject to the rules of competition on an equal footing with private ones. Article 90 reinforces this view by extending the obligation to Member States which might, by confusing their role as guardian of the State and entrepreneur, try to exclude them from the Treaty's ambit.

2.   One of the primary functions of article 90 para 1 is that it imposes an obligation upon Member States to ensure that public undertakings behave in conformance with the Treaty and obey the Treaty rules, in particular those on competition. This is the function of article 90 for which all the commentators are unanimous.

Notwithstanding the fact that under article 5 para 2 States must, in any case, abstain from any measure which could jeopardise the attainment of the Treaty objectives, article 90 is still fulfilling a useful purpose. Except for its practical importance which lies in the Commission's power to issue directives and decisions to Member States under paragraph 3, it further clarifies their obligation in the competition field thus removing any possible doubt as to the subjection of state activities to the competition rules. (19)

The imposition of such obligation upon the Member States was made necessary by the close ties which normally and potentially exist between the State and the public undertakings and the opportunity which the former have to influence the latter as well as the undertakings to which the State grants special or exclusive rights. (20) As Advocate General Reischl stated in his submissions in the case of Italy, France and U.K. v Commission (21) article 90 para 1 was intended to give expression to the fact that the relationship between public authorities and public undertakings is of a particular kind which differs in many respects from the existing relationship between the State and private undertakings. Government undertakings carry, therefore, distinct dangers (22) which the drafters of the Treaty wanted to avoid by removing any doubt (23) as to the obligation of Member States with respect to those undertakings and by granting the Commission a more efficient procedure for the enforcement of this obligation through article 90 para 3.

State influence, which is mostly indirect and through internal measures (24), is not always the result of a conscious state intervention. It may take a variety of forms depending on the instruments used, the diversity of problems involved and the often contradictory attitude of public authorities towards public undertakings. (25) The common denominator of all this kind of state intervention is that it creates a danger that competition is distorted (26) by some state action. Article 90, therefore, by imposing an obligation on Member States, supplements the responsibility which public undertakings themselves have under articles 85 and 86 with that of the Member States which influence them. As Reuter said in connection with the ECSC Treaty, the States do not have the right to provoke by their intervention the economic consequences to which individuals do not have the right to aspire. (27)

Article 90 para 1 does not only limit the legislative and regulatory competence of Member States to enact new measures contrary to the Treaty but, also, imposes upon them a positive and immediate obligation to abrogate all contrary national provisions. (28)

In addition, it follows from the responsibility of States as economic operators, that they are not only prohibited from causing public undertakings to act contrary to the Treaty or tolerate actions violating it. Member States are also under a positive obligation to intervene if public undertakings or undertakings to which they have granted special or exclusive rights violate the Treaty. (29) It is part of the ratio legis of article 90 para 1 that the undertakings referred to therein are not really in a comparable situation with private undertakings since they enjoy a privileged status (particular financial facilities etc.). By imposing an additional obligation upon Member States in connection thereto an equilibrium is attained. (30) This positive duty of the Member States to prevent an infringement of the competition rules by the undertakings which they control is the natural consequence of the privileged position which the Member States themselves have granted to public undertakings and which may induce the latter to disobey the Treaty rules. On the other hand, for the purpose of establishing liability under article 90 para 1, it is immaterial whether the undertakings themselves violate the Treaty. What is important is whether through state measures results contrary to the Treaty are reached although the undertakings may not be responsible. (31)

3. Article 90 para 1 not only prevents Member States from contravening the competition rules through their public undertakings or those to which they grant special or exclusive rights but, in addition, prevents them from using public undertakings in order to avoid the obligations which they themselves have under the Treaty. (32)

As the Commission stated in its 2nd Report on

Competition Policy, one of the primary objectives of article 90 is to avoid Member States that escape the rules by hiding behind the apparently spontaneous behaviour of undertakings which have a particular status or privilege. (33) Article 90 imposes a positive duty upon Member States to ensure that the behaviour of the undertakings subject to it does not have the consequences which, if resulting from state activities, would constitute a violation of the provisions of the Treaty. (34) Those rules to which article 90 refers are those related to the four freedoms (freedom of movement of goods, workers, services and capital). These are necessary conditions for the creation of a Common Market and would be put in great jeopardy if Member States could escape them through the medium of undertakings which they influence or control.

It is therefore obvious that the application of article 90 extends far beyond the area of competition and is wider than articles 85 and 86. It might be said that the primary reason for including the above provision in the chapter relevant to competition was to subject public undertakings to the same rules as private ones, this being a possible explanation for the specific reference to articles 85 and 86 (35) as well as for the granting of the power to address decisions or directives to the Member States concerned. (36) However, article 90 para 1 is finally encompassing the entire Treaty since it prevents the States from enacting or maintaining an act or measure contrary to any rule of the Treaty. This particular function of article 90 para 1 makes clear that this article is only a particular application of article 5 para 2 to public undertakings and those to which the State grants special or exclusive rights.

It is possible that the drafters considered that, just as the State may distort competition through public undertakings and put private firms at a competitive disadvantage at the market level, so it may, through the means of public enterprises and those to which it grants special or exclusive rights, create trade barriers or produce an effect equivalent to quantitative restrictions. Notwithstanding the merits of the argument that, eventually, in such a case a violation of article 30 by public undertakings would automatically be a violation of articles 85 or 86, the general reference to all the rules of the Treaty was still wise. There exist cases where, in view of the influence which Member States exercise over public undertakings, a public undertaking may violate a Treaty provision in circumstances in which a private undertaking would not, without at the same time violating articles 85 or 86. Private undertakings being motivated by profit, are not likely to resort to protectionist measures as the State which combines the functions of sovereign and entrepreneur may. (37)

Moreover, the particular reference to article 7 indicates the general concern of the drafters, which is also a main concern in the present economic crisis, that States have a national tendency to resort to protectionism and to favour their own undertakings and national production. As a corollary to the above, public undertakings and undertakings to which the State grants special or exclusive rights and over which it may exercise control are also likely to behave in such a discriminatory and protectionist manner.

4. The practical importance of article 90 lies in paragraph 3 which enables the Commission to address a decision or a directive against the State in order to prevent a distortion of competition or another violation of the Treaty. This is a very powerful tool in the hands of the Commission which may, thus, oblige a Member State to take certain measures or put an end to a violation without it being necessary to resort to the European Court of Justice and the long procedure that this entails. There has been considerable debate around this paragraph, its objectives, its actual meaning and its efficacy, which shall be dealt with under section 3 of this chapter.

Deringer has also put forward the idea that article 90, in addition to repeating the obligation of article 5 para 2 in a particular context and providing for an efficient procedure, goes also in substance further than 5 para 2 in that it makes clear that it would not be possible to create a Common Market by nationalizing all the industries of a Member State. (38) Such a view, which has been discussed in Chapter Two, cannot, however, be based on a distinction between articles 5 para 2 and 90 para 1. As has already been made clear, article 90 para 1 does not impose upon Member States any obligation to which Member States are not already subject under article 5 para 2.

To summarize the above it could be said that the purpose of article 90 is twofold:

a. To put public undertakings and undertakings to which the State grants special or exclusive rights on an equal

footing with private ones by resorting directly against the State which is the entity holding the strings behind the above undertakings.
b.   To act as vehicle for the application to those undertakings of the other rules of the Treaty, particularly those relating to obstacles to trade and freedom of movement of workers, services and capital, in view of the influence which the State potentially exercises over them.

The above objectives must be understood within the context of the particular interpretation to be given to the terms of article 90 below.

1.3   **Definition of 'public undertaking'**

The term 'public undertaking' combines the element of undertaking by which it is distinguished from public administration and the element of public by which it is distinguished from private undertakings. (1) Both these terms need to be defined in the light of the objectives of the Treaty and of the articles in which they are referred to.

'Undertaking'

Contrary to the ECSC and Euratom Treaties (articles 80 and 196 respectively) the EEC Treaty does not contain a definition of the term undertaking. Notwithstanding the fact that the definitions of the ECSC and Euratom Treaties relate specifically to the Treaty within which they are contained and even if they are sectorial demarcations (2) rather than definitions it is still important to take them into consideration in developing a Community concept of undertaking in view of the absence of any definition in the EEC Treaty.

Article 80 of the ECSC Treaty is particularly restrictive and refers only to 'production' and 'distribution other than sale to domestic consumers or small craft industries'. On the other hand, article 196 of the Euratom Treaty is much wider and defines as 'undertaking' any undertaking or institution which pursues all or any of its activities in the territories of Member States within the field specified in the relevant chapter of this Treaty, whatever its public or private legal status. If the reference to the Euratom Treaty is removed then the breadth of the definition can be seen to be restricted only by the word 'activities'.

It has been observed (3) that the reason why the EEC Treaty contains no definition is that the notion may vary depending on the application of each provision. In fact, such may have been the intention of the drafters which seems to have been followed by the European Court of Justice. The latter has thoroughly avoided, except for its decision in the case of Mannesmann mentioned below, to give an all-encompassing definition of the term 'undertaking' which might prove unduly restrictive in the future. Nevertheless, in view of the fact that it will often be necessary to apply the relevant provisions containing the term 'undertaking', an attempt must be made to pinpoint the necessary elements thereof.

As all notions of the Treaty the term 'undertaking' must be defined in the light of Community law. (4) It is a question of giving the term a Community sense conforming to the objectives of the Treaty. (5) These objectives risk failing if exclusive reference is made to national concepts since those differ to a great extent and show great incoherence even within the same Member State.

The word 'undertaking' is found in articles 52, 80, 85, 86, 90 and 92 of the Treaty. With the exception of the Dutch text (6) the same word is used in all cases, thus indicating the intention of the drafters to use a uniform definition (7) of the term 'undertaking' for the entire Treaty. At least with respect to the articles under the same heading the adoption of a uniform definition is necessary in view of their complementary character and in order to safeguard the equal application of the competition rules. Regard must also be given to the object of article 90 which is to prevent the Treaty from being violated because of the particular legal form of the undertaking or of the fact that the undertaking has a separate legal personality. (8) Moreover, in order to be loyal to the spirit of the Treaty, which is to ensure comparable conditions of competition for all undertakings in the Common Market, the term must be interpreted in the largest possible way. (9)

Franck (10) made a very comprehensive list of factors which he considered as essential to the concept of undertaking and could serve as a basis for the formulation of a definition. These are:

(1) The existence of a definite and unitary body.
(2) A certain permanence and duration.
(3) Possibility to make profit.
(4) Economic activity: production, exchange and distribution of goods and services.
(5) Relations with a clientele and a market.
(6) Subject of law, natural or legal person.
(7) Autonomous administration.
(8) Separate accounts.

It is, however, arguable that the inclusion of all these elements would lead to a narrower definition than was envisaged by the drafters of the Treaty and that the use of such terminology would merely lead to the necessity for further definitions in order to avoid difficulties of interpretation. Such an analysis may also lead to translation difficulties particularly in view of the differing notions of an undertaking apparent throughout the Community.

These difficulties could be resolved if the widest and most simple type of definition were adopted by giving regard to the activities of an undertaking in the market. These activities are what the Treaty mainly aims at 'regulating' in pursuance of the creation of a Common Market where goods circulate freely in conditions of undistorted competition.

As Advocate General Mayras stated in BRT (11), it is important to recall that the authors of the Treaty intended the term to have an economic significance. What is important is the economic activity of the undertaking in the market which may produce the effects which the Treaty considers as illegal if contrary to articles 85 and 86. (12)

In BRT Advocate General Mayras (13) adopted Professor Goldman's description of an undertaking as a coordinated group of people and goods set up for a specific purpose and the activities of which are directed towards the fulfilment of that purpose. We may add that the body must exercise its activity in the area of production, exchange or distribution of goods or provision of services in the market. (14)

We may, therefore, conclude that the term undertaking under the Treaty presupposes, first, an economic entity capable of acting and being the subject of rights and obligations (15) and, second, an activity of this entity aiming towards production and commerce. (16)

The only decision, apart from those involving the

relationship between parent companies and subsidiaries, in which the ECJ expressed itself in general terms on the notion of 'undertaking' was Mannesmann. (17) Therein the Court gave the following definition: 'An undertaking is constituted by a single organization of personal, tangible and intangible elements, attached to an autonomous legal entity and pursuing a given long term economic aim'. (18) This definition has been repeated in later ECSC decisions and has been used by the Commission as a base in its decisional practice.

Apart from the requirement of an 'autonomous legal personality' with which, as we shall explain below, we disagree, the above definition shows that the most important criterion is the pursuit of a definite economic objective in a durable fashion. An economic objective does not necessarily imply an intention to make profit, this, for example, being a specific requirement within the context of article 58 para 2. Furthermore, an activity pursuing an economic objective need not be exercised in a particular legal form. As Advocate General Mayras remarked after citing Mannesmann in his opinion in BRT, the application of the competition law cannot be affected to any great extent by the legal mould in which the undertaking is cast. (19) The objectives of the Treaty can be achieved only if the notion of 'undertaking' covers the most varied forms under which an economic activity may manifest itself. Consistent with this view the European Court and the Commission have held in a series of decisions that an undertaking could be either a physical person exercising an economic activity in his own name (20) or under the name of an establishment, or a legal person or, even, associations (21), professional organizations and cooperatives. (22)

We would also extend the definition of 'undertaking' further than that. While agreeing with the Advocate General in BRT that the application of article 90 cannot depend on the legal form or on the instruments through which the entrepreneurial activity of the State is exercised (23), we do not, nevertheless, understand why he considers the existence of legal personality to be a necessary prerequisite of an undertaking under the Treaty. The existence of a legal personality is a question of national law which tends to vary from one Member State to the other and the adoption of which would, therefore, frustrate the Treaty objectives. (24) As we mentioned above, in defining an undertaking, particularly under the competition rules, it is the economic activity of the agent that matters. (25) Such economic activity may be also carried out by an entity which does not possess an independent legal personality under national law. A group of economic interests without legal personality may thus constitute an undertaking in the sense of the Treaty. The absence of legal personality does not have any effect since those economic entities may be apprehended through the medium of the persons which compose it. So may a government department when pursuing an economic activity. In this respect it is important to note that the fact that under articles 85 and 86 parent and subsidiary may be considered as one undertaking or the subsidiary be exonerated from liability or its acts be imputed to the parent (26), is only for the purpose of establishing responsibility under those articles. It does not deprive the subsidiary of its status as undertaking for the purposes of the other articles of the Treaty.

The issue of independent legal personality is particularly important with respect to the notion of public undertaking under article 90 para 1. The objectives of 90 para 1 are satisfied only if the term undertaking covers every possible participation in the Market on the part of the State. (27) To hold that the notion of 'undertaking' presupposes an independent legal personality is wrong, the legal personality conferred to public undertakings often being a pure juridical technique which the State may confer or not depending on the requirements of good management. (28)

Certain authors who are probably influenced by French domestic law where the notion of 'entreprise publique' presupposes an independent legal personality (29), consider the existence of an autonomous legal personality as a necessary prerequisite. They, thus, believe that the notion of 'undertaking' is exclusive of the notion 'en regie' and of the non-personalized public service administered by the State or the local authorities. (30) Such view, however, is contrary to the preparatory works (31), the declarations of politicians (32), the articles of the Treaty and the opinion of the Commission (33), all of which consider that any activity of the public authorities in the economic field, realized through public undertakings existing in whichever form, is subject to the competition rules. Therefore, the State itself and its subdivisions are undertakings under articles 85 to 90 when they participate in the economy by producing goods and services. (34) In this case the subject of law is the State in the name of which those services are provided. (35)

There are two issues regarding the definition of the notion of 'undertaking', that are particularly relevant in the context of this book and with respect to which disagreement has arisen. These are whether the notion covers, first, the exercise of sovereign activity by the State and, second, the activity of a public authority when buying goods and services for its own needs or to accomplish administrative missions (e.g. construction of roads).

In so far as the exercise of sovereign power is concerned the dominant view, with which we adhere, is that the exercise of sovereign authority by the State, even within the framework of the regulation of commerce, cannot be considered to be the act of an undertaking. (36) The question here is not whether sovereign activity is excluded from the ambit of article 90 para 1, which it clearly is not, but whether it can be considered as the act of an undertaking. If we adopt a uniform definition of the term 'undertaking' in the Treaty, as we already explained such uniform definition being necessary, then the exclusion of the exercise of sovereign activity from the application of articles 85 and 86 necessarily implies that this cannot be considered the act of an undertaking within the context of article 90 either. This does not mean, however, that the State may thus circumvent the application of the competition rules and, as a result, frustrate the objectives of article 90 para 1. On the contrary, all these activities, which because they are sovereign measures do not fall under articles 85 and 86, are particularly encompassed by article 90 para 1 since they are capable of constituting measures under it.

The above view finds support in the ECJ decision in IGAV. (37) In IGAV the Court held that the activities of an institution of a public nature, even if autonomous, fall under the provisions of the Treaty relating to infringements of normal functioning of competition by actions on the part of the States, these being articles 90, 92-94, 101, 102 and 37 and not under articles 85 and 86, to the extent that its intervention takes place in the public interest and these activities are devoid of commercial character. The above statement does not imply a different definition of the term 'undertaking' in articles 85, 86 and 90 but rather indicates that such agencies as the ENCC in the IGAV case are part of the state authorities and any measures taken by them concerning public undertakings or undertakings with special or exclusive rights are subject to article 90 para 1.

The fact, however, that the State or a state department or body purports to be exercising sovereign power does not necessarily imply that the State or the state body cannot be considered to be an undertaking for the purpose of the Treaty. The delimitation of the exercise of sovereign power is in most cases difficult to make and great prudence must be exercised in classifying an act as sovereign. Factors such as the organizational structure, the legal form of the instruments used in conducting a certain activity or the use of business methods are often coincidental and due to historical reasons and are wrong criteria for considering an act as sovereign. (38)

The decisive criterion is the object of the activity which, in order to be classified as the act of an undertaking, must be conducted in the field of production, distribution or sale of goods or services in the market. Such economic activity does not become sovereign merely because it is exercised by a certain body or public administration, nor does it assume such sovereign character merely because it is conducted through statutory instruments or administrative instructions or decisions. As the ECJ held in Sacchi, the fact that a public institution has to serve the public interest does not exclude it from being regarded as an undertaking. (39)

Support for the above view may also be derived from two decisions of the Federal Supreme Civil Court of Germany which, though not authoritative, may be of assistance since they follow the same pattern. The German Court decided, first, that a public radio station, a body organized under public law and fulfilling public duties, may be regarded an undertaking when competing with private cinemas in the purchase of movies (40) and, second, that the Chamber of Medical Doctors, a public body, violated the competition rules by distributing a circular advising its members to boycott an independent laboratory. (41) In both cases the relevant bodies were considered undertakings only in the particular circumstances in which they pursued a market activity.

The caselaw of the European Court, although possibly conflicting on the face of it, also leads to the conclusion that public institutions are subject to articles 85-90 'to the extent that ... performance (of their tasks) comprises activities of an economic nature' (42). On the one hand, in the Benedetti case (43) Advocate General Reischl refused to consider an intervention agency selling cereals at a prescribed price on state instructions with particular social objectives as a public undertaking. He observed that 'such organization does not take part in the economic life and compete as an undertaking does'. He considered it 'more like an administrative organ of the State acting in sovereign capacity' (44). Also the Commission in its observations in the same case accepted that organizations which put into effect mandatory state intervention must be excluded from the concept. (45) Examining a similar agency in the case of the Pigs Marketing Board (46) the ECJ refused to give a precise reply on whether the Board was an undertaking but made clear its position with respect to all cases arising in the context of the Common Agricultural Policy that 'it follows from article 38 para 2 of the Treaty that provisions of the Treaty relating to the Common Agricultural Policy take precedence in case of discrepancy over the other rules relating to the establishment of the Common Market' (47). Following the same pattern in its decision in SAIL (48) the Court did not examine certain Italian milk centres under articles 90 or 37 but exclusively within the context of agricultural rules. (49) All the above mentioned decisions may be distinguished on the ground that they concerned bodies exercising their activity as regulatory agencies in the context of a common organization of the market which, according to well established ECJ caselaw, provides the sole framework in which activities relating to it may be judged and assessed.

On the other hand, in the most recent cases of British Telecom (50) and BNIC v Clair (51) the Court confirmed that the commercial activities of regulatory bodies fall within the scope of the competition rules whatever their form. Although the above decisions did not involve the application of article 90 but that of articles 85 and 86, they are, nevertheless, instructive because they make clear that the regulatory nature of the public body cannot prevent it from being subject to the competition rules. Thus, despite the fact that British Telecom exercised regulatory functions in fixing tariffs and determining certain other conditions of the provision of services to the public, the particular schemes passed by British Telecom in order to prohibit private agencies from using the lower tariffs of the U.K. were held to constitute an activity by an undertaking subject to article 86. As Advocate General Darmon remarked in the same case, if the Italian argument were adopted it would mean that every time an undertaking acts by virtue of a state prerogative the application of the rules guaranteeing the principles of free competition would be avoided. (52)

Similarly, in BNIC v Clair a decision taken within the framework of BNIC was held to constitute an agreement of an association of undertakings although the members of the association represented in BNIC were named by the minister and their decisions were subject to the latter's approval.

With respect to the second issue of discord regarding the extent of the notion of public undertaking Deringer supports the view that a public authority cannot be considered an undertaking when buying goods or services for its own needs or in order to accomplish purely administrative missions (e.g. construction of roads). (53) On the other hand, when the public authority buys not for the accomplishment of administrative tasks but also in order to cover the needs of third parties in accomplishing its tasks (54) then Deringer believes that the public authority must be considered an undertaking in the sense of the 'Rules applicable to undertakings' of the Treaty. In those cases the fact that such supplies are for the accomplishment of an administrative task does not change the private law nature of the agreements with the suppliers. (55)

We do not however accept this view for the following reasons. First, it would be almost impossible to distinguish between supplies made in order to accomplish purely administrative tasks and those made for the purpose of carrying out a certain economic activity. Furthermore it would be impossible to distinguish which supplies would eventually cover the needs of third parties. After all, the construction of roads, which is given by Hochbaum as an example of a purely administrative mission, is, in our opinion, a clear case of an economic activity engaged in by the State. To say, as Deringer does, that the entity which actually carries out the construction of the roads may itself qualify as a public undertaking further shows the difficulty of drawing a line between supplies made for administrative reasons and those forming part of an economic activity.

Second, we believe that independently of the purpose for which public authorities make their supplies, the purchase of goods and services in the market is, as such, an economic activity subject to the rules of competition and the other Treaty provisions. The argument that similar supplies made by an individual for the satisfaction of its own needs do not fall under the competition provisions cannot stand because the reason why this is so is not that the individual is not engaging in an economic activity. Such economic activity affecting an unimportant part of the market cannot give rise to the application of the competition rules. On the other hand any large entity, public or private, whose activities are capable of affecting a large part of the market, must obey the competition rules even when making supplies for the satisfaction of its own needs.

Third, as a corollary of the above, Deringer's view leads to inequality between private undertakings and the administration when the latter exercises an economic activity. The former will always fall under the competition rules even when buying in order to satisfy their own internal needs while similar activities of the latter are not even considered activities of a public undertaking and are, therefore, outside the Treaty's reach. The argument that such supplies by private undertakings also serve their active participation in the market and that private undertakings are capable of passing the expenses to the eventual consumers while public entities are not, is not satisfactory. The drafters of the Treaty intended to subject to article 90 every economic activity of the State in the market, the making of supplies amounting itself to such an activity. Otherwise the States could always invoke that public supplies are made for purely administrative reasons and, thus, circumvent the application of the Treaty provisions. In any case the Treaty contains specific exceptions for reasons of national defence as well as for reasons of general economic interest.

The view that the distinction made by Deringer is illogical also seems to be supported by the Commission in its 5th Report on Competition Policy of 1976. Therein it is expressly stated that if public undertakings become active in the market as suppliers or consumers of goods or services they may be in competition with other undertakings and by their behaviour affect trade between Member States. Furthermore the same approach has been made in article 63 of ECSC. (56)

A different approach was adopted within the framework of GATT where article 17 para 2 excludes from the application of para 1, which imposes an obligation upon the contracting parties to ensure that state trading companies act in a non-discriminatory manner with respect to imports or exports, the imports of products for immediate or ultimate consumption in governmental use. Nevertheless, with respect to such imports each contracting party remains under the obligation to accord to the trade of the other parties fair and equitable treatment. The above GATT provisions cannot, however, be invoked by analogy within an EEC context. The Treaty of Rome aims at creating a real Common Market between the Member States and establishing common rules by which both States and individuals must abide whereas the GATT only aims at facilitating trade between the contracting parties.

'Public'

As was mentioned earlier, the term 'public' needs to be defined in order to delimit state liability with respect to public undertakings as against private ones.

Public undertakings are often driven by non-economic considerations. In every case in which a contravention of the Treaty is detected the Commission must make an appreciation, on the basis of a formula (1), whether the undertaking acted on its own initiative or under the influence of the State. In the latter case and provided the State exercises its influence by virtue of direct or indirect control thereof it is a public undertaking and the Commission can make use of its power under article 90 para 3.

As was stated in the UN Report on the Economy of Europe of 1959, 'the absence of a uniform definition, precise and sufficiently manageable of the notion of public undertaking constitutes one of the principal difficulties'. The reasons are the diversity and multiplicity of forms under which public authorities exercise economic activity in the various States and the variety of national definitions often developed in order to cover particular circumstances. (2) In fact, there exists no official definition of this notion either in national legislation or in the European Communities Treaties. (3)

Within the Common Market itself, except from certain monopolies in the field of public utilities such as postal, telephone and telegraph services and transport which are, to a large extent, common in all Member States, public ownership varies considerably. For example, the revenue producing monopolies of France, Germany and Italy are unknown in the Benelux countries while the production and distribution of electricity which is nationalized in France and Italy, is in Belgium and Germany mostly carried out by joint undertaking groupings of local authorities and private companies. (4) Similar differences exist in the coal and steel sectors which are, however, specifically covered by the ECSC Treaty and not the EEC one.

Not only is public ownership within the EEC so varied but so is the role of public undertakings which, apart from not being defined or clarified, is most often contradictory even within the same Member State. (5) Member States tend to see public undertakings either as subjects of economic life pursuing profit or as objects in pursuit of public priorities. (6) In France the Nora report noted a distinction between public undertakings entrusted with the provision of a public service and those of the competitive sector. As to the latter the report recommended large freedom which would enable them to operate efficiently in the market. However, the Nora report recommendations were not put into effect and the conditions of management and state influence of public undertakings remain blurred. In Italy state participation may be found in virtually all fields and ranges from 100% state ownership of the company to minority state holding. State intervention was originally aimed at curing structural deficiencies of the economy but although in the 50s and 60s the system contributed to the expansion and modernization of the economy since then there has been progressive deterioration. In the U.K. there have been waves of nationalizations starting with the creation of public corporations in 1946 but the degree of state intervention has depended, to a great extent, on the ideology of the government in power. (7)

Except from the above differences in the degree of state ownership and intervention among Member States national legislations also differ in the extent of subjection of public undertakings and public activity to domestic competition rules. Thus, public undertakings are subject to domestic competition rules only in Germany and Denmark while in all other Member States public undertakings are considered to be fulfilling a public function and are not placed on an equal footing with private ones. (5)

In the light of the above contradictions it is obvious that the notion of public undertaking under article 90 cannot depend on national definitions. (9) The term must be interpreted independently of national laws in a way conforming to the spirit of the Treaty and the object of article 90 which is to regulate the influence of public authorities in relation to the functioning of the Common Market, so that it cannot be misused for the purposes of, inter alia, hidden discrimination and distortion of competition. (10)

The definition or, rather, interpretation of the term 'public undertaking' which shall be attempted in this chapter, in no way purports to be a general and comprehensive one. As Advocate General Dutheillet de Lamothe stated in his submissions in the Port of Mertert case, 'it is an economic rather than a legal concept and, in spite of the attention devoted to this question in Brussels (and other Colloquia), it would be dangerous to attempt a general definition in a Community context. The definition may only emerge gradually from caselaw, which, case by case will outline the concept, as also, under Court supervision will Community regulations, directives or decisions'. (11)

This must have been also the intention of the authors of the Treaty who, setting out from the different views prevailing in the Member States on the position, value and necessity of public undertakings, deliberately refrained from defining the concept more precisely. However, as Advocate General Reischl affirmed in the Transparency Directive case, 'such an omission cannot obscure the fact that the term used in article 90 para 1 is a concept of Community law and may, therefore, only be given a uniform interpretation for all Member States on the basis of the purposes of that provision'. (12)

Therefore, with the assumption that the dominant influence of the State is the distinctive mark of public undertakings and should characterize their definition, most commentators agree that are included in the term all undertakings which are dependent, directly or indirectly, on public authorities and are susceptible to be influenced by them, irrespective of the legal form or legal personality of the undertaking. (13) A similar definition has been adopted within the context of the EFTA Convention where the term 'public undertaking' includes 'all central, regional or local authorities, public enterprises and any other organization by means of which a Member State by law or in practice controls or appreciably influences imports or exports'. (14)

It is interesting to note that a similar approach is followed in national legislations. Thus, under para 98 al 2 of the German competition law public undertakings are those which are entirely or partially the property of public authorities or are administered or exploited by the latter. (15) Certain exceptions, particularly in the field of public utilities, carriage of persons and goods and federal railways, are laid down in articles 92-103. Similarly, the French Conseil d'Etat concluded in two cases that undertakings of the public sector are those belonging in totality to the State and other public persons as well as those where the State or other public persons have the majority of capital or seats in their board of Directors, irrespective of whether the undertaking concerned depends directly on those persons or their subsidiaries. (16)

The CEEP definition (17) according to which 'public undertaking is an undertaking having an activity of an economic order in which public authorities have either a majority or play a preponderant role in the management', is also of the same nature.

Therefore, the term 'public undertaking' includes primarily the State and all its subdivisions when they exercise an economic activity (e.g. the Forest Authority) (18) as well as any private undertaking which they control. The control may either exist in law or be exercised in fact. (19)

The essence, therefore, of the definition is to determine the degree of control. On the one hand simple influence exercised by the State by virtue of its role as coordinator of the economic policy or of its prerogative as grantor of a special or exclusive right is not sufficient. The State must be able to exercise its influence upon a public undertaking by virtue of its control thereof which may be due to a structural, contractual, financial or other connection therewith. On the other hand in order to ensure that the competition rules are not circumvented by the States we must adopt a very wide definition of control. Thus, for an undertaking to be 'public' it is sufficient that the public authority be able to exercise a decisive influence over its business decisions without using public power by enacting laws or issuing regulations. This would include in the notion of public undertaking any activity of the State, in its broadest sense, in the field of economic life. What is important is whether the State has the last word, not only the right of decision regarding its formation, organization or dissolution, but also as to its functioning and management and even as to any particular act of the undertaking.

The Advocate General in Port of Mertert adopted a more limited definition. (20) He stated that mere participation in the capital of an undertaking does not, ipso facto, make it a public undertaking and that two factors must be added. First, the establishment of the company must arise from a unilateral act of State, for example a law, and second, that the participation of the State in the management is essential in that the public body must act not as shareholder but by virtue of its imperium.

The additional requirement that the public authority must be acting not only as a shareholder but on the basis of its imperium, appears to have been taken from French law and is unduly restrictive. Mestmäcker argues that some German firms would escape liability since public influence is based only on their position as shareholders. (21) Distinctions based on such abstract notions as 'imperium' cannot be justified since what is important is the possibility of state influence and control however this is achieved.

A wide interpretation seems to be supported also by the European Court which considered the definition of 'public undertaking' adopted by the Commission for the purposes of the Transparency Directive (22) as consistent with the objectives of article 90 para 1. According to the definition of the Directive 'public undertakings are undertakings over which public authorities may exercise, directly or indirectly, a dominant influence by virtue of their ownership of it, their financial participation therein or the rules which govern it. A dominant influence is to be presumed when the public authority holds the major part of the undertaking's subscribed capital, controls the majority of votes attached to the shares issued or can appoint more than half of the members of the undertaking's administrative, managerial or supervisory body'. As the Court stated (23), 'the reasons for the inclusion in the Treaty of the provisions of article 90 is precisely the influence which the public authorities are able to exert over the commercial decisions of public undertakings. That influence may be exerted on the basis of financial participation or of the rules governing the management of the undertaking. By choosing the same criteria to determine the financial relations on which it must be able to obtain information in order to perform its duty of surveillance under 90 para 1 the Commission has remained within the limits of the discretion conferred upon it by that provision'. Moreover, as Advocate General Reischl noted (24) in the same case, 'the danger of influence exists if the Member States control certain economic units outside the framework of general legal ties irrespective of whether that influence is to be ascribed to relations governed by public or private law'.

Notwithstanding the fact that the definition contained in article 2 of the Transparency Directive only tries to establish the criteria in order to delimit the type of undertakings to which the Directive applies, one may conclude from it as well as from the decision of the ECJ that the notion of public undertaking includes undertakings of private law which the State somehow manages or controls. (25) Such control may be direct or indirect through bodies which public authorities control. It may also be held by a variety of public bodies. (26)

Such control need not be of an organic character as Delion argues. (27) Even if in most cases the power of control will be exercised because of the holding of the entire or the majority of capital or the control of the majority of voices on the board, non-organic power of control through contractual clauses (28) or unilateral intervention due to reasons independent of the structure of the undertaking could also make it fall within the ambit of 90 para 1. Undertakings in which the State or public authorities are interested and are subjected to exorbitant rules of private law implying a State dependence are public because the State plays a role of national sovereign. Such might be the case of a private company which is so heavily indebted to a bank controlled by the State that the latter is able to direct its behaviour. In the case in which such a company contravenes the competition rules the State should also be liable under article 90 para 1.

This view is consistent with Delion's own statement describing the present situation, that the 'tendency now is to create big industrial groups of complicated structure often operating within the framework of private law. This imprecise notion which is now taking the place of the classical notion of public undertaking makes more difficult the delimitation of the public economic sector and the definition of its position in the economy'. (29) It is exactly this difficulty that makes the adoption of a very wide definition of control necessary.

Pappalardo has put forward the following interesting view (30): that, nowadays, the establishment of special relationships between States and undertakings is brought about by considerations other than the public ownership of undertakings. According to Pappalardo the dividing line lies no more between public and private companies but between big and midsize or small ones, the former being the privileged instruments of the economic policy and objects of all support measures and special aid. Even if we agree that this is in many respects true, particularly because the collapse of a big industry except from its other adverse economic effects is likely to cause even greater unemployment, we believe that a government's indirect influence and control is not always dependent on the size of the firms. Member States are likely to use the firms which they control in order to carry out their economic objectives independently of the firm's size. Nevertheless, we do not mean by that that the State may not also intervene in the private sector by establishing special relations with private undertakings and impose its wishes upon them possibly in a way frustrating the Treaty objectives. In this connection we do admit that there is a certain inconsistency in the Treaty in providing for the use of the procedure of article 90 para 3 only with respect to measures concerning public undertakings and those granted special or exclusive rights and not with respect to general measures affecting also private undertakings. We shall return to this question in subsequent chapters.

Until now the Court and the Commission have been reluctant to apply article 90 para 1 in order to hold the State responsible for the anticompetitive behaviour of public undertakings. The Commission, instead, has preferred to pursue the undertakings concerned directly, under articles 85 and 86, ignoring the potential application of article 90 para 1 against the Member State which had the power and may have decisively influenced their behaviour. Clear examples of this reluctance are the decisions of the Commission against BNIA (31), BNIC (32) and British Telecom. (33)

In all those cases the Commission found the undertakings concerned liable for anticompetitive behaviour under articles 85 or 86 and in the case of BNIC also imposed a fine which, of course, could not have been extracted under article 90. Both BNIA and BNIC were actually public undertakings since their members and chairman were appointed by the minister and all decisions had to be taken in the presence of a government representative who should either endorse the decision immediately or refer it to the minister. Although the Commission examined whether article 90 para 2 could be invoked there was no mention of whether the undertakings concerned were public undertakings, probably because that was not a relevant issue. In any case, the above mentioned Commission decisions do prove that public undertakings are subject to articles 85 and 86. So does the decision of the Commission in British Telecom where it was specifically mentioned that the U.K. Post Office and the British Telecom were public corporations and economic entities carrying out activities of an economic nature and were, as such, subject to article 86. The BNIC and British Telecom decisions of the Commission have recently been upheld by the ECJ which clearly confirmed that public undertakings are subject to the competition rules to the extent that they pursue economic activities. (34)

1.4 Definition of 'Undertakings to which the State grants special or exclusive rights'

In analysing the concept of an 'undertaking to which the State grants special or exclusive rights' for the purpose of establishing state liability under article 90 para 1 it is necessary first, to define the notion of the grant of such right and consider the effects thereof on the undertaking concerned and, second, to examine the circumstances, if any, in which such grant may be contrary to the Treaty.

Notion of a grant of 'special or exclusive right by the State'

The notion 'undertakings to which the State grants special or exclusive rights' appears simpler than the other terms of article 90 para 1 although one can imagine numerous and diverse ways of according those rights even if there exists a great variety of such rights. (1) Because of this divergence it is preferable, rather than attempting to formulate a precise definition to pinpoint the necessary elements of those rights.

In examining which undertakings may be considered to have been granted special or exclusive rights by the State for the purpose of falling within the ambit of article 90 para 1 regard must be given to the object of article 90 para 1 and the reason for the inclusion of those undertakings in this provision. The notion is, arguably, wider than that of 'public undertakings' and must be interpreted extensively enough in order to encompass all those cases in which the States, by according special or exclusive rights to certain undertakings, enable those to evade the competition rules. (2) State responsibility under article 90 para 1, is inter alia, derived from the assumption of the risk inherent in the deliberate distortion of competition as well as of other Treaty rules by a grant of special or exclusive rights (3) since the undertakings to which those rights are granted may be especially influenced by means other than legislative or administrative acts. (4) What is important is the dependence of those undertakings on the grantor of the right and the power that the latter has to control them. (5) The juridical basis on which control or influence is exercised is immaterial. (6)

Having made clear that for the purposes of article 90 para 1 the common denominator of both public undertakings and those to which the State grants special or exclusive rights is the possibility of influence by the State it is important to note that those terms by no means coincide. Contrary to public undertakings the undertakings to which the State grants special or exclusive rights tend to be private undertakings, completely separate from the State, which became subjected to indirect state influence by reason of the grant and during the time that this lasts. The State therefore does not control those undertakings in as permanent and complete a manner as it does in the case of public undertakings.

Some seem to believe that only private undertakings may benefit from exclusive or special rights. (7) Even if this makes no difference in practice, public undertakings falling within the ambit of article 90 para 1 in any case (8), we do not see any reason why public undertakings may not be granted special or exclusive rights by the State. (9) The ECJ has also ruled implicitly that both public and private undertakings may be the grantees of such rights. (10) The fact that an undertaking is public because it is under the direct or indirect control of the State and therefore actually or potentially under its influence does not necessarily imply that this undertaking has also been granted a special or exclusive right in the sense explained in this chapter which may enable it to be in a privileged position in the market independent of the exercise of state influence. It is true that for the purposes of article 90 para 1 the common denominator of both public undertakings and those to which the State grants special or exclusive rights is the possibility of state influence or control. Nevertheless, it is still important to distinguish between those public undertakings which have and those which have not been granted special or exclusive rights in order to establish whether a contravention of the Treaty rules to which article 90 para 1 refers has actually occurred.

The responsibility of the State for the behaviour of the undertakings to which it grants special or exclusive rights has also been recognized within the framework of the General Agreement on Tariffs and Trade. (11) Article 17 of the said Agreement thus imposes an obligation upon the contracting parties 'if they grant to any enterprise, formally or in effect, exclusive or special privileges' (in the same way as when they establish or maintain a state enterprise), to ensure that 'such enterprise shall in its purchases or sales involving either imports or exports, act in a manner consistent with the general principles of non-discriminatory treatment, prescribed in the Agreement ...'. Colliard seems to consider the GATT formula, which is only cited by way of analogy, acceptable for the purposes of the Treaty of Rome only under the reservation that it must be limited to a legal and not a factual situation. (12) Such a view, which we dispute as creating an unreasonable distinction in circumstances where the responsibility of the State in connection with certain undertakings to which it grants special rights or privileges should be the same, shall be further discussed below.

The next step is to examine when undertakings are deemed to have been granted special or exclusive rights by the State. Special rights have the effect of putting the grantees in a privileged position with respect to their competitors without, however, conceding them exclusivity. Special rights may derive from various acts of the authorities such as authorizations, dispensations, renunciations, admissions etc. Exclusive rights go further than special rights in conferring to the grantees exclusivity and, therefore, a monopolistic position, with respect to the activity for which they are granted. Exclusive rights derive from acts of sovereignty imposed upon undertakings or concessions under the form of a contract or pursuant to a procedure provided in a law, official regulation or 'cahier des charges'. The common denominator of all these must be the dependence of the undertakings on the State and the possibility of influence of the latter upon them. (13)

Colliard, while accepting that national solutions can serve only by way of example, draws analogies from French law and considers the two types of grant existing thereunder as indicative. (14) The one type of grant, which corresponds to the 'concession de service public' existing under French and Belgian law, consists of the exercise of a public service by a private undertaking and makes the latter recipient of particular rights by virtue of the fact that it is a collaborator of the government. The fact that the public service is provided by a private undertaking is only a political choice, such services often being provided by the government departments themselves. The second notion concerns an economic activity exercised by a private undertaking by virtue of a particular permission of the public authorities, e.g. the granting of an exploitation right. The reason for the grant is normally that the activity has its origin in the public domain. However, this is not exclusive, the grant possibly covering an activity previously falling in the private domain. We may say that in the last resort this distinction is immaterial because from the moment the government makes a conscious political decision to grant an exclusive or special right it takes an area outside the private domain by regulating it. We believe that both the above types of grant of right by the State recognized by French law are included in the notion of 'special or exclusive rights' of article 90 para 1. They are also quite illustrative of the wide range of undertakings that the above notion must cover in order to serve the objectives of 90 para 1 best.

The question has arisen whether special or exclusive rights granted under private law are covered or whether the grant must be made by means of a public law act or assignment (i.e. by statute, decree or administrative act). (15) The issue has been raised by German commentators (16) because of its apparent significance in German law. Deringer, for example, would exclude from the application of article 90 para 1 contracts which are exclusively and purely of private law, such as the granting by a commune of all the advertising space to one undertaking. (17) Deringer's view stems from the principle that the grant of the right must serve public ends (18) and, thus, restricts the undertakings falling under article 90 para 1 to those which, as a result of the grant, have been entrusted with duties and privileges normally belonging to the government. We believe that Deringer's view is unduly limited and not justified by the objective of article 90. (19) What serves the public end is a matter of conscious political choice as are the duties and privileges of a government. This is a domain left by the Treaty to be regulated by the State and, therefore, not to be determined at a Community level. However, in carrying out their duties and exercising their privileges Member States remain subject to the Treaty rules including article 90 para 1.

In the light of the above we believe that for the purposes of article 90 para 1 the legal form of the grant is immaterial. (20) All undertakings to which the State or the local authorities confer a particular juridicial position which is exclusive of other undertakings fulfilling the same conditions or gives the undertaking an advantage over the others accompanied by the possibility of state influence are, thus, included in the definition. (21) This is irrespective of whether the right has been granted by an act of public law or under the form of a contract of private law.

There is, therefore, no reason why the State should have the responsibility of ensuring that an undertaking which has been granted the exclusive right of T.V. and cable transmissions (22) or the exclusive right to settle accident claims (23) does not contravene the rules of the Treaty while denying the existence of such state liability for the anticompetitive behaviour of an undertaking which has been granted the exclusive right to use all available advertising space in a Member State. The risk of distortion of competition is the same in all those cases. The fact that the government has decided to grant a special or exclusive right in a certain domain indicates, irrespective of the domain concerned, that the government considers the relevant activity as one with respect to which it has duties or privileges. Government responsibility should be analogous to the degree of its involvement, the functions of a government varying from one Member State to the other. Therefore, the responsibility of the Member States under article 90 para 1 should also vary depending on the degree of regulation and involvement that each government pursues.

At the other end of the scale Mestmäcker advocates a very extensive application of article 90 also to legislation which fixes maximum or minimum prices, quotas etc. Mestmäcker considers that all undertakings to which those measures are addressed are, hoc ipso, holders of an exclusive or special right in the sense of article 90. (24) He, therefore, argues (25) that special or exclusive rights, in the sense of article 90, are granted by a Member State to undertakings to which the State gives the opportunity, guaranteed by law, to escape the application of competition rules. (26) The same was probably the tenor of Van Hecke's view that private undertakings must be deemed to fall under

90 para 1 whenever the special rights granted to them are significant in connection with the Treaty objective of ensuring unadulterated competition (e.g. local monopoly of distribution of electricity, franchised transport protected against competition). (27)

The above view, which may also cause a 'measure' within article 90 para 1 to coincide with the grant of a special right - this being analysed below - is, however, not justified by the objectives of this article and is disputed by the majority of commentators. If a Member State directly restrains competition, through a law, the undertakings concerned may be in a privileged position but are not granted special rights. (28) The relevant undertaking does not necessarily acquire a particular position authorizing it to behave independently of competition. Rather it is the State which restrains the undertakings. Furthermore, such laws do not create any special power of influence or control by the State upon the undertakings concerned.

Independently of the potential liability of the State under article 5 para 2 when combined with the competition rules, article 90 para 1 is only a particular application thereof in circumstances in which the State acts as entrepreneur through the medium of the undertakings which it controls. Therefore, we do not believe that the application of article 90 para 1 may be extended to cover all distortions of competition by the State by interpreting state legislation or regulations fixing maximum or minimum prices, quotas etc. as amounting to a grant of an exclusive or special right. Such rights may be deemed to be granted by the State only when, as result thereof, the grantees may behave independently of their competitors and exercise them in a way which may distort competition or some other Treaty rule.

Mestmacker's view was also implicitly rejected by the ECJ in the case of INNO v ATAB. In a reference for preliminary ruling the national court asked the ECJ whether undertakings to which Member States grant special or exclusive rights within 90 exist where, by means of legislative provisions, the State indirectly gives the manufacturers and importers of certain products, as distinct from those of other products, the possibility of fixing selling prices. The ECJ held that 'since the possibility is open to all, including retailers, who become importers or producers of manufactured tobacco and consequently to an indefinite class of undertakings, it is questionable whether those undertakings can properly be described as having been granted 'special' and, at all events, 'exclusive' rights. (29)

As the Commission stated in its submissions with respect to the above mentioned question, 'the exclusive rights of article 90 para 1 relate to the production or the marketing of goods and services by the person entitled to exercise the rights concerned himself, in other words the access to the market. The relevant Belgian measures (however) did not have this effect since the access to the market was free'. (30)

Therefore, a State is not granting a special or exclusive right when it passes a law or administrative act which only makes an undertaking privileged in comparison to others. It grants a special or exclusive right only when it confers upon the undertaking a position which enables that undertaking to behave independently of competitors in a way contrary to the Treaty and which also allows the Member State to influence the undertaking either because it is correlated to special duties or because it creates some receptiveness of influence. (31) An authorization granted because certain legal predetermined conditions are accomplished is not a special right since all conforming undertakings may obtain it. (32) The test should be whether the authorization, concession etc. is only necessary in order to satisfy certain legal rules for a private activity which is otherwise free, or whether it implies the exclusion of other competitors who also satisfy the condition. (33) Therefore, the so-called 'imperfect' concessions ('fausses concessions') such as professional licences for particular use of public property (taxis, kiosks, petrol stations etc.), do not qualify as special rights within article 90 para 1. (34) Nor are tax advantages such special rights unless combined with duties, nor industrial property rights, for they are open to anybody who fulfils the necessary legal conditions. (35)

Comparison of 'Undertakings to which the State grants special or exclusive rights' with those undertakings falling under article 90 para 2

It has been correctly maintained that the undertakings to which the State grants special or exclusive rights within article 90 para 1 do not automatically fall under article 90 para 2 while the opposite is true. (36) The grant of a special or exclusive right does not necessarily imply that the grantee is entrusted with the operation of a service of general economic interest. On the other hand, the delegation of a public task is normally tied to a particular status but only to the extent that this is necessary for the accomplishment of the task. (37) Franck also argues (38) that if it were otherwise article 90 para 2 would have no reason of being, this probably meaning that otherwise competition would not run the risk of being distorted for an exemption to be provided.

When is a grant of a special or exclusive right contrary to the Treaty

It is implicit in the wording of article 90 para 1 (39) and has also been confirmed by the ECJ in Sacchi (40) and repeated thereafter (41) that 'article 90 para 1 permits, inter alia, Member States to grant special or exclusive rights to undertakings' (42). The European Court of Justice specifically stated that 'nothing in the Treaty prevents Member States, for consideration of public interest of a non economic nature, from removing radio and T.V. transmissions, including cable transmissions, from the field of competition by conferring on one or more establishments an exclusive right to conduct them'. (43) When asked on the compatibility of a public monopoly with the Treaty, the Court replied that 'the interpretation of articles 86 and 90 taken together leads to the conclusion that the fact that an undertaking to which a Member State grants exclusive rights has a monopoly is not as such incompatible with article 86' and that the extension of the exclusive right following a new intervention by the State is not prohibited either. (44) Nevertheless, the Court did not fail to stress that 'for the performance of their tasks these establishments remain subject to the prohibition against discrimination and, to the extent that this performance comprises activities of an economic nature, fall under the provisions referred to in 90 relating to public undertakings and undertakings to which the State grants special or exclusive rights' (45).

The above position of the Court rests on giving a literal interpretation to article 90, which clearly admits the grant of special or exclusive rights. At first sight, it also appears consistent with article 222 which provides that the Treaty shall in no way prejudice the rules in Member States governing the system of property ownership. Even if nationalization does not necessarily imply the grant of a monopoly it is often accompanied by it. It would, thus, arguably, be inconsistent to allow a Member State to acquire an exclusive right by nationalizing a certain sector of the economy while not by granting a right to that effect to a private company. Nevertheless, as the ECJ confirmed in Sacchi and the Commission made clear in its replies to parliamentary questions, (46) this implicit right of the State to grant exclusive rights as well as to nationalize is precisely linked to a duty to respect the competition rules and the other provisions of the Treaty. (47)

The holding of a dominant position by a private undertaking is not incompatible with the Treaty in the private domain either. Article 86 does not prohibit a dominant position but only its abusive exploitation, the exercise of abuse being a question of fact. Yet, in the Continental Can case (48) the ECJ held that abuse may occur if an undertaking in a dominant position strengthens this position in such a way that the degree of dominance reached substantially fetters competition, i.e. that only undertakings remain in the market whose behaviour depends on the dominant one. According to the Court such reinforcement is prohibited by Article 86 whichever are the means used to attain those results. (49)

A different position, however, was adopted by the Court in Sacchi where it held that an extension of an exclusive right following a state intervention is not as such incompatible with articles 86 and 90. (50) The ECJ thus rejected Sacchi's argument which was based on the Continental Can decision.

The obvious inequality created by the above two decisions was raised by Scholten, M.E.P., in a Written Question in the European Parliament. In its reply (51) the Commission denied the existence of a conflict and of different treatment between public and private undertakings by explaining, on the one hand, that the Continental Can decision was not only applicable to private undertakings and, on the other, that the 'reinforcement' of a dominant position by the extension of an exclusive right, which had been allowed by the Sacchi decision, might concern both public and private undertakings.

The above reply, far from giving a satisfactory solution, seems to adopt the Advocate General's position in Sacchi. According to the Advocate General the distinctive feature between the two decisions was that while in the Continental Can case the strengthening of the dominant position had been the result of behaviour on the part of undertaking, in

Sacchi the strengthening of the monopoly only resulted from an extension of the exclusive right by the State. (52) The A.G. considered that if we accept that 'article 90 presupposes the possibility of conferring an exclusive right on certain undertaking, that is, where appropriate, creating a complete monopoly ... it is possible to hold the opinion, particularly in view of the principle of article 222, that a Member State is allowed under 90 to strengthen the market position of such an undertaking, something which is not permitted to dominant undertakings themselves' (53).

We believe, however, that neither the Advocate General's submissions nor the Commission's reply provide an answer for the case in which the creation of the monopoly is not the result of a grant of an exclusive right or an extension of such right by the State but of the strengthening of its position by the undertaking which has been granted special or exclusive rights, under the instigation or influence of the State. In such case it would not be satisfactory to apply the Continental Can decision in order to hold the undertaking responsible while leaving the State undisturbed. Independently of the separate responsibility of undertakings under the competition rules, the absolvement of the State from liability in such a case would mean ignoring the very raison d'etre of 90 para 1, this being to hold States responsible for the behaviour of undertakings which they control.

Despite the decision of the ECJ in Sacchi, which is based on a literal interpretation of article 90, we are of the opinion that the Treaty does not merely regulate the behaviour of firms to which special or exclusive rights have been granted, but that it also limits the power of Member States to grant such rights. This limitation results from the general principles and objectives of the Treaty and the fundamental principles of law which the ECJ has adopted and developed in interpreting Community law. In order to avoid casting doubt on the possibility of nationalization, which might touch the sensitivities of certain existing or future governments of the Member States, we believe that the comparison with article 222 must not be carried too far. One can clearly distinguish the grant of special or exclusive rights from the taking over of the ownership of an industry, the former being not so much a measure of structural reform as a measure of economic and industrial policy. An exclusive or special right affects directly the creation of a Common Market by which Member States have abided, whereas nationalization, even though potentially having the same effect as an exclusive right, is more dependent on the ideology of the government in power and should therefore be left to the State's domain.

The general rules and principles of Community law, which include, inter alia, the prohibition of discrimination and the obligation to ensure that competition is not distorted, as well as the fundamental principles of law adopted by the ECJ, such as the duty to use only proportionate means to achieve certain legitimate aims (54) etc., may pose important limitations to the grant of exclusive rights by the State. In the light of these principles it may be said that Member States may grant special or exclusive rights in a particular economic sector only if what is done is reasonably necessary in order to secure a legitimate objective. In support, reference may be made by analogy to the Sacchi judgment where the Court cited with approval the paragraph of the Commission Directive of 22.12.69 (55) which considered as capable of constituting measures having an effect equivalent to quantitative restrictions those measures governing the marketing of products the restrictive effect of which exceeded the effects intrinsic to trade rules. According to the Court such is the case where the restrictive effects are out of proportion to their purpose. Nonetheless, it must be noted that there is no caselaw of the Court supporting the above argument with reference to the grant of exclusive rights in so far as there is no effect on the circulation of goods.

In fact, in the field of movement of goods the ECJ, implicitly in Sacchi and explicitly in Manghera (56), accepted a limitation to the power of the State to grant an exclusive right, which erodes the absolute character of this power that the Court itself initially proclaimed. By holding that article 37 refers to trade of goods and is, therefore, inapplicable in the case of service monopolies (57) the Court implicitly recognized the prevalence of this article when the grant of an exclusive right has an adverse effect on intracommunity trade. Article 37 which prescribes the progressive adjustment of state monopolies of a commercial character so as to ensure that when the transitional period has ended no discrimination regarding the conditions under which goods are procured and marketed exists between nationals of Member States, was interpreted by the ECJ in Manghera to prohibit all exclusive rights of imports as amounting to discrimination in the sense of this article.

Thus, article 37 raises a serious obstacle to the power of the State to grant exclusive rights in the field of commerce since the ECJ in Manghera clearly established that the adjustment of state monopolies thereunder requires the abolition of all exclusive rights of importation from other Member States. In its subsequent decisions in the cases of REWE (58) and Miritz (59) the ECJ further held that article 37 is not limited to imports and exports which are the direct object of the monopoly but is extended to all actions connected with its existence and having an effect on trade of goods between Member States, irrespective of whether those are subject to a monopoly.

Although article 37 is only applicable to trade of goods we may argue, by analogy, that the power of the State to grant special or exclusive rights should be equally limited by the provisions of the Treaty relating to the other three freedoms which compose the foundations of the Community.

As regards the freedom of movement of persons and services the traditional view is that they may be exercised only to the extent to which this is available to nationals of the Member State. The ECJ in the Van Ameyde case while stating that for discrimination to fall under article 52 and 59 it suffices that it results from rules of whatever kind which seek to govern collectively the carrying out of the business in question, yet it concluded that there is no discrimination if the exclusion of other categories of undertakings is not based on nationality. (60) The same view has been advocated by academics such as Ferrari-Bravo who maintained that the basis of the freedom of establishment as well as of the provisions of articles 62, 67, 71 and 76 is the application to foreigners of the same treatment as to nationals. (61) Thus, if nationals are prohibited from entering the market because the State has established a monopoly, this prohibition cannot be challenged under Community law because it applies equally to nationals and non-nationals. (62)

The above traditional view, according to which the power of Member States to grant special or exclusive rights cannot be limited by the provisions of Title III, is open to challenge as being inconsistent with the Manghera rule and the Treaty principles. One may observe that if a State grants a monopoly, in the same way as when it grants an exclusive right of imports, it grants it in practice almost always to its own nationals or to an enterprise under the control of its nationals. Most monopolies, therefore, are basically discriminatory. The argument that by creating a monopoly the State excludes also its own (other) nationals cannot stand because so does the exclusive right of importation. Furthermore, all such monopolies, being clearly under state control or influence, are more likely to exercise discrimination against the inhabitants of the other Member States in the same way as a holder of an exclusive right of imports may. It may also be argued that when a State closes its market through the creation of a monopoly, while the other States allow free imports, there is a lack of reciprocity in the creation of the Common Market which is similar to discrimination.

The question arises whether there may be circumstances where the creation of monopolies is necessary for public policy reasons. Such could, arguably, be the case with air transport where the grant of exclusive rights on profitable lines is often on the condition that services are provided on other less profitable ones. (Security reasons may also be present). The Treaty itself provides for specific exemptions from the application of its rules both in the field of trade of goods (article 36) and in the area of services (articles 90 para 2 and 223), thus recognizing the prevalence of national interests in certain circumstances.

However, as the ECJ made clear, those provisions of the Treaty which allow derogation from the Treaty rules must be strictly construed and no derogation may be permitted for reason other than those stated therein. (63) Even in those cases where a derogation may potentially be permitted the power of the State to grant special or exclusive rights must still be considered restricted by the general principles of the Treaty which imply that in the pursuit of measures of economic and industrial policy the Member States must choose those instruments which affect least the proper functioning of the Common Market.

Before concluding, analogy may also be drawn with industrial and intellectual property rights despite the fact that the grant of such rights does not fall within the ambit of article 90 para 1. (64) ECJ caselaw concerning those rights shows that there is a distinction between the existence or ownership of such rights under national law, which is protected under articles 222 and 36 of the Treaty, and their exercise which is subject to the Treaty provisions. (65) Also in this field, even if exclusivity is permitted its exercise by the undertakings may engage their responsibility either on the basis of article 85 (66) or on the basis of the free movement of goods. (67) By specifying that the exclusivity accorded in Sacchi was compatible 'as such' it is apparent that it is the possibility of expansion of the above jurisprudence to monopolies and exclusive rights that the Court considered. (68)

It has been argued that even if in legal theory it is impossible to draw the line between existence and exercise of a right, analytically the existence thereof consists of all the ways it may be exercised. In ruling that an important difference rests on a distinction which cannot be clearly drawn the Court has created a very flexible instrument for developing the law. (69) The Court has thus developed the concept of the 'specific subject matter' of the particular kind of industrial or commercial property which sets out the limits of the protection which may be justified. (70) According to this concept the effect of the exercise of such right must not exceed those attached to it and justified by its nature and reason of existence. (71)

By adopting the concept of the specific subject matter for the purpose of determining the limits of the power of the States to grant exclusive rights regard must be given to the reason for granting such an exclusive right and whether what was done was reasonably necessary in order to secure a legitimate objective. If the objective is legitimate then the question arises whether it could be done equally well in another way which would jeopardise the Treaty objectives less. The application of this concept, thus, challenges the absolute power of the States to grant special or exclusive rights and leads to a position similar to the one advocated above.

Therefore, it may be concluded that the grant of an exclusive right, except with respect to imports and exports of goods, is not, as such, contrary to the rules of the Treaty in the sense that it does not constitute 'a measure contrary to those rules' under article 90 para 1. However, in each case an examination must take place of whether such right contravenes any of the rules of the Treaty and, if so, whether such contravention is justified by the general principles and objectives or the particular provisions which provide for certain exemptions from the Treaty (e.g. articles 36 and 90 para 2). In doing so respect must be paid to the principle which has often been proclaimed by the ECJ, that all exemptions from the Treaty rules must be narrowly construed. (72)

1.5 <u>Analysis of the expression '... Member States shall neither enact nor maintain in force any measures contrary to the rules contained in the Treaty and in particular articles 85-94 and 7'</u>

For the purpose of delimiting the application of article 90 para 1 it is important first, to examine the notion of the term 'measures' and define the circumstances under which the State may be deemed to be enacting or maintaining in force such measures and, second, to consider when are those measures contrary to the rules of the Treaty and the ones specifically referred to.

1.5.a <u>Definition of the term 'measures'</u>

For a more complete treatment of the subject regard must be given to two other articles which also contain the term 'measure'. Those are article 5 para 2 of the Treaty, which provides that Member States shall abstain from any measure which could jeopardise the attainment of the Treaty objectives and of which article 90 para 1 is a particular application, and article 30 which prohibits quantitative restrictions or 'measures' having equivalent effect. In view of the fact that all these articles concern and actually prohibit state measures which are contrary to the objectives or particular rules of the Treaty a consistent interpretation of the term must be attempted. This is also made necessary by the fact that those articles are often likely to interact in specific circumstances in the sense that the same state measures may contravene more than one of them.

As all terms of the Treaty the term 'measure' must be interpreted in accordance with the objective of article 90 para 1 which is to prevent Member States from using their influence on public undertakings and those to which they grant special or exclusive rights, on the one hand, in order to avoid their own obligations under the Treaty and, on the other, in order to create unequal conditions between private and public undertakings.

Since the exercise of such influence and control is made possible by the existence of close relations between the States and those undertakings, which make infractions easier to commit, (1) certain commentators have maintained the view that the central issue of article 90 para 1 is not the definition of the 'undertakings' to which it applies but that of 'measures'. (2) In this sense the term 'measure' includes all those acts of influence or control that the States may take with respect to the undertakings with which they have close relations without resorting to legal compulsory acts. If it is the dominant influence of the State over a certain undertaking which is in doubt the very existence of a measure may supply evidence of it. (3) The position that the definition of the term 'public undertaking' of article 90 is based on the notion of measures enables the application of article 90 para 1 to a very wide range of undertakings which the State may control or influence without necessarily owning. (4) This view, which shall be further developed below, is also consistent with the spirit of the Treaty and the objectives of articles 90 para 1. (5)

Almost all commentators agree that in order to attain the objectives of article 90 para 1 the term 'measures' (6) must be interpreted in the largest possible way (7) but there is wide disagreement as to what is included in the term. We may say that (8) 'measure' is any legal or factual influence of the State on public undertakings and those with special or exclusive rights. There are, therefore, included all legislative and administrative acts, Court judgments (9), acts of private law, such as the exercise of shareholders' rights, recommendations (10), mere hints as well as exemptions or approvals. (11)

There are three areas in which disagreement has arisen and which must, therefore, be cleared up in delimiting the term: first, whether acts of private law and mere recommendations or hints by the administration may be classified as measures. Most commentators supporting the inclusion of such exercise of pressure in the definition of 'measures' also believe that the State is responsible for ensuring the application of those provisions. They would, thus, hold the States liable for mere inaction.

Second, certain commentators distinguish between measures adopted by the State in its capacity as public authority ('compulsory' measures) imposing a legal obligation upon public undertakings, and other internal measures of non-obligatory form which a State may take by virtue of its influence and control over certain undertakings. These commentators refuse to consider the former as falling under article 90 para 1. (12) Such a view, although well argued, may lead to inequality and discrepancies between Member States.

Third, few commentators, such as Mestmäcker (13), are willing to extend the application of article 90 para 1 to all laws of general character fixing prices or assigning quotas, etc., irrespective of whether these laws apply to private undertakings or both private and public.

State recommendations and hints. With respect to the first area of discord the view that managerial instructions of the State as shareholder or state recommendations or hints are not measures cannot be maintained and finds very little support. (14) If such internal measures were not included in the definition it would be easy for the Member States to avoid their obligations under the Treaty. (15) If public undertakings are distinguished from private because of the influence that the States may exercise on the former without recourse to authoritative acts, then, it is automatically derived that the drafters of the Treaty could not be referring in article 90 para 1 to authoritative acts alone.

Our view also finds support in the definition of 'measures' adopted by the Commission for the purposes of the Commission Directive No 70/50 of 22.12.69 (16) based on article 33 para 7, as well as on the ECJ decision in the 'Buy Irish' case. (17) Although it is not within the Commission's competence to define the term 'measures' the provisions of that Directive have often been cited, apparently with approval, by the Court (18) and the definition of the term 'measures' contained therein is authoritative and indicative. According to the Commission's view 'for the purposes of article 30 et seq 'measures' means laws, regulations, administrative provisions, administrative practices, and all instruments issuing from a public authority, including recommendations' (19). The French text actually uses the term 'incitation', an 'incitation' in French being even less authoritative than a recommendation. The directive goes on to explain that "recommendation' means any instrument issuing from a public authority which, while not legally binding on the addressees thereof, causes them to pursue a certain conduct'. A similar attitude was adopted by the ECJ in the 'Buy Irish' case. In reply to the Irish government's argument that measures must be binding provisions emanating from a public authority, the Court held that 'even measures adopted by the government of a Member State which do not have a binding effect may be capable of influencing the conduct of traders and consumers in that State and thus of frustrating the aims of the

Community as set out in article 2 and enlarged upon in article 3' (20).

The obvious conclusion to be drawn from the above is that if state actions of non-binding nature fall under the definition of measures of article 30 they do even more so in the case of article 90, the reason for the inclusion in the Treaty of the latter being precisely the influence which the public authorities are able to exert over the commercial decisions of public undertakings. That influence may be exerted on the basis of financial participation or of the rules governing the management of the undertaking'. (21) It does not, therefore, have to be in the form of a legally binding provision.

A serious argument of the few commentators who support the non-inclusion of managerial instructions is that a similar decision by the president of a private concern does not amount to a violation. (22) However, according to ECJ caselaw (23) the acts of a subsidiary may be imputed to the parent in circumstances in which the subsidiary is not autonomous and is under the influence of the parent. The difference with article 90 para 1 is, however, that while a parent company of a private undertaking might be held liable only if it actually exercised its power to influence or control we would also include, as we shall explain in the following sub-section, in the notion of measures even mere inaction on the part of the State and consider the State liable for failing to prevent behaviour of a public undertaking which is contrary to the Treaty. (24)

Inaction. It is assumed that the power and possibility that the State has to influence certain undertakings gives rise to a positive duty to intervene when such undertakings contravene the Treaty rules. (25) The obligation to ensure that public undertakings do not contravene the Treaty stretches the wording of article 90 since it treats failure to act as equivalent to maintenance. Nevertheless, it is also supported by the Commission because it complies with the spirit of article 90 para 1. (26) Thus, in its 6th Report on Competition Policy (27) the Commission stated that it is indispensable that Member States ensure that the behaviour of public undertakings is consistent with the Treaty. The Commission also confirmed that article 90 para 3 allows it to act where a Member State, while possessing the necessary authority, fails to cause a public undertaking to put an end to objectionable practices, i.e. practices which, had they been engaged in by the State itself would have constituted an infringement of the Treaty.

Unfortunately though, most statements made by the Commission or the Court are vague and equivocal and there has been very little discussion on the implications of this view. (28) The wording of the above mentioned statement of the Commission in its 6th Report on Competition Policy could be interpreted to mean that Member States must only intervene when public undertakings engage in practices which Member States are prohibited from engaging in and that they are under no duty to stop an infringement of the rules applicable to undertakings. However, such interpretation must be rejected because it creates unreasonable distinctions. At the same time, no definite conclusions may be drawn from Advocate General Reischl's statement in the Transparency Directive case where he considered the financial relations which are to be regarded as measures within the meaning of article 90 para 1 as including 'any action or failure to act in the financial sphere', (29) the term 'failure to act' probably being used within the limited scope of financial relations. Nonetheless, even general statements, such as the one made by the ECJ in the same case that 'article 90 concerns only undertakings for whose actions the States must take special responsibility by reason of the influence which they may exert' (30), add support to our view that article 90 para 1 imposes a positive duty upon Member States to ensure that the Treaty is not contravened.

Vandencasteele (31) would restrict the obligation of Member States to avoid that the undertakings which they control violate the Treaty only to cases where such undertakings are not autonomous. He believes that to hold Member States liable for mere inaction would create unjustifiable discrimination and maintains that a positive obligation of Member States must be rather based on article 5 para 1 which imposes a duty upon Member States to take to Court the undertakings which so contravene the Treaty.

We believe that the problem with Vandencasteele's position is that, in most cases, it would be impossible to say whether an undertaking which the Member State may potentially influence or control is being managed autonomously. In fact, rather than saying that article 90 para 1 makes Member States liable for the autonomous behaviour of public undertakings it is better to adopt the view which Marenco suggested that if undertakings act contrary to their business interests state intervention is to be presumed. (32)

We may, therefore, conclude that article 90 para 1 must be interpreted to give rise to a positive duty to act and, therefore, also to cover mere failure by the State to put an end to infringements of the Treaty committed by the undertakings which it controls, for the following reasons: first, the difficulty of proving that pressure has been exercised and, second, that some degree of state influence and pressure may always be presumed in view of the fact that the appointment of top managers of public undertakings as well as their financing is dependent upon the State and the state ministers. The same applies to undertakings which have been granted exclusive or special rights by the State since the continuation of such rights also depends upon it. A more restrictive interpretation of the term 'measure' would enable a State to avoid the effects of article 90 by exercising indirect pressure only.

The only disadvantage of the above interpretation of article 90 is that it might make the State interfere with the management of a public undertaking even in circumstances in which it were not willing to do so, in order to avoid a possible liability under that article. Moreover, article 90 might provide an excuse to a state minister for imposing his view upon a manager of a public enterprise who wishes to run the latter as a private enterprise. Nevertheless, in view of the fact that governments almost always declare that their public enterprises are governed as private ones while in fact they do interfere with their management, an extensive interpretation of act or measure is preferable despite the above mentioned danger. In the last resort in each case it is up to the EEC Commission to decide whether for a certain infringement a decision must be addressed to the State under article 90 or to the enterprises concerned under article 85 or 86.

General laws and regulations. The second area of discord is whether legal measures of compulsory character, such as general laws and regulations, should be included in the definition or whether the definition should be limited to public acts and acts of private law relating to the management of public undertakings by public authorities as proprietors.

Pappalardo (33) supports the view that article 90 para 1 does not apply to 'compulsory' measures imposing a legal obligation on the ground that it is illogical to treat a legal compulsory cartel between public undertakings differently from one imposed by the State on private undertakings or both public and private. Therefore, according to this view measure is every state instruction, recommendation or hint addressed to one or more undertakings, by which the State (because of close relations) may determine its or their acts. (34) The measures must concern 'public undertakings' and, in order to fall under article 90, must be easy to adopt, easier than a measure of the same effect adopted in connection with private undertakings. Those measures must arise from the special relationship of supervision and control between the State and undertakings, which exceeds the general opportunity available to Member States with regard to private undertakings. (35)

Marenco, who is of the same view as Pappalardo, admits that the position that legal acts should not be included in the definition of measures presents special problems with reference to the English text of article 90 para 1, which contains the word enact. (36) In the four original languages more neutral words are used (treffen, edictent, emanano, nehmen). Nevertheless, he believes that this restriction is not inherent in the expression used but rather in the raison d'etre of the provision. He, therefore, maintains that if Member States take public law measures concerning public undertakings either (a) these measures are illegal also for private undertakings - which means that the prohibition has its source in another provision and not in 90 para 1 - or (b) these provisions are legal for private undertakings in which case they are also legal for public undertakings and article 90 para 1 is again non-applicable. (37)

Notwithstanding the apparent logic of those arguments and the obvious inconsistency of the EEC Treaty in this respect (38) we disagree with the above view because it runs the danger of leading to an unequal application of article 90 para 1 to Member States since the responsibility of the latter could vary depending on their internal administrative or constitutional structure. (39) It may be the practice in Member States, as it is in France, to issue directives to public undertakings by means of public law acts and in particular by way of decrees or government regulations. (40) If Pappalardo's and Marenco's view were adopted those directives would not fall under the definition of 'measures' in article 90 para 1.

We believe that the exclusion of public law acts of a compulsory character from the definition of measures of article 90 para 1 does not mean that the State may never be held liable for adopting legal acts or regulations which have the effect of distorting competition. Those state measures are potentially prohibited under the combined effects of article 5 para 2 and articles 85 and 86. In such case, however, the use of article 90 para 3 would not be available to the Commission as is actually the case with general measures concerning private undertakings. (41) Furthermore, as we shall explain in Chapter Four, the responsibility of Member States for legal acts and regulations which have the effect of distorting competition has not as yet been sufficiently determined by the Court and the Commission. In spite of the views developed in this thesis, such state legislation concerning exclusively public undertakings might thus remain in force and frustrate the Treaty objectives.

Although we agree that it is somehow inconsistent to treat state measures concerning exclusively public undertakings differently from similar measures concerning both public and private ones, for practical and theoretical reasons we believe that such state legislation or regulations adopted exclusively with respect to public undertakings are included in the definition of 'measures'.

First, from a practical viewpoint if legal and regulatory acts were not covered by article 90 para 1 the objectives of this article would run the risk of being frustrated whenever the State exercised its control over the public undertakings through such acts. In addition to the fact that Member States could thus circumvent article 90 para 3 by giving orders and instructions through public law instruments, the objectives of article 90 para 1 would be also jeopardised by the differences which presently exist between Member States in the management of their public undertakings.

Second, from a theoretical viewpoint we may say that article 90 para 1 was actually intended to apply to the activities of the Member States when acting through the medium of the undertakings which they control, independently of the form in which such activity or control is exercised. What matters is that the relevant measures are adopted exclusively with respect to those undertakings which the State controls and through which it may, as a result, operate in the market.

Pappalardo believes that legal measures forcing separately upon public undertakings a certain anticompetitive behaviour are more theoretical than practical and may only be found in connection with special or exclusive rights, (for example in cases where the State grants a concession by imposing a restriction at the same time). (42) However, assuming that this is true Pappalardo, apparently, did not take those undertakings to which the State grants special or exclusive rights into consideration when excluding legal acts from the definition. (43) Indeed if he had and provided that a grant of such right (which has been held by the ECJ in Sacchi (44) not to be in itself contrary to the rules of the Treaty) coincides with 'a measure' under article 90 para 1 Pappalardo could not have excluded general legislation from the definition.

The ECJ has not taken a clear stand on the issue. The fact that the grant of an exclusive or special right has been held not to be contrary to the Treaty (45) does not mean that such grant is not a measure within the context of 90. Statements such as the one made by the ECJ in the Van Ameyde case that '(by granting an exclusive right) a Member State does not lay down any measure contrary to the rules of the Treaty in particular article 90 in conjunction with articles 85 and 86 so long as such exclusivity does not conflict with the freedom of the insurer ... to rely on another specialized undertaking' (46) may be interpreted to mean that such grant of exclusive right is, in any case, a measure even if not contrary to the Treaty.

Laws and regulations of general character, e.g. price fixing, assigning quotas etc. The third issue which shall be discussed and which is diametrically opposed to the view of Pappalardo discussed above, is whether laws and regulations of general character fixing prices or assigning quotas etc. fall under article 90 para 1 even if they do not apply exclusively to public undertakings. We believe that this interpretation of article 90 para 1, which has been advocated by Mestmäcker (47), would subject to this paragraph all sovereign acts of state, such an extensive application thereof being beyond its wording and contrary to the will of the drafters. According to Hochbaum the importance of article 5 para 2 would be thus diminished and the Commission would find itself with great power to correct the economic policies of Member States, such development being contrary to the spirit of the Treaty. (48)

General laws amount to direct intervention of the authorities in the economic order and must be examined exclusively under articles 30 or 5 para 2 in the same way as compulsory cartels among private undertakings. (49) The difference between articles 30 and 90 para 1 is that while the former concerns acts of the authority of whatever nature creating a general obligation (50), the latter applies to laws concerning strictly public undertakings or undertakings to which the State grants special or exclusive rights. Article 90 para 1 is a particular application of article 5 para 2 in the area of public undertakings and undertakings with special or exclusive rights and, therefore, regulates only the activities of the Member States with respect to those undertakings which they control.

This does not mean that article 90 para 1 may not be applied in conjunction with article 30 to state measures concerning public undertakings which have an effect contrary thereto, article 90 para 1 being a 'renvoi' rule for the entire Treaty. However, it is inconsistent with the general principles of interpretation and the wording of this article to resort to it in order to prohibit state measures to which article 30 specifically applies.

In this respect it may be noted that, in fact, the notion of 'measures' in article 90 para 1 is wider than the one in article 30. Except for the fact that article 30 only applies to measures of equivalent effect to quantitative restrictions while article 90 para 1 refers to all the Treaty rules the latter also comprises, in addition to express state acts, the exercise of influence and abstention.

1.5.b When are measures 'contrary to the rules of the Treaty and in particular articles 85-94 and 7'

The next step is to determine when state measures, in the sense explained above, are contrary to the rules of the Treaty and in particular to those rules provided for in articles 85-94 and article 7. The particular reference to articles 85-94 and 7 may also be considered as indicative of the double objective of article 90 para 1, on the one hand to subject Member States to the competition rules contained in articles 85-94 and, on the other, to prevent Member States from discriminating on the basis of nationality behind the facade of their public undertakings. Article 7 may be deemed to be the common denominator of all the rules contained in Part II of the Treaty which are applicable to States and prohibit any restriction to the free movement of goods, persons, services and capital.

The notion of measures in article 90 para 1 covers two categories of acts. (51) First, those acts which are themselves inconsistent with specific rules, such acts being the granting of an aid, privilege or other facility, and, second, those acts which, though not in themselves contrary to any particular Treaty provision, enable or impose upon undertakings a behaviour contrary to the Treaty. While with respect to the first category of acts the violation is derived from the measure itself, with respect to the second category of acts it is the result which is brought about which is inconsistent with the Treaty.

We believe that at least the illegality of state measures of the first category is not dependent on a behaviour of public undertakings contrary to the Treaty. (52) Even if certain authors have, wrongly, doubted the usefulness of the third paragraph of article 90 in the field of aids, mainly in the light of the existence of article 93 para 2 (53), the subjection to article 90 of those financial benefits and guarantees granted by the States to public undertakings has also been affirmed by the Transparency Directive the legality of which has been upheld by the ECJ. (54) As Advocate General Reischl remarked in connection with the above mentioned Directive, 'if 90 para 1 is to fulfil its purpose at all, such measures must in principle be regarded as including any application of funds or any grant of monetary advantages to public undertakings by the agent of public authorities, that is so to say any action or failure to act in the financial sphere'. (55) According to the ECJ the reason for the inclusion in the Treaty of article 90 is precisely the influence which the public authorities are able to exert over the commercial decisions of public undertakings on the basis of financial participation or of the rules governing the management of the undertakings. Therefore, by choosing the same criteria in performance of its duty of surveillance under 90 para 3 the Commission remained within the limits of its discretion. (56)

The decision of the ECJ in the Transparency Directive case therefore seems to have overruled the position held by certain legal commentators (e.g. Nicolaysen) (57) that aids accorded by the State or through state resources to public undertakings must be judged exclusively under article 92 et seq. Although we admit that in clear cases of aids granted by state authorities the procedure of article 93 para 2 must be followed as being specifically applicable, we think that state aids may also fall under the definition of measures of article 90. Article 90 has enabled the Commission to adopt a complementary procedure in order to investigate and detect the financial relations between the State and public undertakings, this being a necessary prerequisite for the application of the state aid provisions.

Article 90 is, therefore, complementary and subsidiary in character in relation to the provisions of article 92 et seq. of the Treaty. (58) As Advocate General Reischl remarked in the Transparency Directive case, 'if the provision is to have any meaning at all it must mean that on account of the special features of state aids paid to public undertakings, the Commission is to have a power which goes beyond the competence conferred on it in Article 93 and is not identical with the power granted to the Council under article 94 of the Treaty.' (59)

Moreover, article 90 para 1 is a necessary renvoi rule when such aids are granted by public undertakings or undertakings with special or exclusive rights which Member States influence or control. Nicolaysen (60), who interprets article 90 para 1 exclusively as such a renvoi rule, would apply article 90 para 1 in connection with aids only in the case where the public undertaking which the State influences or controls actually proceeds to the granting of aid in contravention of the specific provisions of article 92. In this case behaviour of the undertaking contrary to the Treaty is not a necessary prerequisite. Whether a violation of article 92 must actually be established before article 90 para 1 may be deemed contravened is part of a wider controversy among supporters of a wide or narrow interpretation of article 90 para 1, which shall be discussed below.

In addition to the above, Nicolaysen does not envisage the application of article 90 para 1 in circumstances where the public undertaking grants an aid through the means of state funds, article 92 being alone applicable. However, such distinction, with which we disagree, is, as he himself admits, almost impossible to make.

The main point of controversy arises in connection with state acts which, though not in themselves inconsistent with specific Treaty provisions, give rise to results which are contrary to the general principles and rules of the Treaty.

This controversy actually reflects two conflicting ideologies which are trying to accommodate themselves within the framework of the EEC; one which believes in the operation of the market free of any government intervention and another which considers that economic development as well as the Treaty objectives may only be achieved by active state involvement.

Those who wish to see state activity in the economic field as restricted as possible believe that a wide interpretation is necessary in order to give effect to the objectives of article 90 para 1. They, therefore, consider as a measure contrary to the rules of the Treaty any juridicial or factual intervention by the Member States which has a result contrary to the Treaty, a contravention on the part of the undertakings not being necessary. (61)

At the other end of the controversy are those who believe that the scope of article 90 para 1 should not be overestimated, this provision being a mere reaffirmation in the context of public undertakings of the Community loyalty principle of article 5 para 2. (62) Supporters of this restrictive view are willing to consider article 90 para 1 as a simple renvoi rule. They believe that an extensive interpretation implies that a laissez-faire ideology was actually adopted by all Member States allowing only Community organs to deviate within the scope of their limited powers, such implication being unacceptable to them. (63) While accepting that article 90 is only a reaffirmation of article 5 para 2 in the context of public undertakings we disagree with a restrictive interpretation of either article 90 para 1 or article 5 para 2 for the reasons which we shall explain below in this chapter as well as in Chapter Four.

Those who favour the use of public undertakings in the national plan believe that Member States must be free to decide whether to allow public undertakings to be autonomous or to suppress competition. (64) In support of this position the provisions of the Treaty relevant to economic policy, i.e. articles 2, 6, 105 para 1 and 145 are being invoked. It is argued that these provisions would serve no purpose if one economic policy were propagated by the Treaty (planification or liberal economy) and that, on the contrary, those articles show that it was agreed to leave a wide discretion to Member States and to attempt only a limited coordination of national policies. (65)

The academic differences may be traced back to the

basic question of the autonomous or non-autonomous interpretation of article 90. (66) Is it sufficient for the application of article 90 that state measures have the same effect as an agreement between undertakings or does article 90 cover only measures intended to bring about agreements between undertakings or other behaviour by undertakings which is prohibited by articles 85 and 86?

Nicolaysen (67), who actually advocates the adoption of a narrow interpretation, shows that both views are compatible with the text and even expresses the suspicion that article 90 was intended to cover the differences existing between Member States when the Treaty was signed.

According to a strict interpretation article 90 para 1 is a simple renvoi rule and, as far as the infringement is concerned, subsidiary in character. (68) On the basis of the above, this article forbids state instructions which prescribe or lead to the conclusion of an agreement or concerted practice, the reference in article 90 para 1 to other clauses showing that the state measures must be contrary to specific dispositions. (69)

Nicolaysen would carry the above interpretation to the extreme by arguing that a compulsory cartel is not contrary to article 90 para 1 since, in view of the compulsion, no agreement may be said to have been made and no infringement of article 85 may, thereby, be established. Apart from our general criticism of the restrictive interpretation of article 90 para 1, which we shall develop below, we believe that such extreme formal legalism with regard to article 85 leads to perverse results (70) and its adoption would make article 90 para 1 lose a great deal of its effectiveness. Nicolaysen's view makes the particular reference to articles 85-94 virtually superfluous, since the conditions of article 85 could never be satisfied in those cases in which certain anticompetitive behaviour has been imposed upon public undertakings by means of compulsion. The fact, which Nicolaysen invokes in support of his view, that public undertakings remain obliged to observe articles 7, 30, 34 and 86, is no sufficient guarantee for the maintenance of a system in which competition is not distorted. Even if there is some value in the argument that there is no real competition between public undertakings (71) the problem is not normally one of competition between public undertakings. It is, rather, a question of fair competition between public and private undertakings, the latter often being suppressed for the benefit of the former.

According to a wide interpretation article 90 para 1 prohibits any state measure taken in relation to public undertakings, which is liable to produce effects analogous to those caused by direct infringement of the Treaty by the undertakings. (72) The rationale is that Member States are not permitted to bring about by their own influence results which individuals are prohibited from adopting. (73) An agreement or concerted practice between undertakings is not a necessary prerequisite and for article 90 para 1 to apply it is sufficient to verify that the other conditions have been established. (74) Deringer would extend the application of article 90 para 1 even further than other supporters of the above interpretation are probably willing to. He has put forward the view that the term 'contrary' is wider than 'contravening' and that, therefore, for the application of article 90 no particular infringement is necessary; a consequence brought about by a state measure which is not desired by the Treaty would be sufficient. (75)

We are also of the opinion that a wide interpretation of article 90 para 1 is necessary for the achievement of its objectives and would, therefore, apply article 90 para 1 to the following: first, when the State prescribes or leads to behaviour contrary to the competition rules or the other Treaty provisions.

Second, to mere failure by the State to prevent an infringement of articles 85 and 86 by public undertakings from being committed. In this case, as in all cases where anticompetitive behaviour is not being imposed upon the undertakings by means of legislative or administrative measures, the undertakings committing the infringement may also be held liable. When the issue arises at Community level it will be up to the Commission to decide, after taking into account all relevant factors, whether to act against the undertakings under regulation 17 of 1962 or address a decision to the Member State concerned by virtue of its power under article 90 para 3.

Third, this being the main point of difference with a restrictive interpretation, to measures adopted with respect to public undertakings which, without leaving room for independent behaviour by the public undertakings themselves, produce effects equivalent to the ones brought about by concerted practices or agreements between undertakings. Such measures may be state regulations fixing prices, imposing compulsory cartels, etc.

Such an extensive interpretation of the term 'measures' under article 90 para 1 has been criticized on several grounds.

First, it has been maintained that to interpret article 90 para 1 as prohibiting state measures bringing about results forbidden by articles 85 and 86 is equivalent to saying that Member States are liable if they violate article 3(f). According to these critics articles 85 and 86 do not contain any conditions other than the behaviour of undertakings and the distortion of competition which need to be satisfied, the effect on intracommunity trade being a necessary prerequisite in all cases. Such direct and independent application of article 3(f) is, however, disputed, article 3(f) not being capable of establishing an independent prohibition but being capable merely of anticipating the competition rules and of assistance to their interpretation. (76)

Second, it has been argued that if article 3(f) were so applicable it would be hard to explain why the Treaty contains specific prohibitions such as those relating to free circulation etc., since those would be absorbed in the general prohibition on distortion of competition. It has been said that if it were so article 90 para 1 would not need to refer to any other article of the Treaty except for the competition rules. (77)

Third, in support of their argument the critics of a wide interpretation invoke the ECJ caselaw holding that national regulations imposing minimum or fixed prices are compatible with the EEC rules in so far as prices are not fixed at a level which makes the sale of goods imported from other Member States impossible or more difficult from the sale of similar domestic goods. (78)

The above mentioned arguments against a wide interpretation of the term 'measures' (which shall also be criticized in connection with state liability under article 5 para 2 in combination with the competition rules) in so far as article 90 para 1 is concerned fail to take into account the following elements: First, the fact that a State is liable under article 90 para 1 for acts or instructions etc. in connection with public undertakings, which are likely to produce the results which are prohibited to undertakings, does not imply an autonomous application of article 90 para 1. As Pappalardo rightly remarks (79), even if the violation of articles 85 and 86 by the State is an anomaly it must be accepted that it is inherent in the system established by article 90. The fact that measures must concern public undertakings is an additional guarantee against an unduly extensive application of this article and the interference with the state regulation of the economy must not be overestimated. There is no doubt that article 90 para 1 is a renvoi rule, complementary to the other provisions of the Treaty, and can only be applied in connection with them. (80) Moreover, the particular reference in article 90 para 1 to articles 85-94 indicates precisely that the drafters of the Treaty intended primarily and specifically to subject the Member States to the competition rules.

However, it must be understood that, in view of the fact that the relevant articles of competition apply to undertakings, their application in conjunction with article 90 para 1 automatically implies that the prerequisites (such as agreements etc.) which can only exist in cases of contravention of those rules by undertakings, must be dropped. As the Commission itself replied to the parliamentary question of Graziosi and Sabatini, M.E.P., articles 85 and 86 are not applicable to legal provisions but if the milk centres (which were the subject of the question) were considered as undertakings within article 90 para 1 it remained necessary to examine the compatibility of the Italian legislation with article 90 in connection with articles 85 and 86. (81)

As to the reference in article 90 para 1 to the other Treaty rules applicable to state measures, the same argument applies. The specific provisions of Part II comprising the Foundations of the Community apply with respect to state measures having an adverse effect on the free movement of goods, persons, services and capital and article 90 para 1 is only of assistance in cases in which Member States try to evade their obligations under the Treaty through the means of their public undertakings.

With respect to price regulations, these have been held consistent with EEC law as long as imports are not directly or indirectly hindered. Pappalardo, while admitting that it is difficult to fix general criteria in order to see whether a measure concerns public undertakings, believes that he can draw a clear distinction between price regulation and the attribution of part of the market, the former not falling under article 90 para 1. (82) Perhaps a better view, which would also be consistent with ECJ caselaw upholding state measures regulating prices, would be to make the following distinctions: first, general laws imposing maximum, minimum or fixed prices and applicable to both national and imported products should probably be judged under article 30 or, possibly, under article 5 para 2. Article 90 would be inapplicable in any case, such laws, by definition, also concerning private undertakings.

Second, state measures concerning public undertakings and having the effect of regulating prices in a way which is to the disadvantage of private undertakings should rather be examined under the competition rules and therefore article 90 para 1. With respect to such measures concerning public undertakings alone a further distinction could be made between those imposing a maximum price and those imposing fixed or minimum prices.

Regarding the former there would normally be no problem unless they have the effect of bringing about unfair competition. Such would, for example, be the case if maximum prices were fixed at a level which is so low that sale could be made only at a loss and if public undertakings were able to do so benefiting from state subsidies.

On the other hand state regulations concerning public undertakings alone and setting fixed or minimum prices would have the same effect as an agreement or concerted practice under article 85 and could therefore be prohibited by virtue of article 90 para 3. It is true that similar price regulations applying also to private undertakings could only be apprehended through article 5 para 2, this being an incoherence resulting from the structure of the Treaty, which shall be further discussed below.

We must note that the European Court has not until now directly dealt within the context of article 90 para 1 with state legislative or regulatory measures bringing about an effect equivalent to those prohibited to undertakings under articles 85 and 86. The only relevant cases which came before the ECJ concerned legal acts and regulations of general character, such as the fixing of maximum or minimum prices or price margins. These measures, being of general character, did not give rise to the application of article 90 para 1 but had to be assessed under article 5 para 2 in combination with the competition rules. Those cases are being analysed in detail in the relevant chapter. Since, however, we believe that article 90 para 1 is only a reaffirmation of article 5 para 2 in the field of public undertakings and those to which the State grants special or exclusive rights our views, as developed in that chapter, are also relevant for the interpretation and application of article 90 para 1.

2. DEROGATION FROM THE COMPETITION RULES: ARTICLE 90 PARA 2

Contrary to the first paragraph of article 90, which is addressed to Member States, the second paragraph, being more consistent with the title of the section wherein it is contained - this being 'Rules applying to undertakings' - is addressed to those undertakings which are entrusted with the operation of services of general economic interest or have the character of a revenue producing monopoly. For those undertakings article 90 para 2 permits a derogation from the Treaty rules by providing that they shall be subject to the rules contained in the Treaty, in particular to the rules on competition, in so far as the application of such rules does not obstruct the performance, in law or in fact, of the particular tasks assigned to them. The same section further stipulates that the development of trade must not be affected to such an extent as would be contrary to the interest of the Community.

2.1 <u>Object of article 90 para 2 and comparison with 90 para 1</u>

As we have already indicated in connection with paragraph 1 the fact that paragraphs 1 and 2 are addressed to different persons and concern different categories of undertakings indicates a certain heterogeneity and lack of symmetry and has posed delicate problems of interpretation. (1) Being the result of a real compromise (2) the wording of article 90 admittedly offers room for both the view that article 90 is intended to provide a safeguard against the public sector causing distortion of competition and its opposite which holds that the rules of competition should impede as little as possible the proper functioning of the public sector as an instrument of socio-economic policy. According to this latter view, article 90 para 2 is, first and foremost, a safeguard on behalf of the public sector. (3)

Nevertheless, despite the fervent debate that preceded the adoption of article 90, further consideration of the role of the state-controlled undertakings in the Treaty shows that its significance cannot be reduced to a simple question of the relative weight of the two paragraphs. (4) After all, the entire Treaty has been the result of a compromise and article 90, as most articles of the Treaty, is expressed in general terms in order to accommodate the different ideologies, traditions and practices of the Member States. Its actual application and content have been left to be determined by the practice of the Commission and the caselaw of the Court.

Moreover, as will be shown below, the lack of symmetry between the two paragraphs is only apparent. In fact, article 90 makes a consistent whole enshrining the objective of the drafters to promote the interests of the Community while, at the same time, safeguarding the economic interests of each Member State to accomplish certain particular tasks.

While, therefore, article 90 para 1 makes clear that the public sector is subject to the rules of the Treaty on an equal footing with the private one and considers Member States responsible for the behaviour of the undertakings which they control, article 90 para 2 allows for an exception from those rules in certain limited circumstances where the performance of tasks of general economic interest so requires. However, the primary obligation even of those undertakings entrusted with the operation of services of general economic interest or having the character of a revenue producing monopoly, is to obey the rules of the Treaty. A derogation is allowed only if the performance of the task assigned to them is made impossible by the application of those rules and only to the extent that the development of trade is not affected to a degree that would be contrary to the interest of the Community. The above is derived both from the first paragraph of article 90 and the wording and positive terms in which the second paragraph is formulated.

While recognizing the supremacy of the Treaty rule it was believed that certain undertakings entrusted with the operation of services of general economic interest could not perform their specific duties if they had to obey the rules of the Treaty. (5) There was a need for a realistic appraisal of the impact of the rules of the Treaty and article 90 para 2 was designed to avoid unduly offending national sensitivities (6) by recognizing the right of each State to satisfy its fiscal or public interest objectives through monopoly situations. (7) The object of the clause was, therefore, to regulate the conflict between the public interest to accomplish a mission and the interest of the Community. (8)

It is, therefore, apparent that paragraphs 1 and 2 are closely connected, the exception of paragraph 2 being implicitly available also to Member States and covering to some extent a certain type of activity already subject to paragraph 1. Although article 90 para 2 is, on its face, addressed to undertakings and not to Member States, both the undertakings cited and Member States may resort to this provision. (9) This paragraph limits the obligation of Member States with respect to the undertakings referred to therein in the same way as it limits the application of the Treaty to the undertakings themselves. It, thus, enables Member States to enact measures necessary for the accomplishment, in law or in fact, of the specific missions of the undertakings. (10)

In fact, it depends on who is the addressee of the article from which 90 para 2 allows an exception. As paragraph 1, by its reference to the entire Treaty, indirectly subjects public undertakings and those with special or exclusive rights to those rules of the Treaty imposing obligations upon Member States so does paragraph 2 allow for an exception from the application of those rules to the addressees thereof, if the relevant conditions are fulfilled. For example, an exception from the application of the provisions on aids could only be invoked by Member States, those being the addressees of those provisions. (11)

Furthermore, notwithstanding the different terminology used for the undertakings covered by the first and second paragraphs, it seems that most undertakings to which paragraph 2 is addressed also fall under paragraph 1, the opposite not being necessarily true.

As has been rightly affirmed by the ECJ in its decision in the BRT II case, article 90 para 2 covers both public and private undertakings with or without legal personality. (12) Nonetheless, if a wide definition of public undertakings is adopted - according to which 'public undertaking' means an undertaking the economic behaviour of which public authorities may influence in law or in fact - it appears clearly that most undertakings under article 90 para 2 are public or otherwise accompanied by the grant of special rights. (13) It is in fact difficult to imagine that public authorities would entrust such a task without keeping a power of control. (14) It is possible, therefore, to say that the obligation which is imposed on Member States and undertakings with special or exclusive rights by article 90 para 1 is compensated by the possibility to resort to paragraph 2 of the same article, thus reestablishing an equilibrium. (15)

As was mentioned above, even if undertakings covered by 90 para 2 almost automatically fall under paragraph 1 the opposite is not true. (16) The fact that an undertaking is public or has been granted by the State special or exclusive rights does not mean that it has also been entrusted with the operation of services of general economic interest or that it has been assigned a task the performance of which might result in contravention of the Treaty rules.

However, the right of Member States to give priority to their national interests is not limited. Both the positive form in which article 90 para 2 is formulated and the supremacy of Community interest provided therein indicate that a strict definition of the provision should be adopted. A strict interpretation of this same paragraph has also been advocated by the ECJ in its decision in the BRT case. (17) Such view is also consistent with the decisions of the Commission and the caselaw of the Court with respect to all the articles of the Treaty which allow an exemption from its principles and rules. (18)

Article 90 para 2 cannot, therefore, be applied extensively or by analogy. (19) Its application requires an examination of facts and circumstances in the light of the legal interpretation of its terms. Unfortunately there are very few cases in which either the Commission or the Court have dealt with the issue, thus perpetuating the ambiguity of this section.

2.2 Definition of the terms of article 90 para 2

Having, thus, determined the objectives and general framework of article 90 para 2 an attempt to define or, at least, delimit its terms shall follow. In doing so regard must be given to the principle which has often been reiterated by the ECJ that exceptions or derogations from the rules of the Treaty must be strictly construed.

'Entrusted'

It has been affirmed several times by the ECJ (20) and is the prevailing view among academics (21) that an undertaking (either public or private) coming under article 90 para 2 must be entrusted with the operation of services of general economic interest by an act of public authority. According to the ECJ in the BRT II case this emerges clearly from the fact that the reference to 'particular tasks' applies also to undertakings having the character of a revenue producing monopoly, those being always established by an act of public authority. (22) It may be added that such view is also consistent with the principle that any derogation from the Treaty must be strictly construed. It further shows that a service, in order to be considered of general economic interest for the purposes of article 90 para 2, must be worthy of special protection.

It is, therefore, not sufficient for the application of article 90 para 2 that an undertaking is performing services of general economic interests even if it is subject to the control of public authorities. (23) There is also a clear distinction between authorization, where undertakings are free to choose whether they want to offer the services, and the transfer of positive public duties where article 90 para 2 was intended to apply. (24) There can be no entrustment if an undertaking is conceded a particular protection by a general law (e.g. on copyright) or if the undertaking is managing private interests. (25)

On the basis of the above the Commission held that a collecting society namely GVL, which was engaged in Germany in the exploitation of performers' rights was not so entrusted by an official act or otherwise by a public authority. (26) As the Commission correctly stated in its decision, the granting of authorization is by its nature not an assignment but only a permission to carry out certain activities. (27) Similarly, an undertaking which is obliged by law to fulfil certain financial guarantees (such as a bank) and not to discriminate in its operation cannot be considered to be 'entrusted' in accordance with article 90 para 2. (28)

As the different legal meaning of the terms chosen in the different languages of the Treaty (entrusted, chargees, betrant, incaritato, belast) indicate, the legal nature of the act of entrustment matters little. (29) The entrustment must be made by an act of sovereignty i.e. a law, regulation, administrative act or any other act of public authority. (30) Deringer would include a contract of public law (this being the form in which entrustment is made for example in France or Belgium), but would not extend the definition to include the transfer of a particular task in a certain contract of private law considering the latter too wide an application of 90 para 2. (31)

However, in the light of the several other restrictions of the provision such fear is groundless. Moreover, a comparison between the different legal systems shows that the adoption of Deringer's view might lead to inequalities. (32) It is preferable to adopt a wider view and understand 'entrustment' to mean a 'functional association' so that the juridical form is irrelevant. (33) An entrustment may, thus, be made within the framework of a contract of either public or private law, provided the particular task is made sufficiently specific. It may also be entrusted a posteriori. (34) In conclusion, the test should be one based on an examination of facts rather than of form. There exist cases where such entrustment may be inferred even if there is no formal act of delegation and the character of public service arises out of a de facto management of public tasks. (35) The question is whether, in essence, there has been an entrustment of a public duty by the public authority. (36)

It is now clearly established (37) that national courts are fully competent to decide whether undertakings are entrusted with the tasks mentioned in the first paragraph as well as whether the tasks so entrusted prevent, in law or in fact, compliance with the material obligations as laid down by national courts under 85 or 86 or any clear self executing provisions.

'Operation of services of general economic interest'

One of the most important requirements of article 90 para 2 is that the undertaking must be entrusted with the operation of services of general economic interest.

'Services'. As to the notion of the term 'services', it is generally agreed that it does not only cover services in the sense of article 60 but that it also includes the production, transformation and distribution of goods. (38)

Such definition is also consistent with the objectives of article 90 para 2, the latter being the only provision of the Treaty permitting an exception from the Treaty rules if the economic interest of the Member States so requires and all the other conditions of the section are fulfilled. It would be unreasonable to hold that a Member State could promote its own interests by entrusting an undertaking with the provision of services in the strict sense of the word, while not by entrusting it with the production, transformation or distribution of goods. Support for a wide definition may also be derived from the fact that the exemption also applies to revenue producing monopolies, those most often having as their object the production, transformation and distribution of goods.

A wider definition than that of 'services' of article 60 may also be deduced from the fact that article 90 para 2 does not speak of 'services' but of 'operation of services', probably in an attempt to differentiate the two. (39) A wide definition also results from the definition of services existing in French, Belgian and Italian law, national laws being by no way binding and resort to them being made only by way of assistance. (40)

General economic interest. The term 'general economic interest' finds no equivalent in domestic legal systems. It is extremely broad and has apparently for this reason been preferred to more traditional, but also narrower concepts of national laws such as the French notions of 'service public' or 'service public à caractère industriel et commercial'. (41) Another reason for the non-use of an existing notion was that the drafters wanted it to have an autonomous meaning. (42)

There are two important issues which arise with respect to the notion of 'general economic interest'. First, whether it is the general economic interest of Member States or that of the Community and, second, who is competent to decide whether it is served.

As to the first issue, despite the original divergence of opinion which existed among commentators (43) it is now generally agreed that the general economic interest is that of Member States. This does not mean that the general economic interest of a Member State and that of the Community may never coincide. An undertaking pursuing an objective of community interest may also be dispensed from the strict observance of the Treaty rules in conformance with article 90 para 2. Nevertheless, since the undertaking must be entrusted with the operation of services of general economic interest by an act of public authority it is finally within the competence of the Member State to decide whether to entrust an undertaking with the operation of services of general economic interest - Community or national - and assign it with tasks for the achievement of which the Treaty rules may be put aside provided the other conditions of article 90 para 2 are also satisfied. The view that it is a purely national notion finds support both in a literal and a logical interpretation of article 90 para 2.

Literally, it may be argued that since the section puts revenue producing monopolies which can only be established by the State, on the same footing as undertakings entrusted with the services of general economic interest, the establishment of the latter must also be a State's option.

Logically, the general economic interest cannot be that of the Community as opposed to that of the Member States because at the present stage of Community integration the adoption of a Community definition, even if it were possible, would defeat the object of 90 para 2 which is to recognize the interests of Member States in certain limited and well defined circumstances. (44) A Community notion cannot take into account the economic realities and it is possible for an activity to be of general economic interest in one Member State and not in another. Nor is there any value in the argument that all notions of the Treaty are Community notions (45), an example of such national notion being the 'security of State' in article 223.

As the Commission supported in its pleadings before the ECJ in the case of SAIL, the definition of general economic interest must take account of the various situations peculiar in each Member State. (46) In that case both Advocate General Roemer (47) and the Commission (48) took the view that the distribution of consumer goods, carried out in the interests of the citizens as a whole, comes within the concept.

That the general economic interest is a national notion may also be inferred from the decision of the ECJ in the Port of Mertert case. There it was held that article 90 para 2 involves an appraisal of the requirements, on the one hand, of the particular task and, on the other, of the protection of the interest of the Community, this appraisal depending on the objectives of the general economic policy pursued by Member States under the supervision of the Commission. (49)

If the view is adopted that the general economic interest is a national concept it is hard to conceive the disagreement which still exists as to who is competent to define it. Supporters of a Community definition have also themselves noted the difficulty of a comprehensive and abstract definition, the general economic interest being a political decision varying depending on the period and the needs. (50)

The view that the general economic interest is a national notion to be defined each time by the Member States in accordance with their political choices also finds support in the statements of the Commission and the decisions of the Court. Thus, in the 6th report on Competitive Policy it was stated that 'the Commission may in a constructive and realistic manner recognize the legitimate interest of Member States to safeguard the accomplishment of a particular task while assuring the good functioning of the Common Market'. (51) Moreover, the statement of the ECJ in its decision in Sacchi that 'if Member States treat undertakings entrusted with the operation of T.V., even as regards their commercial activities, in particular advertising, as undertakings entrusted with the operation of services of general economic interest the same prohibitions apply, as regards their behaviour within the market, by reason of article 90 para 2, so long as it is not shown that the said prohibitions are incompatible with the performance of their tasks' (52) clearly shows a deference by the Court to the views of Member States.

At the same time that same statement of the ECJ in Sacchi reaffirms the preeminence of the Treaty provisions. It thus provides an answer to the supporters of a Community definition whose main argument is that if each Member State were allowed to declare that a certain activity is of general economic interest, it would be easy to fall within the exemption and article 90 para 2 might be unduly extended. Deringer has even argued that if a Community definition were not adopted States could always invoke article 90 para 2 in nationalizations. (53)

However, the danger of abuse should not be overestimated. There exist the following important limitations and guarantees (54):

First, for an undertaking to fall under the exception of 90 para 2 it is not enough that it is entrusted with the operation of services of general economic interest. As will be shown below, the undertaking must also be assigned with a task the accomplishment of which must be made impossible by the application of the rules of the Treaty. The positive form in which article 90 para 2 is framed clearly shows that undertakings entrusted with the operation of services of general economic interest are, first and paramount, subject to the Treaty rules. The Sacchi decision, mentioned above, reaffirmed that view.

Second, the wording of this same paragraph also affirms the prevalence of the Community interest, this providing additional support to the positive formulation of its terms. (55)

Third, article 90 para 3 allows the Commission to exercise control in so far as the assessment of the general economic interest is concerned. As has been observed by the ECJ in the British Telecom case, the application of article 90 para 2 is not left to the discretion of the Member State which has entrusted an undertaking with the operation of services of general economic interest. Paragraph 3 assigns to the Commission a task of surveillance under the control of the Court against the exercise of which task the Member States may bring an action for annulment under article 173 para 1. (56)

The Court thus rejected the argument of the Commission that since article 90 para 2 raises matters of fact and judgment peculiar to the Member State which has entrusted the undertaking in question that Member State is alone competent to decide whether the application of the Treaty rules would prevent the accomplishment of the tasks so entrusted. Contrary to Advocate General Darmon who seems to have followed the Commission's view the Court accepting the admissibility of the Italian claim under article 173, went on to examine the reasons offered by the Italian government in support of its assertion that the Commission's decision against British Telecom would prejudice the accomplishment of the latter's tasks but rejected them on the grounds of lack of evidence. Until now the Commission itself has rarely exercised this control but it is an option which it could take more advantage of in the future. (57)

Fourth, Member States may also agree on an approximation of their laws through article 100 or agree to coordinate their economic policies under articles 6 or 147, economic integration also leading to harmonization.

Despite the fact that the definition of the concept of general economic interest falls upon the Member States it is possible to put forward certain general criteria which may, somehow, delimit it. Although it is a political question varying according to the circumstances and up to the government to decide, in general terms the concept can be said to coincide with the defence of the interests of the 'collectivité'. (58)

Deringer (59) has suggested criteria such as the

imposition of a duty which cannot be varied unilaterally, the importance of the service, the retention of supervisory powers, the fact that it is a service that the State would provide itself and the availability of the service to all users on the same basis and conditions. These criteria may be taken into consideration by the Commission when the latter exercises its supervisory powers.

The interest must be general, this meaning that there is no question of general economic interest when the services are provided to a particular group (e.g. churches) or to a particular branch or industry (e.g. management of intellectual rights protected by law). (60)

On the other hand, the interest is still general when affecting only one region. (61) What is important is that the activity is serving the general interest. This must not necessarily be the interest of the State as a whole but may also be the interest of a subdivision thereof, as long as this is not characterized by geographic criteria. (62)

In the light of the use of the term 'economic' it has been argued that undertakings with social, cultural and charitable objectives are excluded. (63) However, as has been rightly pointed out, the use of the term 'economic' adds nothing since there is often a close relationship between social and cultural interests and those of an economic nature. (64) What is important is the nature of the activity inherent in the service and not the object of the service (this being important with reference to the particular task). (65) To the extent that an undertaking with social, cultural and charitable objectives is engaged in an economic activity it is difficult to detect a justification for less favourable treatment. (66)

'Revenue producing monopoly'

A revenue producing monopoly is an undertaking which exercises its activity in a closely defined and reserved sector and the purpose of which is to collect revenue for the budget. (67) As is the case with the undertakings entrusted with the operation of services of general economic interest, in order to benefit from the exception of article 90 para 2 a revenue producing monopoly must also be entrusted with its task by an act of public authority. (68)

Since the establishment of such a monopoly involves the concession of an exclusive right (69) it also automatically falls under article 90 para 1. For the purposes of article 90 para 2, however, the concession of the monopoly must also permit the undertaking to exploit a particular source of revenue for the State. (70) It is, therefore, not sufficient if a monopoly of production is created, even if this is obliged to give the profit to the State. (71) Nor is it sufficient if some undertakings to which exclusive rights are granted are also entrusted with a fiscal mission such as to collect a tax and give it to the State. However, there does exist such a fiscal monopoly if the undertaking is allowed to fix a margin particularly high and, therefrom, obtain budgetary revenue (similar to consumption tax). (72) This is, for example, the case with the French and Italian tobacco monopolies and the German alcohol monopoly (whose revenue is serving to finance the national organization of agricultural alcohol).

It may, therefore, be concluded that a revenue producing monopoly exists only if the concession of the monopoly is motivated uniquely by fiscal reasons and is granted in order to exploit a particular source of revenue for the State.

There is a close relationship between article 90 para 2 and article 37, the latter stipulating the progressive adjustment of state monopolies of a commercial character so as to ensure that when the transitional period has ended no discrimination regarding the conditions under which goods are procured and marketed exists between nationals of Member States. In fact, article 37 was originally placed by the drafters of the Treaty in the section containing the competition rules, but it was then decided that it is more akin to quantitative restrictions and has finally been included in the part comprising the foundations of the Community.

In the Member States most of the commercial monopolies falling under article 37 para 1 are also considered fiscal monopolies because, at the same time, they collect revenue for the State. This does not mean, however, that they automatically fall under the exception of 90 para 2. (73) They can benefit from it only with respect to their fiscal element and only in so far as the application of the rules would prevent the accomplishment of their fiscal objective.

There has been some dispute among academics as to which of the articles 90 para 2 and 37 prevails. (74) However, this is a wrong approach, the actual application of either article depending on different conditions. The Commission has taken the view that there is no reason why the application of article 37 would prevent a task from being accomplished. (75) According to the Commission, fiscal revenue obtained through a monopoly of commercial character can always be collected in some other way, such as through taxes, that does not affect trade.

This interpretation, which appears to have been adopted by the Court in the Manghera (76) decision where the exclusive right of import was held incompatible with article 37, has had the effect of reading article 90 para 2 out of the Treaty in so far as it applies to revenue producing monopolies. Indeed, by its very nature, the only way in which a revenue producing monopoly can perform the particular task assigned to it is by ensuring a particularly high margin for the sale of its product and this, in turn presupposes that it has the possibility to exclude the import of lower-priced products from other Member States. Saying that the revenue can be collected through taxes means, in effect, that there is no room for fiscal monopolies in the Community. The attempt made by Italy to invoke article 90 para 2 with regard to its tobacco retail monopoly in a recent case brought by the Commission against it before the ECJ, found no response by the Court which decided the case in Italy's favour making, however, no mention of article 90 para 2. (77)

'Shall be subject ... Community interest'

To those undertakings which are entrusted with the operation of services of general economic interest or have the character of a revenue producing monopoly - in the sense explained above - article 90 para 2 permits a derogation from the Treaty rules only if the following two conditions are satisfied: first, the application of the rules must obstruct the accomplishment of the particular task assigned to them and, second, the development of trade must not be affected to a degree contrary to the Community interest.

Both the exceptional character of article 90 para 2 and its positive structure make clear, first, that, as all other undertakings as well as Member States (article 5), the undertakings of 90 para 2 are obliged to respect the Treaty rules and, second, that the above conditions justifying a derogation must be strictly construed. (78)

'Shall be subject to the rules contained in this Treaty ... in so far as the application of such rules does not obstruct the performance, in law or in fact, of the particular task assigned to them' (79). In order to allow an undertaking take advantage of the exception, the application of the Treaty rules to that undertaking must actually obstruct the accomplishment of the particular task, the term 'obstruct' having received a very strict interpretation. (80) It is, therefore, not enough if the accomplishment of the task is rendered more difficult by the application of the rules. (81) A simple obstacle is not sufficient. (82) The derogation is only allowed if the task assigned becomes so difficult to perform that it would be unreasonable to expect that the Treaty rules are obeyed in every respect. The undertaking must have no other feasible means, technically and economically, to accomplish the particular task without violating the Treaty. (83) Whether this is so depends on a case by case examination (84) where account must be taken, on the one hand, of the duties assigned to the undertakings and, on the other, of the relevant rules of the Treaty. (85)

Moreover, a derogation is permitted only to the extent that the application of the rules obstructs the accomplishment of the particular task assigned. As for the rest of their activities, the undertakings mentioned in article 90 para 2 remain subject to the Treaty rules. (86) In its recent decision in Campus Oil the ECJ noted that article 90 para 2 does not exempt a Member State which has entrusted an undertaking with the operation of services of general economic interest from the prohibition of adopting, in favour of the undertaking and with a view to protecting its activity, measures that restrict imports from other Member States contrary to article 30 of the Treaty. (87)

Therefore, before resorting to 90 para 2 it must be established, first, whether and which is the particular task assigned and, second, whether there exist other means of accomplishing it without violating the Treaty and the ease with which such means can be employed. The burden of proving the impossibility to realize the mission otherwise falls upon the one invoking the exception. (88) In the light of the above one may conclude that article 90 para 2 is not applicable if it is possible to obtain an exemption under article 85 para 3 or 93 para 3. (89)

As the relevant treaty rules are based on very normal current economic aims and methods the chance that the application of the rules would prevent such fulfilment appears remote. (90) It is also difficult to see how a contravention of a Treaty rule, such as the imposition of unfair or discriminatory prices amounting to abuse of dominant position, could be indispensable to the accomplishment of a task. On the other hand, state subsidies under articles 92-94 could be authorized under 90 para 2 if they were necessary for the accomplishment of a mission.

The question obviously arising is whether a subsidy which would normally be denied under the relevant aid provisions could be justified under article 90 para 2 if it is granted to an 'entrusted undertaking'. It may be said that in cases in which the conditions of article 90 para 2 are fulfilled the need for the accomplishment of the particular task must be taken into consideration by the Commission when examining an aid under article 93 para 3. (91)

In most cases until now the Commission has refused to allow an exemption under article 90 para 2 in circumstances in which the parties wanted to avoid liability by invoking it. In its decisions in the cases of BNIA (92), ANSEAU-NAVEWA (93) and British Telecom (94) the Commission, while accepting that the undertakings under discussion had been entrusted with the operation of services of general economic interest, held that the application of the Treaty rules would not obstruct the performance of their duties in an efficient and economic way. Thus, in ANSEAU-NAVEWA the establishment of discriminatory conditions was held not to be necessary for the accomplishment of the tasks of the Water Supply Companies and so was the prohibition which constituted a quantitative restriction of trade in BNIA. In its British Telecom decision the Commission, while accepting in its broadest sense the view that international cooperation and the honouring of international commitments are essential features in the provision of international communications in an efficient and economic way, held that the cooperation should not go so far as to violate the Treaty rules on competition.

'The development of trade must not be affected to such an extent as would be contrary to the interests of the Community'. This condition, while affirming the supremacy of the Community interest over the interest of the Member States even in circumstances where the application of the rules would obstruct the accomplishment of particular tasks, is very vague, wide and ambiguous and very difficult to apply. The Commission and the ECJ have contributed little in clarifying the notion. Thus, in the cases before the Commission where article 90 para 2 was invoked by the parties (95) the Commission has either simply referred to the Community interest as a necessary condition without explaining it any further or decided that it was unnecessary to consider it, the other conditions for the application of the exemption not having been fulfilled. Similarly, in the Port of Mertert case the ECJ simply limited itself to restating it as one of the requirements to be taken into account when examining the application of 90 para 2. (96)

Therefore, without any guidance by the Commission or the Court and taking into account that the term is insusceptible to an abstract definition (97) an attempt shall be made to delimit it within the context of article 90 para 2. Regard shall be given to the aim of the provision and the role of the 'Community interest' within it.

It may be derived from the wording of article 90 para 2 that the drafters did not consider any effect on trade sufficient. (98) For the 'Community interest' to come into play the development of commerce must be seriously affected to an extent much greater than the effect on trade envisaged in articles 85 and 86 because, otherwise, article 90 para 2 would have no reason of being.

Notions similar to the 'Community interest' are actually spread out in the Treaty. The 'interest of the Community' is thus akin to expressions such as the 'common European interest' of article 92 para 3(b), 'common interest' of article 110, 'common concern' of articles 103 para 1 and 107 para 1, as well as to the interest of the 'Common Market' as institution, found in articles 85 para 1, 86 38, 67 and many other articles of the Treaty. (99)

The use of the term 'Community interest' has been taken to indicate an intention to create a hierarchy of interests. (100) Even though it would be difficult, if not impossible, to hierarchise all these interests, such hierarchy being in fact unnecessary, the mere use of distinct terms in the same Treaty cannot be without explanation. It rather shows that the drafters did not intend all these expressions to have the same meaning.

Notwithstanding the existence of common traits between those notions it would be possible to differentiate them by interpreting the 'common interest' and 'common concern' as corresponding to the sum or average of individual interests of all Member States for the attainment of the Community objectives, while the 'Community interest' as referring to the interest of the Community as entity. (101) The use of the term 'concern' in the English text actually supports such an interpretation. Moreover, the Community interest cannot be identified with that of the Common Market as institution, the latter in fact being promoted and achieved by the particular rules of the Treaty from which a derogation is allowed. Such identification of the two notions, the interest of the Common Market being enshrined in the development of free trade, would also be contrary to the wording of article 90 para 2.

It is true that references to the interest of the Community as entity (102) or to the interest to achieve the general objectives of the Treaty (103) do not sufficiently contribute to concreticize the notion. It must, however, be noted that the drafters intended the concept of 'Community interest' to be vague. It is important to keep in mind that article 90 was a political compromise and that the second paragraph thereof was intended to provide a very limited exception from the Treaty rules in deference to certain economic or fiscal priorities of the Member States. In this context the written affirmation of the preeminence of Community interest provides the ultimate guarantee against abuse by Member States giving priority to their national interests and needs. The Community interest is, therefore, something over and above the interest of the Common Market as institution which, as already explained above, is enshrined in the particular Treaty rules. Neither can the Community interest be the same as the common interest of the Member States, article 90 para 2 itself permitting Member States to take certain activities outside the ambit of common interest. (104)

The term Community interest must, therefore, be interpreted in the light of the general objectives of articles 2 and 3 of the Treaty notwithstanding the ambiguity that this entails. The burden of clarifying the concept and of supervising its application rests upon the Commission. (105)

As the Court stated in its decision in the Port of Mertert case, article 90 para 2 does not lay down an unconditional rule but involves an appraisal of the requirements, on the one hand, of the particular task and, on the other, of the protection of the interest of the Community. (106) It is not a simple question of balancing the interest of the undertaking or the Member State with that of the Community. (107) The issue of the 'Community interest' comes into play only when the other conditions are fulfilled. (108)

2.3 Supervision of the application of article 90 para 2 at Community and national level

Having, thus, concluded that article 90 para 2 provides an exemption from the Treaty rules and having determined and defined the strict conditions under which it may be invoked the question arises of who is competent to safeguard and control the restrictive application of the exemption and prevent its abusive use by Member States.

Such control may be exercised at two levels, the Community and the national level. In view of the fact that the ECJ has held that article 90 para 2 is not at the present stage directly applicable by national courts - the issue of direct applicability being dealt with below - the exercise of supervision at the Community level becomes of primary importance.

At the Community level

At the Community level the primary responsibility for the application of article 90 para 2 by Member States falls upon the Commission. This responsibility is much greater than the general duty that the Commission has with respect to the entire Treaty and the promotion of the Treaty objectives under article 4. This is derived both from the wording of the third paragraph of article 90, which expressly empowers the Commission to address appropriate decisions and directives to Member States, and from the rulings of the ECJ.

In fact, the first practical conclusion to be drawn from the European Court's decision in the Port of Mertert case, as well as from subsequent decisions which affirmed that article 90 para 2 does not produce direct effect in national laws, was that, since the Commission was the only competent to interpret article 90 para 2, it should abandon its relatively passive wait and see attitude and take positive steps with respect to the interpretation and effective application of article 90. (109)

At least in principle, the Commission has accepted the responsibility by expressing, in its 6th Report on Competition Policy, its intention to safeguard the full application of the exemption while, concurrently, adopting a strict interpretation. This allows it to recognize constructively and realistically the legitimate wish of Member States to safeguard the effectiveness of public undertakings assigned with particular tasks while at the same time ensuring that the Common Market functions smoothly. (110)

In its role as guarantor of the application of article 90 para 2 within the Treaty framework the task of the Commission is twofold:

On the one hand, its duty is to issue appropriate directives and decisions in order to clarify the terms of the section and assist in its application and interpretation. The authority of the Commission to explain the constituent elements of article 90 para 2 through an implementing decision under paragraph 3, has actually been confirmed by Advocate General Mayras in the BRT II case. (111) Considering that article 90 para 2 was the result of a compromise, its exact content having been left to be determined in the future, the power of the Commission to define its terms in a binding manner without Council approval is of legislative nature and extends far beyond its other powers under the Treaty. The interpretation of the terms of the exemption as well as any other guidelines issued under article 90 para 3 are, of course, subject to the final control of the ECJ.

On the other hand, in respect of individual cases the Commission is competent to decide whether the conditions for the application of article 90 para 2 are fulfilled and, if not, to take the necessary steps in order to stop any infringement of the Treaty in the process of being committed. Until the present time article 90 para 2 has only concerned the Commission in the context of investigations of contraventions of the competition rules by undertakings under Council regulation No. 17 of 1962. In all the decisions taken in this context the Commission dismissed the application of article 90 para 2 either because the undertakings were not entrusted with the operation of services of general economic interest or because the undertakings had not proven that the non-observance of the rules of the Treaty would prevent the accomplishment of their tasks. The competence of the Commission to decide over the application of article 90 para 2 was affirmed by the ECJ in its decision in the British Telecom case. There the Court held that a Commission decision rejecting article 90 para 2 as inapplicable may be challenged by a Member State only through an action for annulment under article 173 para 1. (112) As the ECJ made specifically clear, the application of article 90 para 2 cannot be left to the discretion of the State which has entrusted the undertaking with the operation of services of general economic interest.

Until the present time the Commission has been reluctant to exercise its power under article 90 para 3 in order to clarify the use of the exception by Member States by addressing directives or decisions to them. It has found it safer to deal with article 90 para 2 only in the context of individual cases concerning undertakings which are used as tools for the contravention of the Treaty rules. The Commission has thus failed to assist in the interpretation and use of article 90 para 2. The reason is that at the present stage of economic crisis and protectionism the Commission refrains from entering the field reserved for Member States by issuing guidelines with respect to concepts such as the general economic interest for which the views of Member States may differ considerably.

A similarly passive attitude may be observed in the decisions of the ECJ, the ECJ having also failed to provide the Commission with any guidelines for the interpretation and application of article 90 para 2. It is true that concepts such as the 'general economic interest' and the 'Community interest' are in a state of flux and that only the Commission is competent to balance them by taking into account, in each particular case, all the prevalent conditions and surrounding circumstances. Nevertheless, some further guidance by the Court would give the Commission, which is subject to political pressure, the necessary authority and stimulus to proceed.

At the national level

In the light of the above the possibility of application of article 90 para 2 by national courts becomes of considerable importance. The issue of the direct effects of article 90 para 2 in the national legal system first arose before the ECJ in the Port of Mertert case. In reply to the question of the national court, 'whether in this field rights are conferred directly by the Community on individuals subject to national law', the European Court held that article 90 para 2 does not lay down an unconditional rule and cannot at the present stage create individual rights which national courts must protect. (113) As the Court stated, article 90 para 2 involves an appraisal of the requirements, on the one hand, of the particular task and, on the other, of the protection of the interest of the Community. Such appraisal national courts are not competent to make since it depends on the objectives of the general economic policy pursued by the States under the supervision of the Commission.

The judgment of the Court is far from satisfactory, this being partly due to the way in which the question was framed by the national court, the referring court having failed to specify the provisions of the Treaty it considered relevant. (114) The ECJ treated the request as one for the interpretation of article 90 para 2 and, thinking that the Port, as well as similar undertakings, could fall under this provision, erroneously considered that section as lex specialis in relation to such undertakings and drew the conclusion that it is not directly applicable. The Court, thus, ignored that article 90 para 2 does not apply independently but that it is likely to be invoked in context of directly applicable provisions, such as those of articles 85 or 86.

As a result, the ECJ judgment does not only deny that article 90 para 2 is self executing but also implies that articles 85 and 86, as well as any other provision of the Treaty, cannot have direct effects whenever the exemption of article 90 para 2 is being invoked. (115) On that basis it would be easy for the parties, by invoking article 90 para 2, to take the consideration of many cases outside the competence of the court, article 90 para 2 arguably containing conditions preventing its direct applicability by national courts. (116) The above approach cannot be accepted. In those cases the national court should, at least, be competent to examine whether the undertaking concerned has been entrusted with the operation of services of general economic interest. To the extent that the exception is available to an undertaking in proceedings before the national court it should unquestionably be of direct effect, in that the effect of its availability would be to deny direct effects to an otherwise directly enforceable provision. (117)

Subsequent cases have limited the scope of the decision in the Port of Mertert case. Thus, in its decision in BRT II the ECJ, without overruling Port of Mertert, held that 'it is the duty of the national courts to investigate whether the undertakings claiming derogation are so entrusted'. (118) However, the Court did not touch the main problems raised by article 90 para 2. Having made the preliminary statement that the task of the particular undertaking had been conferred upon it by its members and not by a public authority the Court held that article 90 para 2 was not relevant. The BRT decision may be interpreted to mean that the competence of the national judge is restricted to the existence of a formal act of public authority and cannot concern the appreciation of the general economic interest. Such interpretation, however, would not cure the obvious defects of the general statement in the Port of Mertert decision. The self executing effects of many Treaty provisions might still be denied in the case of undertakings which, although entrusted with a duty by an act of public authority, are not operating services of general economic interest.

What is important is to distinguish between the question concerning the nature and source of the obligation of article 90 para 2 (misleadingly described as question of direct effects) and the question concerning the operation of the exception. (119) In this respect the BRT decision must be taken to have made it clear that the first question is for the national court to decide. If the answer to the first question is negative then the issue of the exception does not arise. If the application of article 90 para 2 is not clear the national judge would have to refer to the ECJ under article 177 or, possibly, if the case is also before the Commission, interrupt the proceedings until the latter has issued a decision. (120)

The issue of direct applicability has not been dealt with by the ECJ in more recent cases. However, the Advocate Generals in IGAV (121) and Sacchi (122) reiterated the principle of the Port of Mertert decision, thus partly indicating that this is still the rule, at least with respect to the exception. The Court did not deal with the issue at all in IGAV, nor did it address it directly in Sacchi. In Sacchi the ECJ, while holding that article 86 is directly effective even within the framework of article 90, also stated that national courts must in each case ascertain the existence of abuse and that the Commission has to remedy it within the limits of its power. (123) The statement concerning the Commission's duty to remedy should not be taken to mean that national courts are not competent to ascertain the existence of an abuse or impose sanctions under national law. Rather, it should be interpreted to imply that if such abuse is committed by Member States the Commission should issue an appropriate directive or decision.

In the light of the BRT decision and the recent

tendency to consider national courts competent to decide at least on whether an undertaking claiming a derogation under article 90 para 2 is entrusted with the operation of services of general economic interest, the blunt invocation of the Port of Mertert principle by the ECJ in the recent case of Inter-Huiles sounds out of place. (124) On the other hand, Advocate General Mme Rozès, considering the applicability of article 90 para 2 in the particular case, concluded that even if the undertakings approved for the collection and disposal of waste oils could be regarded as 'undertakings entrusted with the operation of services of general economic interest' the prohibition on exports was not essential for the accomplishment of their task. (125) The opinion of Mme Rozès is more in line with the modern tendency and objectives of article 90 para 2, as explained in this chapter. It is also possible, however, that the Court did not expand on article 90 para 2 because it did not consider it immediately material or, in any case applicable, for the same reasons as the Advocate General.

3. ENFORCEMENT OF ARTICLE 90 THROUGH 90 PARA 3 AT COMMUNITY AND NATIONAL LEVEL

The primary importance of article 90 lies with its third paragraph which provides that the Commission shall ensure the application of the provisions of this article and shall, where necessary, address appropriate directives or decisions to Member States. While the first part of this article is of no particular significance, since it merely reiterates the general duty of the Commission with respect to all the Treaty rules under article 155 (1), the last part thereof is of paramount importance because it grants the Commission the power to issue directives and decisions. This power extends far beyond the normal competence of the Commission under article 155 to formulate recommendations or deliver opinions and to assist the Council in the formulation and implementation of the rules laid down by the latter.

3.1 Advantages of article 90 para 3

The special power of the Commission to address directives and decisions to Member States contributes to the enforcement of the relevant Treaty provisions both at

Community and national level.

At the Community level
At the Community level article 90 para 3 confers upon the Commission, in the exercise of its duty of surveillance, the following advantages. First, it provides the Commission with a fast and effective procedure to suppress an infringement of the provisions of article 90 committed by a Member State. In the absence of paragraph 3 the only solution for the Commission would be to engage against the Member State the procedure of article 169. The latter, however, is long and cumbersome and most often unduly prolonged by the Member State committing the infringement.

Although it is true that if the State does not conform with the Commission's decision resort to article 169 becomes necessary, the binding nature and moral weight of a Commission decision or directive cannot easily be ignored by Member States. (2) After all, compliance with an ECJ decision is also up to the Member State's discretion. In view of the absence of the possibility of execution of a Community decision against a Member State the entire edifice of the Common Market and the achievement of its aim is, in the last resort, dependent on the good faith of its members and their confidence in its institutions.

Second, article 90 para 3 enables the Commission, in its role as guardian of the Treaty and as supervisor of the application of article 90, to take precautionary measures of a general nature in order to prevent an infringement from happening. The power of the Commission to issue directives was challenged by three Member States in connection with the Commission directive on Transparency (3) but was finally affirmed by the ECJ in its decision of 6.7.82. (4) Both the Transparency Directive and the ECJ decision upholding it shall be discussed below.

At the national level
The use by the Commission of its power under Article 90 para 3 is likely to facilitate and promote the enforcement of the provisions of article 90 also at the national level. In a national context the importance of a Commission directive or decision cannot be reduced to a simple question of extra moral weight. Any decision or directive issued by the Commission under article 90 para 3, in addition to

facilitating the interpretation and enforcement of the provisions of article 90 by the state authorities, may also have direct effects in national law and create individual rights which national courts must protect. Such direct effects are produced provided the relevant provisions are sufficiently clear, unconditional and unequivocal and do not allow the exercise of discretion by Member States. (5) In view of the ambiguity and disagreement over the direct applicability of article 90 itself, any directive or decision assisting in its interpretation or containing elements or provisions directly applicable in national laws, is likely to promote the application and enforcement of the provisions of this article.

3.2 Explanation of the existence of article 90 para 3

Before dealing with the tasks of the Commission under article 90 para 3 we must, first, inquire into the reason for the existence of article 90 para 3. The obvious question arising is why this special power is granted to the Commission only with respect to state measures concerning public undertakings and those with special or exclusive rights while in the case where similar measures also apply to private undertakings resort to article 169 is necessary.

The most widespread explanation for the granting of a special power to the Commission under article 90 para 3 is the existence of close relations between Member States and certain undertakings which enable and may induce the former to use their influence over the latter. This close relationship increases the danger of infringements and makes them, in addition, difficult to detect. (6)

While, however, the existence of close relations between Member States and the undertakings concerned does explain the need for preventive action by the Commission it does not sufficiently justify the different treatment, which may result from the use of 90 para 3, between existing state measures concerning exclusively public undertakings and measures concerning both public and private undertakings or exclusively private ones. While with respect to the former the Commission may use article 90 para 3 for the purpose of addressing a decision to the State concerned, with respect to the latter resort to article 169 is necessary.

It is for the purpose of consistency and in order to

bypass the above discrimination that certain commentators have interpreted the term 'measures' of article 90 para 1 as not covering legally compulsory acts. These commentators maintain that legal or administrative acts can only be suppressed by resorting to the Court under the procedure of article 169 even when they concern exclusively public undertakings. (7) The rationale behind this view is that such legal acts are not justified by the existence of close relations. It is, therefore, believed that there is no reason for treating differently a legal compulsory cartel among public undertakings from one also including private ones or exclusively among private undertakings. According to this theory the special power of article 90 para 3 has been granted to the Commission only in order to detect and suppress state acts of influence or pressure in view of their frequency and easy adoption.

Notwithstanding the logic of the above rationale, as has already been explained in the relevant section, the exclusion of legal acts from the definition of the term 'measures' cannot be accepted for various reasons. First, it is likely to lead to inequality in other respects by inducing Member States, which wish to avoid the effects of article 90 para 3, to influence the behaviour of their public undertakings through overt legal acts. Furthermore, the inclusion of legal acts in the definition of measures also accommodates the traditional differences that exist between Member States in the management of the undertakings which they control, certain Member States directing the activities of those undertakings through administrative measures while others do so through informal directives and orders. In any case, even if the use of article 90 para 3 were restricted to informal acts contravening the Treaty, arguably once those acts have been detected the mere existence of close relations does not justify the adoption of a faster procedure for their suppression.

While, therefore, the existence of close relations between the Member States and the undertakings with respect to which measures are taken is a prerequisite for the application of article 90, the possibility of influence is only an incident of the exercise of state activity in the economic field. It does not yet, by itself, sufficiently justify the special power granted to the Commission under article 90 para 3.

The explanation for the existence of article 90 para 3 must be traced back to the real objective of this article which is to subject the entrepreneurial activities of the State to the rules of the Treaty. It is, therefore, the capacity in which the State acts which is material and not the form. If a wide definition of the term 'public undertaking' is adopted to include every undertaking, either public or private, which Member States control or influence, then it may be said that article 90 was intended to cover all the circumstances in which the State acts in an entrepreneurial capacity. This should be irrespective of whether the State does so through legal or administrative acts or informal orders and hints. The existence of close relations in all these cases does not mean that only indirect pressure should be controlled, Member States often managing their undertakings through legal or administrative acts.

In the light of the above the following explanation may be given for the power of the Commission to take actions of a repressive character under article 90 para 3.

First, taking into account the position of article 90 under the rules of competition it may be said that, originally, such power was granted to the Commission for reasons of consistency. Thus, considering that article 90 makes clear that the entrepreneurial activities of a Member State are subject to the rules of the Treaty and in particular the rules of competition, the third paragraph thereof enables the Commission to address directives or decisions to Member States in order to ensure compliance with the rules of the market in the same way as it may address decisions to undertakings under regulation 17. (8) The reason why the procedure for addressing a decision to undertakings has been left by article 87 of the Treaty to be contained in a regulation was probably that more details had to be specified in that case in view of the direct power of enforcement granted to the Commission over the subjects of the Member States. This was not necessary for a decision addressed to the signatories of the Treaty themselves, since there is no possibility of execution of a Community decision against a Member State anyway.

The fact that the scope of article 90 extends beyond the competition rules and empowers the Commission to address a decision to Member States, even when the undertakings which they control contravene the remaining rules of the Treaty, may also be explained on the basis of the above mentioned rationale. In view of the fact that Member States combine their role as regulators of the economy and participants in it there exists the danger that they use their influence over their public undertakings in order to carry out their economic activities in a protectionist manner, thus contravening the rules of the Treaty relevant to the establishment of the Common Market. In doing so States continue to act within the framework of their entrepreneurial activities even if they also act in pursuance of purely nationalistic and protectionist objectives. Therefore, the power of the Commission to put an end to an infringement by addressing a decision to the Member State concerned is consistent with its power to see to it that the rules of the market are being obeyed by its participants.

The reason why the Commission does not have a similar power to address a decision to a private undertaking is probably that the drafters of the Treaty had not envisaged the possibility of contravention of those rules by private undertakings. Private undertakings are profit motivated and could have no reason to protect the national market as such. Furthermore, a contravention by private undertakings of the rules of the Treaty establishing the free movement of goods, services, persons and capital is most likely to amount also to a contravention of the competition rules. After all, all these rules have a common objective, the creation of one Common Market where goods, services, persons and capital circulate freely and undertakings, both public and private, are free to operate under conditions of undistorted competition. While Member States are most likely to jeopardise that objective by creating obstacles at national level for the purpose of protecting their national market, private undertakings are most likely to distort the proper functioning of competition by taking measures to protect the market of their own product.

3.3 Tasks of the Commission under article 90 para 3

In the light of the above we may, therefore, conclude that the task of the Commission under article 90 para 3 is twofold. On the one hand, it is its duty 'to ensure that in the case of the said undertakings the Member States do not maintain in force any measure which is incompatible with the EEC Treaty, which means that it must ensure that measures already in existence are abolished. On the other hand, it has to ensure that the Member States do not enact any like measure, that is to say do not adopt such measure in the future. Thus, in article 90 para 3 the task is clearly conferred on the Commission of taking both reactive and preventive action in order to prevent infringements of the Treaty' (9).

This dual function of the Commission may also be derived from the choice offered by article 90 para 3 between the use of a decision and that of a directive, those instruments being of a repressive and preventive character respectively.

Obligation of the Commission to take repressive action

Certain commentators (10) believe that article 90 para 3 could not be used for reasons of urgency in a case where the normal proceedings under article 169 could be instituted in order to terminate the infringement immediately and in its entirety. They have, therefore, argued that the power of the Commission to take steps of a repressive nature under article 90 para 3 should be limited to those complex situations where the Commission would have to set out in detail what Member States should do in order to eliminate the distortions and what time limits should be observed to bring about the necessary changes, thereby authorizing the temporary maintenance of situations which are eventually to be eliminated.

However, neither the Commission nor the Court have indicated that they consider the Commission's power so limited. On the contrary, in its 6th Report on Competition Policy, the Commission has expressed its intention to make use of article 90 para 3 for the purpose of suppressing state measures contrary to article 90 para 1. Therein it made clear that article 90 para 3 allows it to act when the State orders or instigates an anticompetitive behaviour as well as when a Member State, while possessing the necessary authority, fails to cause a 'public undertaking' to put an end to objectionable practices, irrespective of whether the State has or has not got the necessary authority to correct such behaviour. (11)

Furthermore, the Commission proceeded for the first time to use article 90 para 3 as basis for a decision (12) by holding incompatible with article 90 para 1, read in conjunction with articles 52, 53, 5 para 2 and 3(f), certain Greek legislative provisions which reserved exclusively for the public sector the insurance of all public property and obliged Greek state-owned banks to recommend to their customers to take out insurance with public sector companies. In order to supervise the enforcement of its above mentioned decision the Commission asked Greece to inform it within two months of the measures it had taken to comply. Failure by Greece to comply would amount to a breach of its duty to cooperate under article 5 para 1 and could open the way to an action under article 169 on that ground alone. In view of the lack of executory power against Member States compliance with any Community decision eventually depends on the goodwill of the infringing Member State.

At the same time, however, the above mentioned Commission decision contributes to the enforcement of the relevant Community provisions at the national level by making clear that, to the extent that such provisions are themselves directly applicable, they may be relied upon by individuals before the national courts. The latter are, therefore, obliged to apply the relevant Community provisions, despite the absence of compliance by the State, by leaving aside any contrary national provisions.

Obligation of the Commission to take preventive action

The second task of the Commission under article 90 para 3 is to take preventive steps. This means that the Commission can have procedures and approaches initiated which are not necessarily linked to specific departures from the Treaty but which will serve gradually to prevent them from happening. (13) It is with this purpose that the Commission adopted the 'Transparency Directive' (14) in order to overcome the difficulties involved in applying the provisions of article 90 caused by the lack of transparency in the accounts of some public undertakings. (15) The power of the Commission to take such preventive steps under article 90 para 3 has been challenged by three Member States but has been upheld by the Court in a judgment which cleared the way for a greater and more efficient use of article 90 para 3 in the future. The Transparency Directive as well as the issues that arose during the annulment proceedings shall be further discussed below.

Another aspect of this preventive task of the Commission is to issue directives and decisions assisting in the interpretation of the provisions of article 90 and, therefore, facilitating their enforcement as well as the observance and fulfilment of the obligations of the States and the undertakings under article 90. Thus, for example, the Commission may, where necessary, address appropriate directives, decisions or recommendations to Member States calling upon them to cause their public undertakings, by sector or separately, to take the necessary measures in order to ensure the observance of the Treaty provisions. (16) Such directives, although envisaged by the Commission, have not been issued yet.

3.4 **The Commission Directive on transparency**

The first and only directive issued by the Commission on the basis of article 90 para 3 is the one concerning the transparency of the financial relations between Member States and public undertakings which was adopted on 25 June 1980 (17). In essence this Directive imposes upon Member States the obligation to ensure that the financial relations between public authorities and public undertakings are transparent as provided in the Directive and requires Member States to keep information concerning those financial relations at the disposal of the Commission for a period of five years and make it available upon request.

Both the background history of the Transparency Directive and the events that followed its adoption indicate that its promulgation was not an easy process. The Financial Times (18) described it as 'a direct and unprecedented challenge to governments' sovereignty ...' and as an 'attempt to usurp the power of the Council of Ministers', these statements probably reflecting the views of the three Member States which directly challenged the validity of the Directive by the institution of annulment proceedings before the ECJ. In view of the limited scope of the final draft the reaction of the Member States may be considered slightly exaggerated and must be traced to an obvious worry that this Directive may be only the beginning of an increasing use by the Commission of its powers under article 90 para 3.

The Directive was finally upheld by the ECJ which, thus, opened the way for a more efficient supervision by the Commission of the governments' involvement in the economic field. However, in order better to understand the reaction which the Directive provoked, before proceeding to analyse its content and the decision of the European Court we shall first examine its background.

Background of the Directive

The Commission has been driven to the adoption of the Directive by the need to apply the rules governing state aids to assistance to the public sector. (19) As has already been made clear by the ECJ, the aid rules of the Treaty are applicable to assistance to public and private undertakings alike. (20) It is obvious from the wording of the aid provisions that it is not all state aids which are incompatible with the Treaty. Thus, state aids are justified if they fall within one of the permissible categories of aids in articles 92 para 2 and 3 or if they are granted to undertakings entrusted with the operation of services of general economic interest and are necessary for the fulfilment of their tasks as provided by article 90 para 2. Moreover, article 222 allows in principle the establishment of public undertakings or the investment of funds in existing private undertakings in so far as this power is not used in a manner which 'would be incompatible with article 92'. (21) In all those cases it is up to the Commission to make the necessary appraisal.

However, it soon became apparent that, in view of the economic crisis, government assistance to undertakings which could not survive otherwise was increasing and that the Commission was not in a position to assess the compatibility with the Treaty of assistance to public undertakings which were supported by public funds for a long period of time and were, thus, competing on an unequal level with private ones. As the Commission observed on several occasions (22) and also mentioned in the preamble of the Directive, the supervision of the provision of aids to public undertakings was becoming increasingly difficult for two main reasons: first, the failure of Member States to notify those aids in accordance with the procedure laid down in article 93 para 3 and second, the lack of transparency in the financial relations between Member States and public undertakings. (23) Member States were, thus, exploiting the opportunities which the lack of transparency offered them in order to circumvent articles 92 to 94 by conferring unfair competitive advantages upon their undertakings which the Commission was not able to detect. Some action on the part of the Commission, therefore, became necessary if the system of undistorted competition was to be maintained.

Although the Commission for the first time in its 5th Report on Competition Policy for the year 1975 indicated its intention to take measures which would put it in a better position to check on compliance with the Treaty by Member States operating through their public undertakings and by the undertakings themselves (24), it was only in 1980 that the Transparency Directive was finally adopted. The long period of time that elapsed between the conception of the Directive and its final adoption shows the difficulty of agreeing on its legal basis and the Member States' strong reaction to an extension of the Commission's power and to the involvement of the latter in the management of their public undertakings.

In an attempt to reconcile the different views as well as for reasons of practicality, the final draft imposes limited but concrete obligations upon Member States which should provide an effective starting point for the implementation by the Commission of the rules on aids to assistance to the public sector. The 'on request system' of informing the Commission, which was finally adopted in article 5, is preferable to the initial proposal which envisaged the institution of a pre-notification system whereby Member States were to be obliged to inform the Commission in sufficient time for it to examine the compatibility of the proposed allocation following the procedure provided by article 93 para 3. Such a pre-notification system would have been unworkable and ineffective in view of the limited resources which the Commission has to examine the compatibility of all the proposed allocations. (25) As the Commission itself stated in its 9th Report on Competition Policy, the 'on request' system would avoid any superfluous provisions of information and enable it to concentrate on the most important cases. (26)

Analysis of the contents of the Directive

The Directive is addressed to the Member States (article 9) which were to comply with its requirements by 13.12.81 (article 8). It imposes upon the Member States (article 1) a duty to ensure that the financial relations between public authorities and public undertakings are transparent 'so that the following emerge clearly:

(a) public funds made available directly by public authorities to the public undertakings concerned;
(b) public funds made available by public authorities through the intermediary of public undertakings or

financial institutions; and

(c) the use to which these public funds are actually put'.

By way of example of 'making available' article 3 quotes:

(a) the setting off of operating losses;
(b) the provision of capital;
(c) non-refundable grants, or loans on privileged terms;
(d) the granting of financial advantages by forgoing profits by the recovery of sums due;
(e) the forgoing of a normal return on public funds used;
(f) compensation for financial burdens imposed by the public authorities.

Therefore, assistance may take the form of both the actual transfer of funds to the undertaking and the forgoing of transfers from the undertaking to the State which would normally take place. As Advocate General Reischl stated in his opinion in the proceedings for the annulment of this Directive, 'if article 90 is to fulfil any purpose, such measures must in principle be regarded as including any application of funds or any grant of monetary advantages to public undertakings by the agent of public authorities, that is to say any action or failure to act in the financial sphere.' (27)

While information on some of the aspects listed in article 3 would enable the Commission to discover the existence of an undisclosed aid, there may often be cases, such as the provision of capital, where it will be impossible to decide whether a state aid is involved. The test of assessing what a private investor would do in a similar situation is by no means easy to apply. However, in adopting the Directive the Commission was aware of the difficulties of administering it. This awareness is reflected by the statement in the preamble that the Directive 'must be applied in close cooperation with the Member States and where necessary be revised in the light of experience'.

Article 5 requires the Member States to keep available for five years information concerning the financial relations in question and to supply such information to the Commission where it so requests.

For the purposes of the application of the Directive article 2 defines as 'public authorities' the State and other regional or local authorities and as 'public undertakings' any undertaking over which the public authorities may exercise directly or indirectly a dominant influence by virtue of their ownership of it, their financial participation therein or the rules which govern it. A dominant influence is to be presumed when the public authorities directly or indirectly hold the major part of an undertaking's subscribed capital, control the majority of votes attaching to shares issued or can appoint more than half of the members of the undertaking's administrative, managerial or supervisory body.

Although the definition of the term 'public undertakings' is widely drawn, the number of public undertakings whose financial relations were originally affected by the Directive was considerably limited by article 4. This excluded from the Directive small undertakings or undertakings which supply services not liable to affect intra-Community trade and undertakings in the water and energy areas, including in the case of nuclear energy the production and enrichment of uranium, the reprocessing of irradiated fuels and the preparation of materials containing plutonium. Transport, posts, telecommunications and credit institutions were also exempt. The exclusion of public credit institutions and the energy and transport sectors being in principle temporary (28), the Commission recently amended article 4 by including the above mentioned undertakings within the ambit of the Directive and limiting the exemptions thereto to the following: first, public undertakings as regards services the supply of which is not liable to affect trade between Member States to an appreciable extent; second, central banks; third, public credit institutions, as regards deposits of public funds placed with them by public authorities on normal commercial terms; and fourth public undertakings with total turnover for two financial years of less that 40 million ECU and, with respect to public credit institutions 800 million ECU. (29)

Under articles 6.1 and 7 of the Directive the Commission is under an obligation of professional secrecy with regard to information disclosed to it and is required regularly to inform the Member States of the results of the operation of the Directive.

3.5 **The appeal brought by the French, Italian and U.K. governments**

The validity of the above Directive was challenged in September 1980 by France, Italy and the U.K. mainly on the grounds of lack of competence. Germany and the Netherlands intervened in support of the Commission. (30) The ECJ upheld the validity of the Directive by a judgment of 6.7.82.

The decision of the ECJ is of paramount significance because it confirms the legislative power of the Commission and thereby strengthens its effectiveness as guardian of the Treaty and in particular as supervisor of the provisions of article 90. (31) The power of the Commission to take preventive measures under article 90 para 3 is indispensable for the effective exercise of its functions. (32) Moreover, according to the Advocate General 'there is further evidence against a mere repressive action in the individual case in the fact that article 90 para 3 of the EEC Treaty is not intended to replace the procedure provided for in article 169 of the EEC Treaty in the event of an infringement, but that it is instead the purpose of that provision by providing clear procedural rules to avoid the necessity of initiating such a procedure in connection with an infringement of the Treaty'. (33)

At the same time, the balance of power, fundamental to the EEC Treaty, is clearly taken into account by the fact that the Commission's law-making power is limited to the application of the provisions of this article. (34) Its narrowly-defined competence within the framework of article 90 para 3 guarantees that, contrary to the fears expressed by the applicants, the Commission may not claim a general power to lay down a special status for public undertakings. The Commission itself admitted this limitation of its power by stating in its submissions that its powers under article 90 are limited to monitoring the observance of the rules of the Treaty and that it is not entitled to amend substantive provisions. (35)

In the light of the above it is clear that article 90 para 3 is of a nature which is complementary to the power of the Commission under article 169. (36) If a state measure relating to a public undertaking is contrary to the Treaty the Commission has the option either to apply the normal repressive rules or, if it considers that the particular measures may not be apprehended under those substantive and procedural rules, the Commission may resort to the power contained in article 90 para 3. In the context of its role as guardian of the Treaty the Commission has specific powers under that provision to take preventive action by addressing directives to Member States.

The Court also made clear that there is a distinction between the objectives of article 90 para 3 and those of article 94 as well as between the conditions for their respective application. (37) It pointed out that while article 94 regulates the sphere of aids granted by States, regardless of the form and recipients of such aids, article 90 is concerned only with those undertakings for whose actions States must take special responsibility by reason of the influence which they may exert over them. Article 90 imposes on the Commission a duty of surveillance in respect of States, and this duty may, where necessary, be discharged by the adoption of directives or decisions addressed to Member States. As to the conditions for their application, these too are different: the powers of the Council under article 94 are to be exercised in connection with the application of articles 92 and 93 while the powers of the Commission under article 90 para 3 are to be exercised in the context of the duty of surveillance.

To have denied to the Commission the power to adopt the Transparency Directive could have had adverse consequences for the maintenance of a system of undistorted competition within the Community and the supervision of state aids. It would also have greatly hindered the Commission in the performance of its duty of surveillance under article 90 para 3. Grants to public undertakings do not, like financial aid by a private company to an undertaking, come from the private property of those companies which are subject to commercial risk but, directly or indirectly, from resources of the state budget. As a result, commercial considerations which a businessman would take into account do not always come into play and most often those aids are given in forms which are difficult or impossible for outsiders to identify. (38)

The above special problems make the Commission's supervisory task considerably more difficult or even impossible, and, therefore, justify the issuance by the Commission of rules which leave the substantive provisions of article 92 et seq of the Treaty unaffected and only create the technical preconditions enabling it to carry out its obligations. (39)

The Court rejected the contention of the French and Italian governments that the Directive was not necessary to enable the Commission to perform its task of surveillance on the ground that the funds available to public undertakings appear in any case in legislative budgetary measures as well as in annual accounts and reports of undertakings. (40) Instead, the Court accepted the Commission's argument that, in view of the diverse forms of public undertakings in the various Member States and the ramifications of their activities which also make their financial relations with public authorities very diverse and complex and therefore difficult to supervise, there is an undeniable need for the Commission to seek additional information of those relations by establishing common criteria for all the Member States and for all the undertakings in question. (41) The allegation of breach of proportionality was also rejected on the ground that the Commission had not exceeded the limits of its discretion, the terms of the Directive being those required to deal with the particular difficulty it sought to regulate. (42)

As the Commission had rightly remarked, in order to be in a position to form an opinion at a later stage, the Commission must also be entitled to a margin of discretion and have access to a wide spectrum of financial activities so as to distinguish between profitable activities and those activities which fall within article 92 et seq. (43)

The French and Italian governments also attempted to turn the principle of equality between public and private undertakings against the validity of the Directive by claiming that the Directive imposed heavy obligations on public undertakings which did not apply to private ones. Such argument, however, failed to see that there are fundamental differences between grants to public undertakings and those to private ones, which provide objective justification and for a differential treatment if equality between public and private undertakings in the field of competition is ever to be achieved. The Court therefore rejected the argument by succinctly stating that the principle of equality of treatment presupposes comparable situations which do not exist in the case of public and private undertakings. (44)

As the Court rightly pointed out, the elements of profitability which play an important role in the determination of the industrial and commercial policy of private undertakings is most often lacking from the formulation of the policy of public undertakings which, in view of the influence of public authorities, tend to pursue public interest objectives. As a result, there exist between those undertakings and public authorities financial relations of a special kind different from those existing between public authorities and private undertakings. These relations make the taking of special measures in the case of the former necessary.

The Court rejected the submission that the Commission had attempted without any legal foundation to define the concept of public undertaking and determine the financial relations which, in the Commission's opinion, may constitute state aids. As the Court stated, the list of 'financial relations' to which article 2 of the Directive relates was not expressed to be a list of state aids. It was only a list of financial transactions of which the Commission considered it should be made aware in order to carry out its duty of surveillance and to check whether state aids have been granted by Member States without complying with the obligation to notify the Commission under article 93 para 3. (45)

It is obvious that in many cases it will be very difficult, if not impossible, for the Commission to decide whether a grant made by a public authority to a public undertaking is a state aid or a normal investment. There are no objective criteria for taking such a decision which most often depends on the businessman's own mentality and risk avertness. On the other hand, the risk of failing which is always present in the mind of the private investor is lacking in the case of public undertakings which may, thus, with the support of the public authorities, continue to operate indefinitely and seriously distort competition. In the light of the above difficulty but also in view of the real danger that exists, it is important that the Commission has access to the widest possible range of financial relations between public authorities and public undertakings in order to decide, by taking into account all the relevant circumstances, whether a state aid has been granted.

Although the Court emphasized that the object of article 2 of the Directive was not to define the concept of public undertaking as it appears in article 90 but only to establish the necessary criteria to delimit the group of undertakings which were to be subject to the Directive, it also proceeded to approve of the criteria used as serving the objectives of article 90 and therefore potentially being of a much wider application. (46) There can be no doubt that the definition given in the Directive will have a considerable influence in the future interpretation of the term. (47)

4. DIRECT APPLICABILITY OF ARTICLE 90 PARA 1

The direct applicability of article 90 para 1 has not yet been directly dealt with by the European Court and, as a result, has been the object of some controversy. The ECJ decision in the Port of Mertert case (1), while authority for the proposition that article 90 para 2 cannot at the present stage produce direct effects, does not warrant the conclusion that article 90 para 1 contains no elements whatever which national courts must protect. (2)

Despite the attempts that have been made to interpret the judgment as authority against the direct applicability of article 90 para 1 regard must be given to the opinion of Advocate General Dutheillet de Lamothe in the same case. The Advocate General, while adopting the same approach as the ECJ with respect to article 90 para 2, expressly distinguished the two paragraphs and even proceeded to state that the decision against the direct effects of article 90 para 2 in no way prejudices the direct applicability of article 90 para 1. (3)

The opposite view has been advocated by Advocate Generals Reischl and Trabucchi in their opinions in Sacchi (4) and IGAV (5) where they denied direct effects to article 90 para 1 on the ground that it is difficult to draw the line between paragraphs 1 and 2, their execution being dependent on the issue of a Commission decision. (6) Supporters of this view believe that the interpretation of article 90 para 1 requires decisions of political relevance and an evaluation of facts and circumstances which national courts are not, at the present stage, qualified to make under article 177. (7) However, as a corollary to this, they do not exclude the possibility that at a later stage article 90 para 1 may become capable of creating individual rights if the Commission defines the meaning of the provision under article 90 para 3. (8)

The above theory, apart from failing to take into account the fact that the use of article 90 para 3 is only discretionary, does not find support in recent caselaw which seems to have adopted the Commission's view that article 90 para 1 is directly effective independently of article 90 para 3. (9)

Those who doubt that article 90 para 1 is self-executing fail to see that this article does not contain any substantive rules of law but is only intended to ensure that the other provisions of the Treaty do not remain without effects. The issue of direct applicability never arises with respect to article 90 para 1 alone but only in connection with the other provisions of the Treaty to which article 90 refers. The legal protection afforded to individuals would, therefore, be seriously weakened if direct effects were denied to otherwise directly enforceable provisions only because they had to be applied together with article 90. (10) On the basis of this rationale it becomes obvious that article 90 para 1 can yield direct effects when the articles in conjunction with which it is applied are themselves directly applicable.

Following this approach in Sacchi the ECJ implicitly considered article 90 para 1 in conjunction with article 86 to be directly applicable by stating that even within the framework of article 90 article 86 produces direct effects which national courts must safeguard. (11) The statement of the Court that national courts must in each case ascertain the existence of abuse and that the Commission has to remedy it within the limits of its power (12) must not be interpreted as restricting the competence of national courts to ascertaining the abuse. It rather stresses the responsibility of the Commission for a more effective application of the provision. (13)

The ECJ decision in IGAV also followed the same pattern. After stating that it is a matter for the individuals and national courts to take appropriate measures in so far as the intervention of the State or its decentralized agencies might infringe such rules as might be directly invoked in legal proceedings, thus indirectly advocating the direct applicability of article 90 para 1 in conjunction with directly enforceable provisions, it proceeded, like in the Sacchi judgment, to stress that it is up to the Commission to see that the relevant provisions of the Treaty are respected by the authorities of the Member States. (14)

The above decisions lead to the conclusion that the ECJ, while realizing that to deny direct effects to article 90 para 1 would mean denying the application of otherwise directly enforceable provisions, is also aware of the controversy that the application of article 90 creates. This is derived from the fact that the ECJ did not fail to note each time the obligation of the Commission to issue guidelines in order to assist and facilitate its interpretation and enforcement by the authorities of Member States.

The most recent ECJ decisions of Van Ameyde (15) and INNO (16) also seem to be based on the assumption that article 90 para 1 has direct effects when the relevant state measures contravene directly enforceable Treaty rules. Thus, in Van Ameyde the ECJ expressly stated that it is for national courts to decide whether the conditions for the application of article 90 in conjunction with article 86 are fulfilled. (17) Also in INNO the Court implied such direct applicability by holding that in assessing the compatibility with the Treaty of fixing retail selling prices national courts must take into account all the conditions for the application of the provisions of Community law which have been referred to. (18)

It may therefore be concluded, quoting Advocate General Reischl in INNO, that since Sacchi it has been clear that article 90 para 1 in conjunction with directly applicable provisions definitely has direct effects. (19) Since article 90 para 1 can never apply alone a general statement that article 90 is not directly applicable must not be considered as intended to have any independent value but only as implying that article 90 para 1 itself cannot confer direct effects to otherwise non directly enforceable provisions to which it refers.

NOTES

1.	Marenco, 'Public sector and Community Law', (1983) 20 C.M.L. Rev. 495 at p. 513.

2.	Van Hecke, 'Government Enterprises and National Monopolies under the EEC Treaty', (1970) C.M.L. Rev. at p. 452.

3.	Deringer, Bruges (1968), op. cit. at p. 393.

4.	Ipsen, 'Offentliche Unternehmen in Gemeinsamen Markt', (1964) 17 N.J.W. at p. 2338, Huth, 'Die Sonderstellung der Offentlichen Hand in den Europäischen Gemeinschaften', Hamburg (1965) at p. 334. Buttgenbach, Rapport International, Colloque de Bruxelles (1963), Rivista di Diritto Industriale (1963) I at p. 229, Pappalardo, 'Regime de l'article 90 du Traité CEE. Les aspects juridiques' in Semaine de Bruges (1968) at p. 80, Deringer, 'Les règles de la Concurrence au sein de la CEE, (Analyse et commentaires des articles 85 à 94 du Traité)', (1966-7) Nos 87-97 and 98-

108, R.M.C. at p. 765 (1966), Deringer, Bruges (1968) op. cit. at p. 394, Schindler, 'Public Enterprises and the EEC Treaty', (1970) 7 C.M.L. Rev. at p. 59, Van Hecke, op. cit. at p. 452 Marenco, op. cit. at p. 514.

5. Mestmäcker, 'Offene Märkte im System unverfälschten Wettbewerbs in der EWG' in Festchrift Böhm, Karlsruhe (1965) at p. 383.

6. Avis 1/61; Receuil GH VII at p. 529, cited by Deringer, Bruges (1968) at p. 394.

7. See Vygen, 'Offentliche Unternehmen im Wettbewerbsrecht der EWG', Köln-Berlin-Bonn-München (1967) at p. 27.

8. INNO, (1977) ECR at p. 2145, cited supra.

9. INNO, (1977) ECR at p. 2146, cited supra.

10. Marenco, op. cit. at p. 513.

11. Hochbaum in 'Les ententes et les positions dominantes dans le droit CEE' by Thiesing, Schröter and Hochbaum, Paris (1977) at p. 281.

12. Hochbaum, ibid at p. 281. Contra: Mestmäcker, Europäischen Wettbewerbsrecht, München (1974) at p. 652.

FUNCTIONS AND SCOPE OF ARTICLE 90

1. Colliard, 'Le régime des Entreprises Publiques', Les Novelles, Droit de CEE, Bruxelles (1969) at p. 853.

2. Ipsen, (1964), 17 N.J.W., op. cit. at p. 2336 et seq and Huth, op. cit. at p. 317. Also Lipstein, 'The law of the European Economic Community', (1974), at p. 239, note 6 and Marenco, op. cit. at p. 505.

3. Page, 'Member States, Public Undertakings and Article 90', (1982) E.L. Rev. at p. 22.

4. Pappalardo, Bruges (1968), op. cit. at p. 79.

5. Joliet, 'Contribution à l'étude du régime des entreprises publiques dans la CEE', Ann. Faculté Droit Liège (1965) at p. 49.

6. Franck, Congrès de Düsseldorf (1961) de la Ligue Internationale contre la Concurrence Déloyale, Annuaire (1962) at p. 336.

7. Baron Snoy et d'Oppuers at the end of the debate of the Colloque de Bruxelles organized in 1963 by the Belgian Branch of the Ligue Internationale contre la Concurrence Déloyale. Cited by Franck, 'Les entreprises visées aux articles 90 et 37 du Traité CEE', Semaine de Bruges (1968) at p. 23.

8. Baron Snoy et d'Oppuers, (1963) Riv. Dir. Ind. at p. 248.

9. Page, op. cit. at p. 20.

10. Verloren Van Themaat, 'A case involving article 90 of the EEC Treaty', in European Competition Policy (1973) at p. 243-4.

11. Hochbaum, op. cit. at p. 275.

12. There is judicial support for the view that article 90 can be partially applied in relation to undertakings covered by the ECSC and Euratom Treaties since the scope of the EEC is general and is restricted by the sectorial Treaties only in so far as they regulate a given problem, see Joined Cases 188-190/80, France, Italy and U.K. v Commission (also referred to herein as Transparency Directive Case), (1982) ECR 2545, 2579-80. See also the opinion of Advocate General Reischl at p. 2598-2599 and the submissions of the Commission at p. 2558-9.

13. Hochbaum, op. cit. at p. 274. Also see Waelbroeck, Le droit de la Communauté Economique Européenne, Commentaire vol. 4, Concurrence, Bruxelles (1971) at p. 83 et seq. Member States would be induced to vary the effects of the rules on their undertakings by altering the system of ownership governing them: Deringer, 'The interpretation of article 90 of the EEC Treaty', (1964-65) 2 C.M.L. Rev. at p. 130.

14. Colliard, Les Novelles, op. cit. at p. 853.

15. Page, op. cit. at p. 24. He adds, however, that this is not its sole or, arguably, most important function.

16. See Chapter Five.

17. Waelbroeck, op. cit. at p. 82, Buttgenbach, Colloque de Bruxelles, op. cit. at p. 39, Van Gerven, 'Traitement égal d'entreprises privées et publiques en droit belge', FIDE (1978) at p. 2.2, Delion, R.M.C., op. cit. at p. 79.

18. Marenco, op. cit. at p. 499.

19. See also section 1.1 of this chapter.

20. See Pappalardo, Bruges (1968), op. cit. at p. 81, Deringer, Bruges (1968), op. cit. at p. 395, Deringer, R.M.C., op.cit. (1966) at p. 662, 765, Page, op. cit. at p. 21.

21. (1982) ECR at p. 2588.

22. See Van Hecke, op. cit. at p. 452.

23. See Marenco, op. cit. at p. 510.

24. Pappalardo, 'Tendances actuelles de l'initiative industrielle publique en France, au Royaume Uni et en Italie', in Reflets et perspectives de la vie Economique,

Bruxelles (1978) at p. 317 et. seq., Schindler, op. cit. at p. 59.

25. Pappalardo, ibid at p. 317 et seq.

26. Commissioner Vouel before the European Parliament, 16 November 1977, cited by Deringer, 'Equal treatment of public and private enterprises', FIDE (1978) at p. 1.11.

27. Reuter, 'La Communauté Européenne du Charbon et de l'Acier', Paris (1953), p. 200.

28. See Colliard, Les Novelles, op. cit. at p. 855, Hochbaum, op. cit. at p. 284, Catalano, 'Application des dispositions du Traité CEE (et notamment des règles de concurrence) aux entreprises publiques' in Festschrift für Otto Riese (1964) at p. 135.

29. Hochbaum, op. cit. at p. 284, Deringer, FIDE (1978), op. cit. at p. 1.11, 1.17-1.20.

30. Mathjisen, 'Egalité du traitement des enterprises dans le droit des CEE', FIDE (1978) at p. 11.6

31. Pappalardo, Bruges (1968), op. cit. at p. 79, Deringer, FIDE, Equal Treatment, op. cit. at p. 1.17. See also Section 1.5 of this chapter.

32. See, Pappalardo, Bruges (1968), op. cit. at p. 78, Hochbaum, op. cit. at p. 274-5, Deringer, FIDE, Equal Treatment op. cit., at p. 1.17, Page, op. cit. at p. 22.

33. Second Commission Report on Competition Policy (1972) at p. 132.

34. Ibid at p. 132.

35. See Pappalardo, Bruges (1968), op. cit. at p. 77. The sedes materie and the reference to the rules of competition indicate that the provision aims at preventing that state intervention has the effect of distorting competition.

36. See Section 3 of this chapter.

37. France, Italy and U.K. v Commission, (1982) ECR at p. 2577.

38. Deringer, Equal Treatment of Public and Private Enterprises, FIDE (1978) at p. 1.11.

DEFINITION OF 'PUBLIC UNDERTAKING'

1. See Deringer, FIDE, Equal Treatment, op. cit. at p. 1.3. See also Delion, 'La notion d'entreprise publique', L'Actualité Juridique - Droit Administratif, Paris, Avril 1979, No 4 at p 3.

2.   Franck, Bruges (1968), op. cit. at p. 26.
3.   Franck, Bruges (1968), op. cit. at p. 26.
4.   Deringer, R.M.C., op. cit. (1966) at p. 818.
5.   Joliet, op. cit. at p. 60.
6.   The Dutch text distinguishes in article 90 para 1 between the public 'bedrijven' and the 'ondernemingen' which have been granted special or exclusive rights. For all other purposes the term 'ondernemingen' is used.
7.   See Deringer, R.M.C., op. cit. (1966) at p. 766, Catalano, op. cit. at p. 137, Monaco, op. cit. at p. 31.
8.   Catalano, op. cit. at p. 137.
9.   Buttgenbach, op. cit. at p. 228.
10.   Op. cit. at p. 29.
11.   Case 127/73, BRT v SV SABAM and NV FONIOR, (1974) ECR 313, 322.
12.   See Catalano, op. cit. at p. 138. Opposite view by Monaco, op. cit. at p. 32. As the ECJ reaffirmed in ANSEAU-NAVEWA, article 85 para 1 of the Treaty applies also to associations of undertakings in so far as their own activities or those of the undertakings affiliated to them are calculated to produce the results which it aims to suppress, Joined Cases 96-102, 104, 105, 108 and 110/82, (1983) ECR 3369.
13.   (1974) ECR at p. 322, cited supra.
14.   See also Deringer, R.M.C., op. cit. (1966) at p. 766, Franck, op. cit. at p. 35. According to Delion the term undertaking does not include the provision of administrative services concerning the adoption, application etc. of a regulation even in the economic field. See also the definition of the term 'public' in this section.
15.   Gide, Loyrette et Nouel, 'Le droit de la Concurrence de la CEE' at p. 18, Deringer, R.M.C., op. cit. (1966) at p. 766 and FIDE, Equal Treatment, op. cit. at p. 1.4.
16.   Deringer, R.M.C., op. cit. (1966) at p. 766 and FIDE, Equal Treatment, op. cit. at p. 1.4. It is interesting to note that in Danish law where the legal notion of undertaking is unknown, the notion of entrepreneurial activity is used in the meaning of an economic activity exercised by non-wage earning persons with a view to obtaining an economic advantage. Reference in Deringer, ibid. at p. 1.3.
17.   Case 19/61, Mannesmann AG v High Authority, (1962) ECR 357.
18.   Ibid at p. 371.

19. (1974) ECR at p. 322. According to Advocate General Sir Gordon Slynn in BNIC v Clair, 'for the purposes of applying article 85 an 'undertaking' is to be understood as an economic unit whatever its legal form and whatever the economic activity in which it is engaged', Case 123/83, (1985) ECR 402. See also Commission Decision 82/861/EEC in British Telecom, O.J. No L 360/36 of 21.12.82 and Case 41/83, Italy v Commission, (1985) ECR 881.

20. E.g. Commission Decision 76/29/EEC in A.O.I.P.-Beyrard, O.J. No L 6 of 13.1.76, p. 8.

21. E.g. BNIC v Clair, cited supra.

22. E.g. Commission Decision 74/634/EEC in Re Franco-Japanese Ballbearings, O.J. No L 343 of 21.12.74, p. 19 and Case 61/80, Stremsel, (1981) ECR 851.

23. See Marenco, op. cit. at p. 500, Deringer, FIDE, Equal Treatment, op. cit. at p. 1.7.

24. See also Catalano, op. cit. at p. 137.

25. Gide, Loyrette et Nouel, op. cit. at p. 18.

26. E.g. Commission Decision 69/195/EEC in Christiani and Nielsen, J.O. No L 165 of 5.7.69, p. 12, Commission Decision 70/332/EEC in Kodak, J.O. no L 147 of 7.7.70, p. 24. See also Cases 15/74, Centrafarm v Sterling Drug, (1974) ECR 1147, 16/74 Centrafarm v Winthrop, (1974) ECR 1183 and 22/71, Beguelin, (1971) ECR 949.

27. Deringer, FIDE, Equal Treatment at p. 1.5, Waelbroeck in Megret-Louis-Vignes-Waelbroeck, op. cit. at p. 82, Emmerich, 'Das Wirtschaftsrecht der offentlichen Unternehmen', (1969) at p. 372.

28. See Delion, 'La notion d'entreprise publique', L'Actualité Juridique - Droit Administratif, Avril 1979, No 4, p. 14. Nevertheless, Delion believes that for both legal and administrative reasons the term public undertaking must be reserved for bodies with a sufficiently homogeneous regime so that the concept may refer to precise legal rules, ibid at p. 14, 15.

29. In France the term 'entreprise publique' does not correspond to a comprehensive term used with regard to state economic activity.

30. See Delion, ibid at p. 15. However, Delion was not consistent with his own theory when, while excluding the undertakings 'en regie' from the competition rules, admitted that government branches such as the Bundespost and the Bundesbahn in West Germany possess sufficient autonomy in order to qualify as undertakings under article 90, ibid at p. 6.

31.   Even the Resolution of Messina (1 and 2 June 1955) provided for the subjection of public undertakings to the competition rules. See also Franck, Bruges (1968), op. cit. at p. 33-4.

32.   See, for example, M. Larock, Minister of Foreign Trade of Belgium, in the Exposé des Motifs de la loi Belge du 9.5.57, cited by Franck, Bruges (1968), op. cit. at p. 33.

33.   Von der Groeben, 'La Politique de Concurrence, integral part of the economic policy of the Common Market', (Speech delivered at the European Parliament on 16.5.65) at p.9.

34.   Deringer, R.M.C., op. cit. (1966) at p. 767.

35.   Joliet, op. cit. at p. 64.

36.   Deringer, R.M.C., op. cit. (1966) at p. 766, Hochbaum, op. cit. at p. 278, Franck, Bruges (1968), op. cit. at p. 35.

37.   Case 94/74, IGAV v ENCC, (1975) ECR 699.

38.   Deringer, FIDE, Equal Treatment at p. 1.6.

39.   Sacchi, (1974) ECR 409, cited supra.

40.   BGHZ 37, 1, 17, cited by Deringer, FIDE, Equal Treatment, op. cit. at p. 1.7.

41.   BGH 22.3.76, WuW/E BGH 1469, cited by Deringer, FIDE, Equal Treatment, op. cit. at p. 1.7.

42.   Advocate General Reischl in Sacchi, (1974) ECR at p. 430, cited supra.

43.   Case 52/76, Luigi Benedetti v Munari Filli, (1977) ECR 163.

44.   Ibid at p. 191.

45.   Ibid at p. 177.

46.   Case 83/78, Pigs Marketing Board v Raymond Redmond, (1978) ECR 2347.

47.   Ibid at p. 2368.

48.   Case 82/71, Publico Ministero Italiano v SAIL, (1972) ECR 119.

49.   See also IGAV, cited supra.

50.   Italy v Commission (British Telecom), cited supra.

51.   BNIC v Clair, cited supra.

52.   Advocate General Darmon in Commission v Italy, cited supra.

53.   Also Hochbaum, op. cit. at p. 279.

54.   Report of the Bundeskartellamt (1959) at p. 14.

55.   A similar view was adopted by the German Federal Supreme Court in connection with the supply of elastic stocking by the Social Insurance. Judgment of 26.10.61, WuW/BGH 449, cited by Deringer, R.M.C. (1966),

op. cit. at p. 767.

56.   See also Annual Report of the Bundeskartellamt (1971) at p. 23.

'PUBLIC'

1.   Deringer, R.M.C. op. cit. (1966) at p. 818.
2.   See Franck, Bruges (1968), op. cit. at p. 30 et seq.
3.   Hochbaum, op. cit. at p. 276.
4.   See Van Hecke, op. cit. p. 450.
5.   Pappalardo, 'Tendances actuelles de l'initiative industrielle public en France, au R.U. et en Italie', op. cit. at p. 319.
6.   Ibid at p. 319.
7.   Ibid at p. 321 et seq.
8.   See Deringer, FIDE, Equal Treatment, op. cit. at p. 1.4. et seq.
9.   Nicolaysen, 'Le secteur public dans le cadre d'un plan national', Semaine de Bruges (1968) at p. 330. According to Advocate General Dutheillet de Lamothe in the Port of Mertert case, the concept of public undertaking is derived from the Anglo Saxon notion of 'public corporation'. Case 10/71, Ministère Public of Luxemburg v Hein, (1971) ECR 723, 738. However, no conclusions must be drawn from the origin of the term.
10.   Advocate General Reischl in the Transparency Directive Case, (1982) ECR at p. 2596, cited supra. The same principle of non-discrimination is enshrined in article 58 of the Treaty, this being the only other article of the Treaty in which reference to a legal person of public law is made and according to which legal persons of both private and public law may benefit from the provisions relevant to the right of establishment.
11.   (1971) ECR at p. 738, cited supra.
12.   (1982) ECR at p. 2596, cited supra.
13.   Catalano, op. cit. at p. 137, Pappalardo, Bruges (1968), op. cit. at p. 81, Hochbaum, op. cit. at p. 277, Deringer, R.M.C., op. cit. (1966) at p. 819, Buttgenbach, op. cit. at p. 227, Monaco, op. cit. at p. 34.
14.   Article 14 of the EFTA Convention.
15.   See Buttgenbach op. cit. at p. 35, Deringer, R.M.C., op. cit. (1966) at p. 819.
16.   Delion, 'La notion d'entreprise publique', op. cit. at p. 6.

17. Cited by Hochbaum, op. cit. at p. 277.
18. Deringer, R.M.C., op. cit. (1966) at p. 767.
19. Gleiss-Hirsch in EWG Kartellrecht, Heidelberg (1963), p. 231, argues that the control must exist in law. However, most commentators believe that control in fact is sufficient. See also Pappalardo, Bruges (1968), op. cit. at p. 82.
20. (1971) ECR at p. 738, cited supra.
21. Mestmäcker, Europäisches Wettbewerbsrecht, (1974) at p. 649, cited by Deringer, FIDE at p. 1.13.
22. Commission Directive No 80/723, O.J. No L 195/35 of 29.7.80 as amended by Commission Directive No 85/413/EEC, O.J. No L 229/20 of 28.8.85.
23. Transparency Directive Case, (1982) ECR at p. 2579, cited supra.
24. (1982) ECR at p. 2596.
25. Also called companies of mixed economy derived from the German term 'Gemischte Wirtschaft'. See also Delion, op. cit. at p. 12.
26. Delion, ibid at p. 17.
27. Delion, ibid at p. 16.
28. See Hochbaum, op. cit. at p. 277.
29. Delion, 'Entreprises Publiques et CEE', (1966), R.M.C. at p. 70 et seq.
30. In 'Position des Monopoles publics par rapport aux monopoles privés', Semaine de Bruges (1977), ed. Van Damme, p. 538.
31. Commission Decision 76/684 of 26.7.76, O.J. No L 231/24 of 21.8.76.
32. Commission Decision 82/896 of 15.12.82, O.J. No L 379/1 of 31.12.82.
33. Commission Decision 82/861 of 10.12.82, O.J. No L 360/36 of 21.12.82. The Commission Decision has been upheld by the ECJ in its judgment of 20.3.85, cited supra.
34. Case 123/83 BNIC v Clair, (1985) Rec 391, Commission v Italy, cited supra.

DEFINITION OF 'UNDERTAKINGS TO WHICH THE STATE GRANTS SPECIAL OR EXCLUSIVE RIGHTS'

1. Franck, Bruges (1968), op. cit. at p. 36.
2. Deringer, R.M.C., op. cit. (1966) at p. 871.
3. Wyatt and Dashwood, 'The Substantive Law of the EEC', (1980) at p. 368.

4. Deringer, FIDE, Equal Treatment, op. cit. at p. 1.14.

5. Franck, op. cit. at p. 36.

6. Nicolaysen, op. cit. at p. 331.

7. See Colliard, ibid at p. 857, Huth, 'Die Sonderstellung der öffentlichen Hand in den Europäischen Gemeinschaften' op. cit. at p. 328 et seq. Bull. Fabrimetal No 673 of 25.5.59; Ligue Européenne de Cooperation Economique, Rapport introductif concernant les règles de concurrence applicable aux enterprises à l'interieur de Marché Commun, 15.11.57, p. 36 cited by Franck, op. cit. at p. 37.

8. Deringer, R.M.C., op. cit. (1966) at p. 871.

9. Franck, op. cit. at p. 37.

10. For example in Sacchi, (1974) ECR 409, RAI, the undertaking which was granted the exclusive right for cable transmissions, was also a public undertaking.

11. GATT, Basic Instruments and Selected Documents, Vol. III, Nov. 1958.

12. Colliard, Les Novelles, op. cit. at p. 858.

13. Franck, op. cit. at p. 37.

14. Colliard, Les Novelles, op. cit. at p. 858.

15. Catalano considers that the grant may be made by law or custom, op. cit. at p. 134. According to Huber (cited by Deringer, R.M.C., op. cit. at p. 871) the delegation of administrative powers to an entrepreneur is only possible in the form of public law.

16. See Schindler, op. cit. at p. 64.

17. Deringer, R.M.C., op. cit. (1966) at p. 871.

18. Ibid at p. 871.

19. See Schindler, op. cit. at p. 64-5.

20. Hochbaum, op. cit. at p. 279-80, Deringer, R.M.C., op. cit. (1966) at p. 871.

21. Hochbaum, ibid at p. 279.

22. Sacchi, (1974) ECR 409, cited supra.

23. Case 90/76, Van Ameyde v UCI, (1977) ECR 1091.

24. Mestmäcker, op. cit. at p. 389.

25. Mestmäcker, ibid at p. 387.

26. Similarly Van Hecke, op. cit. at p. 453.

27. Van Hecke, op. cit. at p. 453.

28. Hochbaum, op. cit. at p. 280.

29. (1977) ECR at p. 2146 cited supra.

30. (1977) ECR at p. 2134, cited supra.

31. Ipsen, 'Europäisches Gemeinschaftsrecht', (1972) at p. 663, Deringer, FIDE, Equal Treatment, op. cit. at p.

1.14, Hochbaum, op. cit. at p. 280-1.

32. Hochbaum, op. cit. at p. 279.
33. Deringer, R.M.C., op. cit. (1966) at p. 872-3.
34. Schindler, op. cit. at p. 64, Deringer, R.M.C., op. cit. (1966) at p. 872.
35. Deringer, R.M.C., op. cit. (1966) at p. 873. See also Franck, op. cit. at p. 37-8.
36. Franck, op. cit. at p. 39, Mathijsen, FIDE, Equal Treatment, op. cit. at p. 11.8.
37. Deringer, R.M.C., op. cit. (1966) at p. 871-2.
38. op. cit. at p. 39.
39. Hochbaum, op. cit. at p. 280, Küyper, 'Airline Fare Fixing and Competition: An English Lord, Commission Proposals and US parallels', (1983) C.M.L. Rev. at p. 207.
40. Sacchi, (1974) ECR at p. 409, cited supra.
41. E.g. Van Ameyde, (1977) ECR 1091, cited supra, Case 26/75, General Motors Continental NV v Commission, (1975) ECR 1367, Case 172/82, Syndicat National des Fabricants Raffineurs d'Huile de Graissage v Groupement d'Intérêt Economique 'Inter-Huiles', (1983) ECR 555.
42. Sacchi, (1974) ECR at p. 429, cited supra.
43. Ibid at p. 429.
44. Sacchi at p. 430, cited supra.
45. Ibid at p. 430.
46. See, for example, Commission's reply to Written Questions No 1012/81 of Herman, M.E.P., O.J. No C 53/3 of 1.3.82 and Nos 1208, 1210, 1213, 1215, 1217, 1220, 1222, 1224, 1226, 1228, 1230, 1232, 1234, 1235/81, O.J. No C 305/3 of 15.3.82.
47. Sacchi, (1974) ECR at p. 430, cited supra.
48. Case 6/72, Europemballage Corporation and Continental Can Co. Inc. v Commission, (1973) ECR 215.
49. Ibid at p. 245.
50. Sacchi, (1974) ECR at p. 430, cited supra.
51. Written Question No 384/75, O.J. No C 67 of 22.3.76, p. 12-13. In connection with the compatibility of the two decisions see also Pappalardo, 'Position des Monopoles publics par rapport aux monopoles privées', Bruges (1977), op. cit. at p. 538.
52. (1974) ECR at p. 442, cited supra.
53. Ibid at p. 443.
54. See Hauer, (1979) ECR 3727, cited supra.
55. O.J.L. 13/29 of 19.1. 70.
56. Case 59/75, Manghera, (1976) ECR 91.
57. Sacchi, (1974) ECR at p. 428, cited supra.

Confirmed in Case 271/81, Amélioration de l'élevage v Mialocq, (Artificial Insemination), (1983) ECR 2057, 2072. In this case the Court did not rule out the possibility that a monopoly over the provision of services may have an indirect influence on trade in goods between Member States if, for example, such monopoly leads to discrimination against imported products as opposed to products of domestic origin.

58. Case 45/75, Rewe, (1976) ECR at p. 181.
59. Case 91/75, Miritz, (1976) ECR 217.
60. Van Ameyde, (1977) ECR at p. 1127, cited supra.
61. Ferrari-Bravo, Bruges (1968), op. cit. at p. 430-1.
62. See Costa v ENEL, (1964) ECR 585, cited supra.
63. See Case 229/83, Association des Centres Distribiteurs Edouard Leclerc v Au Blé Vert, (1985) ECR 17 and Case 231/83, Henri Cullet v Centre Leclerc à Toulouse, (1985) ECR 315.
64. Some commentators argue the contrary. For example, see Waelbroeck, op. cit. at p. 680 and Franck, op. cit. at p. 37-8.
65. Case 56 & 58/64, Consten and Grundig v Commission, (1966) ECR 299, Case 24/67, Parke, Davis v Probel (1968) ECR 55, Case 51/75 EMI v CBS, (1976) ECR 811.
66. Case 40/70, Sirena, (1971) ECR 69.
67. Case 78/70, Deutsche Grammophon, v Metro, (1971) ECR 487, Case 15/74, Centrafarm v Sterling Drug, (1974) ECR 1147. See Vandencasteele, 'Libre Concurrence et intervention des Etats dans la vie économique', Cahiers de droit Européen (1979) at p. 552. In subsequent cases the Court was concerned more with the rules regarding the free movement of goods. See Korah, 'An Introductory Guide to EEC Competition Law and Practice', (1981) at p. 74.
68. See Vandencasteele, op. cit. at p. 553.
69. Korah, op. cit. at p. 73.
70. In applying this concept in Centrafarm v Sterling Drug, (1974) ECR at p. 1162, cited supra, the Court held that with regard to patents the specific subject matter of industrial property is, inter alia, to ensure to the holder, so as to recompense the creative effort of the inventor, the exclusive right to utilise an invention with a view to the manufacture and first putting into circulation of industrial products, either directly or by the grant of licences to third parties, as well as the right to oppose any infringement. In the case of Keurkoop, Case 144/81, (1982) ECR 2853,

Advocate General Reischl expressed the view that for the purpose of article 36 the specific subject matter of a right in a design for the protection of which barriers to trade may be permitted can only be determined within the context of the relevant national legislation regard being given to the specific structure and content thereof and not by reference to a uniform model. However, the Court avoided to examine whether the protection of an exclusive right in a design was justified altogether, estimating that in the absence of Community standardization or harmonization of laws the determination of the conditions and procedures under which protection of designs is granted is a matter for national rules.

71. See Case 51/75, EMI v CBS, (1976) ECR 811, 849.
72. In this respect see Section 2 of this chapter.

ANALYSIS OF THE EXPRESSION '... MEMBER STATES SHALL NEITHER ENACT NOR MAINTAIN IN FORCE ANY MEASURES CONTRARY TO THE RULES CONTAINED IN THE TREATY AND IN PARTICULAR ARTICLES 85-94 AND 7'

1. Pappalardo, Bruges (1968), op. cit. at p. 81, Deringer, R.M.C., op. cit. (1966) at p. 765.
2. Pappalardo, Bruges (1968), op. cit. at p. 79, Marenco, op. cit. at p. 515.
3. Marenco, ibid at p. 515.
4. Pappalardo maintains that the measures provided for in article 90 para 1 can only be adopted in connection with certain undertakings which the State controls or influences and cannot, therefore, include compulsory laws and regulations which may be adopted in all circumstances, Bruges (1968), op. cit. at p. 80. But see below Section 1.5.a of this chapter.
5. See also Section 1.3. of this present chapter.
6. Both articles 5 para 2 and 90 para 1 actually refer to 'any measure' while article 30 to 'all measures', all three references indicating the width of the term that the drafters intended.
7. Deringer, R.M.C., op. cit. (1966) at p. 873, Pappalardo, Bruges (1968), op. cit. at p. 85, Catalano, op. cit. at p. 136, Hochbaum, op. cit. at p. 282-3, Schindler, op. cit. at p. 65, Waelbroeck in Megret-Louis-Vignes-Waelbroeck, op. cit. at p. 87.

8.   Deringer, FIDE, Equal Treatment, op. cit. at p. 1.15.

9.   According to the caselaw of the European Court of Justice with respect to articles 30-36 of the Treaty. Cited by Deringer in FIDE, Equal Treatment, op. cit. at p. 1.16.

10.   Waelbroeck, in Megret-Louis-Vignes-Waelbroeck, op. cit. at p. 87.

11.   Such as progress contracts in Belgium; mentioned by Deringer FIDE, Equal Treatment at p. 1.16. Vygen would not include in the definition of measures managerial instructions of the State as shareholder because in such a case the State acts like a private owner; in "Offentiche Unternehmen im Wettbewerbsrecht der EWG', Köln-Berlin-Bonn-München (1967) at p. 76.

12.   Gamm, cited by Deringer, R.M.C., op. cit. (1966) at p. 873, Pappalardo, Bruges (1968), op. cit. at p. 88 et seq., Marenco, op. cit. at p. 513, Nicolaysen, op. cit. at p. 344-5.

13.   'In Offene Märkte im System unverfälschten Wettbewerbs in der EWG', in Festschrift Böhm, Karlsruhe (1965), p. 383. et seq.

14.   E.g. Vygen, op. cit. at p. 76.

15.   Huth, op. cit. at p. 257.

16.   J.O. No L 13/29 of 19.1.70.

17.   Case 249/81, Commission v Ireland, (1982) ECR 4005.

18.   E.g. in Sacchi, (1974) ECR 409, cited supra, INNO v ATAB, (1977) ECR 2115, cited supra, and Case 13/78, Eggers Sohn & Co. v Frei Hansenstadt Bremen, (1978) ECR 1935.

19.   Commission Directive 70/50 at p. 17, cited supra.

20.   (1982) ECR at p. 4023, cited supra.

21.   France, Italy and U.K. v Commission, (1982) ECR at p. 2579, cited supra.

22.   See Vygen, op. cit. at p. 76.

23.   E.g. Cases 6,7/73, I.C.I. and Commercial Solvents Corporation v Commission, (1974) ECR 223.

24.   Deringer, FIDE, Equal Treatment, op. cit. at p. 1.18, Hochbaum, op. cit. at p. 284, Page, op. cit. at p. 24, Schindler, op. cit. at p. 65. According to Hochbaum, ibid, it follows from the responsibility of States as economic operators that they are obliged to interfere if public undertakings under their influence violate the Treaty.

25.   According to Deringer in FIDE, Equal Treatment, op. cit. at p. 1.19, the obligation of Member States to

prevent public undertakings from contravening the rules of the Treaty corresponds to the 'Einwirkungspflicht' of public authorities on public undertakings in German law.

26. Page, op. cit. at p. 24. See also Wyatt and Dashwood, op. cit. at p. 368.

27. At p. 145.

28. The Commission has as yet been reluctant to apply article 90 para 1 even in circumstances in which there has been obvious state control over certain undertakings. Instead, it has preferred to turn against the undertakings themselves and hold them liable under article 85 without mention of state responsibility. E.g. Commission Decision of 21.7.76 in Pabst & Richarz/BNIA, O.J. No 231/24 of 21.8.76 and Commission Decision of 15.12.82 in AROW/BNIC, O.J. No 379/1 of 31.12.82. In this respect see also Section 1.3.b. of this chapter.

29. (1982) ECR at p. 2593, cited supra.

30. Ibid at p. 2575.

31. Op. cit. at p. 549.

32. Marenco, op. cit. at p. 511. Such view also conforms with the 2nd Report on Competition Policy where the Commission spoke of 'apparently spontaneous behaviour of the undertakings with special status or prerogatives'.

33. Bruges (1968), op. cit. at p. 86 et seq.

34. Ibid at p. 88.

35. Nicolaysen, op. cit. at p. 331, Marenco, op. cit. at p. 512-3, Huth, op. cit. at p. 327 et seq.

36. Op. cit. at p. 513. See also Brothwood, FIDE, Equal Treatment, op. cit. at p. 10.13, for whom the problem is to interpret article 90 so as to encompass instructions.

37. Marenco, ibid, at p. 513.

38. Further discussion of this issue below in Section 4 of this chapter. See also Chapter Four.

39. Catalano, op. cit. at p. 136.

40. Huth, op. cit. at p. 334.

41. Marenco does not exclude that public law measures may in special circumstances be forbidden by the Treaty because of their anticompetitive characteristics. However, he is willing to consider the State liable only when this extends to third parties the obligations incurred by a restrictive agreement or when it promotes or facilitates agreements under article 85 or abuse under article 86, op. cit. at p. 514.

42. Bruges (1968), op. cit. at p. 77.

43. See Schindler, op. cit. at p. 67.

44. Sacchi, (1974) ECR 409, cited supra.
45. ECJ in Sacchi, ibid.
46. Van Ameyde v U.C.I., (1977) ECR at p. 1124, cited supra.
47. In Festschrfit Böhm, op. cit. at p. 389.
48. Op. cit. at p. 281.
49. Ibid at p. 281.
50. See Nicolaysen, op. cit. at p. 332.
51. Pappalardo, Bruges (1968), op. cit. at p. 82.
52. Hochbaum, op. cit. at p. 282, Deringer, Bruges (1968), op. cit. at p. 396. Page, op. cit. at p. 23-4, Pappalardo, Bruges (1968), op. cit. at p. 91 et seq.
53. Pappalardo, Bruges (1968), op. cit. at p. 93.
54. Transparency Directive Case, (1982) ECR 2545, cited supra.
55. Ibid at p. 2593.
56. Transparency Directive Case, ibid at p. 2579.
57. Op. cit. at p. 360-65.
58. Advocate General Reischl in the Transparency Directive case, (1982) ECR at p. 2586, cited supra.
59. Ibid at p. 2589.
60. Nicolaysen, op. cit. at p. 363-5.
61. Deringer, Bruges (1968), op. cit. at p. 396, Pappalardo, Bruges (1968), op. cit. at p. 91 et seq, Hochbaum, op. cit. at p. 282.
62. Marenco, op. cit. at p. 513, 514.
63. Marenco, ibid. at p. 508.
64. Nicolaysen, op. cit. at p. 355.
65. Nicolaysen, ibid at p. 356-8.
66. Schindler, op. cit. at p. 66.
67. Op. cit. at p. 347.
68. Marenco, op. cit. at p. 513. In support of his view Marenco invoked the Advocate General's characterization of article 90 para 1 as subsidiary in the Transparency Directive case, (1982) ECR at p. 2589, cited supra. However, Marenco failed to mention that the complementary nature of article 90 para 1 was also stressed by the Advocate General in the same case.
69. Nicolaysen, op. cit. at p. 346.
70. Küyper, op. cit. at p. 213.
71. Nicolaysen, op. cit. at p. 348.
72. Deringer, Bruges (1968) at p. 397, Pappalardo, Bruges (1968), op. cit. at p. 93-7, Mestmäcker, Festschrift Böhm, op. cit. at p. 385, Vygen, op. cit. at p. 35-8, 77-84.
73. Reuter, 'La Communauté Européenne du Charbon

et de l'Acier', Paris (1953), p. 200.

74.   Deringer, Bruges (1968), op. cit. at p. 396.

75.   R.M.C. (1966), op. cit. at p. 873.

76.   Nicolaysen, op. cit. at p. 335, Marenco, op. cit. at p. 508.

77.   Marenco, ibid at p. 508-9.

78.   See, for example, Case 82/77, Van Tiggele, (1978) ECR 25, Case 13/77, INNO v ATAB, (1977) ECR 2115, Case 231/83, Cullet v Centres Leclerc, (1985) ECR 315.

79.   Bruges (1968), op. cit. at p. 94-5. However, it must be noted that Pappalardo does not include legal compulsory acts in the definition of measures of article 90 para 1. According to Pappalardo for the application of article 90 para 1 the undertakings to which the measures are directed must form part of the instrumentarium that the State disposes in order to achieve its objectives.

80.   Also confirmed by the Commission's reply to Written Question No 149/68 of Deringer, M.E.P., O.J. No C 109/5 of 23.10.68, where the Commission stated that a breach of the prohibition contained in article 90 para 1 only arises when some other provision of the Treaty, such as articles 7, 37, 85, 86 or 92, is contravened.

81.   Written Question No 29 of 17.6.65, J.O. no 201 of 25.11.65, p. 3021.

82.   Bruges (1968), op. cit. at p. 94. Pappalardo believes that while in the case of attribution of part of the market there is a clear link between the measure and the undertakings, the latter being the destinators of the measures, in the case of price fixing the measure concerns essentially the product and must, therefore, be excluded from the application of 90 para 1.

DEROGATION FROM THE COMPETITION RULES: ARTICLE 90 PARA 2

1.   Marenco, op. cit. at p. 505, Colliard, Les Novelles, op. cit. at p. 853.

2.   Neri-Sperl, op. cit. at p. 224.

3.   Verloren Van Themaat, op. cit. at p. 244.

4.   Page, op. cit. at p. 20.

5.   Sunberg-Weitman, 'Discrimination on Grounds of Nationality' (1977), p. 214.

6.   Ipsen, 'Offentliche Unternehmen im Gemeinsamen Markt', (1964) 17 N.J.W., p. 2338. According to Marenco, op.

cit. at p. 516, the idea that there are some economic activities which cannot be properly performed by fully respecting the competition rules is also enshrined in article 42 concerning the production and trade in agricultural products and, to a more limited extent, in article 77 concerning transport. The same idea underlies the power conferred upon the Council under article 87 para 2 (c) 'to define, if need be in the various branches of the economy, the scope and the provisions of article 85 and 86'.

7.   Baron Snoy et d'Oppuers, op. cit. at p. 249.

8.   Mestmäcker, 'Europäisches Wettbewerbsrecht', München (1974) at p. 653.

9.   Dominant view supported by Deringer, R.M.C., op. cit. (1967) at p. 317, Waelbroeck, op. cit. at p. 88, Barounos-Hall-James', EEC Anti-Trust Law', 1975 at p. 248, Catalano, Festschrift Riese, op. cit. at p. 139, Pappalardo, Bruges (1968), op. cit. at p. 695, Hochbaum, op. cit. at p. 47.

10.   Catalano, op. cit. at p. 138-9, Ferrari-Bravo, op. cit. at p. 422, Hochbaum, op. cit. at p. 47.

11.   Deringer, R.M.C., op. cit. (1967) at p. 319.

12.   Case 127/73, BRT v SADAM, (1974) ECR 313. Also Pappalardo, Bruges (1977), op. cit. at p. 542, Colliard, Les Novelles, op. cit. at p. 859, Hochbaum, op. cit. at p. 286.

13.   Hochbaum, op. cit. at p. 286.

14.   Pappalardo, Bruges (1977), op. cit. at p. 543.

15.   Mathijsen, FIDE, Equal Treatment, op. cit. at p. 11.8.-11.9. Frank, op. cit. at p. 39, has even maintained that if article 90 para 2 did not concern undertakings subject to 90 para 1 it would have no reason of being.

16.   Deringer, R.M.C., op. cit. (1966) at p. 871-2.

17.   (1974) ECR at p. 318, cited supra.

18.   For example articles 36 and 116 of the Treaty of Rome. Also Catalano, op. cit. at p. 134.

19.   Catalano, ibid at p. 134.

20.   E.g. BRT II, (1974) ECR 313, cited supra and Case 172/80, Züchner v Bayerische Vereinsbank A.G., (1981) ECR 2021.

21.   E.g. Deringer, R.M.C., op. cit. (1967) at p. 261, Hochbaum, op. cit. at p. 289, Catalano, op. cit. at p. 141.

22.   (1974) ECR at p. 318, cited supra.

23.   Hochbaum, op. cit. at p. 289, Waelbroeck, op. cit. at p. 90, Pappalardo, Bruges (1968), op. cit. at p. 693.

24.   Buttgenbach, Manuel de Droit Administratif, Larcier, Bruxelles (1959) at p. 238.

25.   Hochbaum, op. cit. at p. 289-90. Commission Decision No 81/1030 of 29.10.81 in GVL, O.J. No L 370/49 of 28.12.81.

26.   GVL at p. 58, cited supra.

27.   Ibid at p. 58.

28.   Advocate General Mayras in BRT, (1974) ECR at p. 327, cited supra, quoting with approval Commission Decision No 71/224/EEC in GEMA, J.O. No L 134/15 of 20.6.71.

29.   Hochbaum, op. cit. at p. 289.

30.   Deringer, R.M.C., op. cit. (1967) at p. 261, Hochbaum, op. cit. at p. 289, Catalano, op. cit. at p. 141. For a different view see Schindler, op. cit. at p. 68-9.

31.   Deringer, R.M.C., op. cit. (1967) at p. 261.

32.   See Schindler, op. cit. at p. 69. Schindler further maintains that since the final wording of article 90 para 2 originated in a French draft it may be concluded that a public service concession should not be treated otherwise than as a de facto service.

33.   Ipsen, (1969) 17 N.J.W., op. cit. at p. 2338. Also Huth, op. cit. at p. 330.

34.   Hochbaum, op. cit. at p. 289.

35.   Schindler, op. cit. at p. 69.

36.   In this context a question which might arise is whether the entrustment of an undertaking with the operation of services of general economic interest could be made by the authorities of the Community themselves. Despite the fact that such direct entrustment is not within the latter's competence it may be, for example, the indirect result of community industrial policy. Furthermore, a practical example thereof could be found in the case of joint undertakings established under article 45 of the Euratom Treaty. An undertaking entrusted with the operation of services of general economic interest in this way should also be covered by article 90 para 2. In such case the general economic interest would be that of the Community. See also under 'General Economic Interest' in this section.

37.   BRT II, (1974) ECR 313, cited supra. See also discussion on direct applicability of article 90 para 2 in Section 2.3 of this chapter.

38.   Franck, op. cit. at p. 41, Hochbaum, op. cit. at p. 287, Deringer, R.M.C., op. cit. (1967) at p. 95.

39.   Deringer, R.M.C., op. cit. (1967) at p. 95.

40.   Deringer, R.M.C., op. cit. (1967) at p. 95, Hochbaum, op. cit. at p. 287, who, therefore, concludes that

the term 'operation of services' covers not only railways and the post but also the distribution of gas and electricity.

41.   Advocate General in Port of Mertert, (1971) ECR at p. 739, cited supra. See also Colliard, Les Novelles, op. cit. at p. 859, Hochbaum, op. cit. at p. 287, 88.

42.   Colliard, ibid at p. 859.

43.   A Community definition has been supported by Francescelli in the Colloque de Bruxelles of 1963, Rivista di Diritto Industriale (1963), Ribolzi, 'Aspetti giuridici delle essenzioni suggettive alle regule sulla concorrenza nella Communita Economica Europa' Rivista di politica economica (1963), p. 1824 et seq (both cited by Pappalardo, Bruges (1968), op. cit. at p.99) and Ferrari-Bravo, op. cit. at p. 424. A national definition has been advocated by Pappalardo, Bruges (1968), op. cit. at p. 98 et seq, Grassetti in the Colloque of 1963 (cited by Pappalardo, ibid at p. 99), Catalano, Manuel de droit de Communautés Européennes (1965) p. 491, Franck, Bruges (1968) op. cit. at p. 42, 43 and Catalano, op. cit. at p. 141. Deringer, Bruges (1968), op. cit. at p. 404, while admitting that it is primarily up to the States to decide, nevertheless, maintains that as the term 'Community interest' is contained in the Treaty it primarily represents a Community notion and cannot be interpreted very differently by the different Member States. In any case the task falls upon the Commission to ensure that no distortion of competition occurs as a result of the divergent interpretations of this term.

44.   See Catalano, op. cit. at p. 141-2.

45.   Deringer, Bruges (1968), op. cit. at p. 404.

46.   Case 82/71, SAIL, (1972) ECR 119.

47.   Ibid at p. 144.

48.   Ibid at p. 132.

49.   (1971) ECR at p.730, cited supra.

50.   Del Marmol, cited by Franck, op. cit. at p. 42. Jeze, a French jurist cited by Delion in 'Entreprises Publiques et CEE', (1966) R.M.C. at p. 81, defined 'public services' as the needs of general interest that at a certain moment the governors of a certain country decide to satisfy by means of the provision of a public service.

51.   6th Commission Report on Competition Policy (1976) at p. 114.

52.   Sacchi, (1974) ECR at p. 430, cited supra. Such deference can also be inferred from the decision of the ECJ in Port of Mertert, (1971) ECR 723, cited supra.

53.   Deringer, Bruges (1968), op. cit. at p. 404.

54.   Pappalardo, Bruges (1968), op. cit. at p. 102-103, Catalano, op. cit. at p. 143.

55.   Ferrari-Bravo tried to separate the general economic interest, with respect to which he advocated the adoption of a Community definition, from the particular task which he considered a national notion; op. cit. at p. 424-6. Such separation, however, is not possible, the notions being virtually identical.

56.   Case 41/83, cited supra.

57.   This task of the Commission was also stressed and somehow raised in importance by the Court in its decision in the Port of Mertert case where article 90 para 2 was denied direct applicability, (1971) ECR 723, cited supra.

58.   The Belgian Minister of Economic Affairs during the discussion of a bill against the abuse of economic power, Ann. Parl. Senat, 18.12.59, p. 143, cited by Franck, op. cit. at p. 42.

59.   Deringer, R.M.C., op. cit. (1967) at p. 97.

60.   Hochbaum, op. cit. at p. 288. See also BRT(II), (1974) ECR 313, cited supra.

61.   Hochbaum, op. cit. at p. 288. Franck, op. cit. at p. 43. Opposite view by Schindler, op. cit. at p. 70.

62.   However, the view of the Commission in Case 90/76, Van Ameyde v UCI, that the national insurers' bureau was not entrusted with the operation of services of general economic interest 'since its activities do not benefit the whole of the national economy' (1977) ECR 1091, 1117, was described as too restrictive; Wyatt and Dashwood, op. cit. at p. 377.

63.   See Hochbaum, op. cit. at p. 288. Hochbaum cites in support Commission Decision No 71/224/EEC in GEMA, O.J. No L 134 of 20.6.71 p. 15.

64.   Waelbroeck in Merget-Louis-Vignes-Waelbroeck, op. cit. at p. 89. Mestmäcker, Europäisches Wettbewerbsrecht, op. cit. at p. 664.

65.   Deringer, R.M.C., op. cit. (1967) at p. 96.

66.   Page, op. cit. at p. 28.

67.   Hochbaum, op. cit. at p. 290, Colliard, Les Novelles, op. cit. at p. 859.

68.   Hochbaum, op. cit. at p. 290.

69.   A typical example is the concession of a power belonging to the State. In this respect see Mestmäcker, Europäisches Wettbewerbsrecht, op. cit. at p. 194.

70.   Waelbroeck in Magret-Louis-Vignes-Waelbroeck, op. cit. at p. 90, Hochbaum, op. cit. at p. 290.

71.   Hochbaum, op. cit. at p. 291.
72.   Hochbaum, ibid. at p. 291.
73.   Hochbaum, ibid. at p. 291.
74.   Franck, op. cit. at p. 65, quotes Dubouis, 'Les Monopoles dans le Marché Commun', p. 156, as supporting the preeminence of 90 para 2 while Champaud and Houssiaux support the contrary. According to Franck it depends on whether it is the commercial or the fiscal element which prevails.
75.   Advocate General Roemer in SAIL, (1972) ECR at p. 144-5, cited supra.
76.   Case 59/75, Manghera, (1976) ECR 91.
77.   Case 78/82, Commission v Italy, (1983) ECR 1955.
78.   See also the ECJ decision in Sacchi where it was held that, by reason of article 90 para 2, the prohibitions of articles 86 and 90 also apply to undertakings entrusted with the operation of services of general economic interest as regards their behaviour in the market, so long as it is not shown that the said prohibitions are incompatible with the performance of their tasks; (1974) ECR at p. 430, cited supra.
79.   Baron Snoy et d'Oppuers, one of the Belgian negotiators and signatories of the Treaty, revealed that the word 'obstruct' was a compromise between the French and the German delegations, the former having preferred the wording 'make impossible' while the latter the wording 'make intolerably difficult', op. cit., p. 250-51. The Germans were thus ready to accept a larger exception than the French.
80.   Advocate General Roemer in SAIL, (1972) ECR at p. 144, cited supra.
81.   Page, op. cit. at p. 30.
82.   Deringer, R.M.C., op. cit. (1967) at p. 318.
83.   Hochbaum, op. cit. at p. 293, Pappalardo, Bruges (1968), op. cit. at p. 696, Spaak Report, op. cit. at p. 15. Also see Commission Decision No 82/371 of 17.12.81 in ANSEAU-NAVEWA, O.J. No L 167/39 of 15.6.82.
84.   Hochbaum, op. cit. at p. 293, Catalano, op. cit. at p. 141, Deringer, R.M.C., op. cit. (1967) at p. 318.
85.   Commission in SAIL, (1972) ECR at p. 132-3, cited supra.
86.   See Page, op. cit. at p. 30, Deringer, R.M.C., op. cit. (1967) at p. 317, Schindler, op.cit. at p. 67-8.
87.   Case 72/83, Campus Oil Ltd v The Ministry of Industry and Energy, (1984) ECR 2727.

88. Deringer, R.M.C., op. cit. (1967) at p. 318.
89. Deringer, FIDE, Equal Treatment, op. cit. at p. 1.24, Waelbroeck in Megret-Louis-Vignes-Waelbroeck, op. cit. at p. 88, Mestmäcker, Europäisches Wettbewerbsrecht, op. cit. at p. 664. Such exemption under article 85 para 3 was granted by the Commission to the International Energy Agency, in Commission Decision No 83/671 of 12.12.83, O.J. No L 376/30 of 31.12.83.
90. Van der Esch, 'French Oil Legislation and the EEC Treaty', (1970) C.M.L. Rev. at p. 41.
91. The Commission in its answer to Written Question No 48 of Burgbacher, M.E.P., stated in 30.7.63 that State subsidies fall under articles 92-94 irrespective of whether they are granted to private or public undertakings or those undertakings covered by article 90 para 2; J.O. No 125 of 17.8.63 p. 2235.
92. Commission Decision No 76/684 of 26.7.76 in Pabst and Richarz/BNIA, O.J. No L 231/24 of 21.8.76.
93. Commission Decision No 82/371 of 17.12.81 in ANSEAU-NAVEWA, O.J. No L 167/39 of 15.6.82. In joined Cases 96-102, 104, 105, 108 and 110/82 the ECJ upholding the Commission Decision made no mention of article 90 para 2; (1983) ECR 3369.
94. Commission Decision No 82/861 of 10.12.82 in British Telecommunications, O.J. No L 360/36 of 21.12.82. In an action by Italy for the annulment of the British Telecom Decision, the ECJ upheld the Commission's view; Case 41/83, Italy v Commission, cited supra.
95. See, for example, Commission Decisions in BNIA, ANSEAU-NAVEWA, and British Telecom, cited supra.
96. Port of Mertert, (1971) ECR at p. 730, cited supra. Same approach by Advocate General Roemer in SAIL, (1972) at p. 145.
97. Page, op. cit. at p. 31.
98. Deringer, R.M.C., op. cit. (1967) at p. 319, Hochbaum, op. cit. at p. 293, Page, op. cit. at p. 31.
99. Hochbaum, op. cit. at p. 294, Deringer, R.M.C., op. cit. (1967) at p. 415, Baron Snoy et d'Oppuers, op. cit. at p. 251.
100. Page, op. cit. at p. 31.
101. Deringer, R.M.C., op. cit. (1967) at p. 415. As Hochbaum stated in op. cit. at p. 294, the 'common interest' cannot go further, at least in aids, than the 'European common interest' in 92 para 3(b) or the 'common interest' of 92 para 3(c) since those provisions permit a derogation from

the principle of free movement of goods.

102. Deringer, R.M.C., op. cit. (1967) at p. 415.

103. Deringer, ibid at p. 415, Deringer, Bruges (1968), op. cit. at p. 405, Hochbaum, op. cit. at p. 294-5.

104. Port of Mertert, (1971) ECR at p. 730, cited supra. Baron Snoy et d'Oppuers, op. cit. at p. 254.

105. Advocate General Mayras in BRT II, (1974) ECR at p. 327, Advocate General Reischl in Sacchi, (1974) ECR at p. 443 and Advocate General Trabucchi in IGAV (1975) ECR at p. 723, cited supra.

106. (1971) ECR at p. 730, cited supra.

107. Deringer, R.M.C., op. cit. (1967) at p. 416.

108. Commission Decision in ANSEAU-NAVEWA, cited supra.

109. Verloren Van Themaat, op. cit. at p. 244.

110. 6th Commission Report on Competition Policy, (1976) at p. 144.

111. (1974) ECR at p. 328, cited supra.

112. Italy v Commission, cited supra.

113. Port of Mertert, (1971) ECR at p. 730.

114. Page, op. cit. at p. 32, Verloren Van Themaat, op. cit. at p. 244, 247.

115. Verloren Van Themaat, op. cit. at p. 248.

116. Ibid at p. 248.

117. Wyatt and Dashwood, op. cit. at p. 373.

118. (1974) ECR at p. 318, cited supra. Advocate General Mayras, implying the same, considered it necessary to examine whether, in fact, SABAM's functions corresponded to the general economic interest, ibid at p. 327.

119. Page, op. cit. at p. 31.

120. Deringer, FIDE, Equal Treatment, op. cit. at p. 1.32.

121. (1975) ECR at p. 723, cited supra.

122. (1974) ECR at p. 443.

123. Ibid at p.430.

124. Case 172/82, Inter-Huiles, (1983) ECR 555, 567.

125. Ibid at p. 581.

ENFORCEMENT OF ARTICLE 90 THROUGH 90 PARA 3 AT COMMUNITY AND NATIONAL LEVEL

1. Article 155 of the Treaty of Rome provides the following: 'In order to ensure the proper functioning and

development of the Common Market, the Commission, shall:
- ensure that the provisions of this Treaty and the measures taken by the institutions pursuant thereto are applied;
- formulate recommendations or deliver opinions on matters dealt with in this Treaty, if it expressly so provides or if the Commission considers it necessary;
- have its own power of decision and participate in the shaping of measures taken by the Council and by the Assembly in the manner provided for in this Treaty;
- exercise the powers conferred on it by the Council for the implementation of the rules laid down by the latter'.

2.   See Pappalardo, Bruges (1968), op. cit. at p. 81 and Schindler, op. cit. at p. 71. However, Pappalardo's remark, ibid at p. 81, that it is difficult to say to which extent the moral weight of a directive or decision is greater than that of a recommendation, fails to take into account that, after all, the entire Treaty has only a moral weight upon Member States.

3.   Commission Directive No 80/723 of 25.6.80 on the Transparency of financial relations between Member States and public undertakings, O.J. No L 195/35 of 29.7.80. Amended by Commission Directive No 85/413 of 24.7.85, O.J. No L229/20 of 28.8.85.

4.   Joined Cases 188 to 190/80, France, Italy and the U.K. v Commission, (1982) ECR 2545.

5.   On direct effects see, for example, Case 26/62, Van Gend en Loos, (1963) ECR 1, Case 6/64, Costa v ENEL, (1964) ECR 585, Case 57/65, Lütticke v Hauptzollamt Saarlouis, (1966) ECR 205.

6.   Pappalardo, Bruges (1968), op. cit. at p. 79 et seq.

7.   E.g. Pappalardo, Bruges (1968), op. cit. at p. 85 et seq. See also Section under 'General Laws and Regulations' in Section 1.5.a of this chapter.

8.   Council Regulation No 17, J.O. 204/62 of 21.2.62, Spec. Ed. (1959-1962) at p. 87. See Mathijsen, FIDE, Equal Treatment, op. cit. at p. 11.9-11.10.

9.   Advocate General Reischl in the Transparency Directive Case, (1982) ECR at p. 2586-7, cited supra. See also Mathijsen, FIDE, Equal Treatment, op. cit. at p. 11.10.

10.   E.g. Marenco, op. cit. at p. 522.

11.   6th Commission Report on Competition Policy (1976) at p. 144-5.

12.   Commission Decision No 85/276/EEC of 24.4.85

concerning the insurance in Greece of public property and loans granted by Greek state-owned banks, O.J. No L 152/25 of 11.6.85.

13.   6th Commission Report on Competition Policy at p. 145. See also 5th Commission Report on Competition Policy (1975) at p. 117.

14.   See Section 3.4 of this chapter.

15.   6th Commission Report on Competition Policy at p. 145-6.

16.   6th Commission Report on Competition Policy at p. 146.

17.   Cited supra.

18.   27 June 1980.

19.   See Page, 'The new Directive on transparency of financial relations between Member States and public undertakings', (1982) E.L. Rev. at p. 492.

20.   Case 78/76, Firma Steinike und Weinlig v Germany, (1977) ECR 595.

21.   See 2nd Commission Report on Competition Policy (1972) at p. 127.

22.   Thus, while in its 2nd Report on Competition Policy at p. 131, the Commission stated that its responsibilities included, inter alia, ensuring 'that the Member States do not grant these undertakings aids incompatible with the Common Market - aids which may be difficult to detect, masked as they are by the special relations between the Member States and the undertakings', in its 5th Report on Competition Policy at p. 117, the Commission noted that 'the work of its departments in this field were often hampered by the lack of transparency in the financial links between governments and undertakings ... whose conduct may be influenced by governments'. Member States were made aware of those problems encountered by the Commission in its Communication of 30.9.1980, O.J. 1980 C 252/2 headed 'The Notification of state aids to the Commission pursuant to Article 93(3) of the EEC Treaty; the failure of Member States to respect their obligation'. Also in reply to Written Question No 701/77 of Muller-Hermann, M.E.P., the Commission stated that because of the lack of transparency it had not been able formally to establish any violations of article 90 in conjunction with article 92 et seq or indeed any other provisions of the Treaty, O.J. 1978, No C 42/23.

23.   O.J. No L 195 of 29.7.80 at p. 35, cited supra.

24.   Fifth Commission Report on Competition Policy

at p. 117-8.

25. See Page, 'The Transparency Directive' at p. 499, cited supra.

26. 9th Commission Report on Competition Policy at p. 131.

27. (1982) ECR at p. 2593, cited supra.

28. The decision of the Commission to leave those sectors outside the ambit of the Directive, even if only in order to examine the desirability of preparing further transparency measures adapted to the particular problems of those undertakings, was not left without any criticism. See Brothwood, 'The Commission Directive on transparency of financial relations between Member States and public undertakings', (1981) C.M.L. Rev. at p. 207, where the author noted that the exclusion of certain industries such as aviation and shipping and public credit institutions, while showing caution on the part of the Commission was a matter of some regret.

29. Commission Directive No 85/413 of 24.7.85 amending Directive 80/723/EEC on the transparency of financial relations between Member States and public undertakings, O.J. No L 229/20 of 28.8.85.

30. See (1982) ECR at p. 2565-71, cited supra.

31. See also Brothwood, 'The Court of Justice on article 90', op. cit. at p. 343.

32. Advocate General Reischl, (1982) ECR at p. 2587, cited supra.

33. (1982) ECR at p. 2587, cited supra.

34. A.G., ibid. at p. 2589.

35. Commission's reply to France, ibid at p. 2557.

36. Commission submissions, ibid at p. 2554.

37. ECJ, (1982) ECR at p. 2575, cited supra.

38. A.G., (1982) ECR at p. 2591-2, cited supra.

39. A.G., ibid. at p. 2592.

40. ECJ, (1982) ECR at p. 2576-7, cited supra.

41. Commission, ibid at p. 2553-4.

42. ECJ, ibid at p. 2577.

43. Commission submissions, (1982) ECR at p. 2557-8, cited supra. Affirmed by the A.G., ibid at p. 2594.

44. ECJ, ibid at p. 2577-8.

45. ECJ, (1982) ECR at p. 2578, cited supra.

46. ECJ, (1982) ECR at p. 2578-9, cited supra.

47. See Brothwood, 'The Court of Justice on Article 90 of the EEC Treaty', op. cit. at p. 344.

DIRECT APPLICABILITY OF ARTICLE 90 PARA 1

1.   Port of Mertert, Case 10/71, (1971) ECR 723.
2.   Verloren Van Themaat, op. cit. at p. 246.
3.   (1971) ECR at p. 739-40, cited supra.
4.   Sacchi, (1974) ECR 409, cited supra.
5.   IGAV v ENCC, (1975) ECR 699, cited supra.
6.   Advocate General Reischl in Sacchi, (1974) ECR at p. 443, cited supra.
7.   Advocate General Trabucchi in IGAV, (1975) ECR at p. 723, cited supra. See also Deringer, FIDE, Equal Treatment, op. cit. at p. 1.31.
8.   Deringer, ibid at p. 1.31.
9.   See Commission submissions in Port of Mertert, (1971) ECR at p. 728 and in Sacchi, (1974) ECR at p. 415, cited supra.
10.   See Page, 'Member States, Public Undertakings and article 90', (1982) E.L. Rev. at p. 31.
11.   (1974) ECR at p. 430, cited supra.
12.   (1974) ECR at p. 430, cited supra.
13.   See Page, 'Member States, Public Undertakings and article 90', op. cit. at p. 35.
14.   (1975) ECR at p. 713, cited supra.
15.   Van Ameyde v UCI, (1977) ECR 1091, cited supra.
16.   INNO v ATAB, (1977) ECR 2116, cited supra.
17.   Van Ameyde, (1977) ECR at p. 1125-6, cited supra.
18.   INNO v ATAB, (1977) ECR at p. 2145, cited supra.
19.   (1977) ECR at p. 2168.

Chapter Four

STATE INTERVENTION IN THE PRIVATE SECTOR: APPLICATION OF THE COMPETITION RULES

While article 90 makes clear that in respect of public undertakings and undertakings to which the State grants special or exclusive rights Member States may not enact or maintain in force measures contrary to the rules of the Treaty, and in particular those of competition, there exists no particular Treaty provision specifically prohibiting Member States from enacting or maintaining general measures producing comparable anticompetitive effects. (1) The absence of such a provision, however, should not be taken to indicate the lack of any state responsibility in this field, article 90 being only a particular application of certain general principles which bind the Member States. (2)

The responsibility of Member States for their intervention in the market through general measures which have the effect of distorting competition must, therefore, be traced elsewhere in the Treaty. It must be borne in mind that in such case where state responsibility is not established under article 90 para 1 the use of article 90 para 3 is also not available. As we have already explained (3), the importance of article 90 para 1 lies with article 90 para 3 which grants the Commission a special power, over and above its general power under the Treaty, to address directives and decisions to Member States when those contravene the Treaty rules by acting through the medium of undertakings which they influence or control. It goes without saying that the objectives of article 90 will be best served by the adoption of the widest possible definition of the terms 'public undertakings' and 'measures' in order to cover every potential participation of the State in the market as entrepreneur. (4)

Nonetheless, even the adoption of the widest possible definition of the term 'public undertaking' cannot extend the application of article 90 (including its third paragraph) to all cases of distortion of competition by the State. It is true that private undertakings no longer formulate their policy and strategy as independently from the State as they used to. Their relations with the State have become closer and are often obscure, particularly when they occupy important sectors of the economy or face serious economic problems. (5) However, the existence of such relations cannot always justify the subjection of those undertakings to article 90 para 1 even if the widest possible criteria were adopted.

The State is nowadays present and somehow influences every kind of economic activity without exercising control or influence as entrepreneur in the sense of article 90. At the same time, in an attempt to cure unemployment or other structural problems or also for purely ideological reasons, Member States tend to adopt general measures which affect both public and private undertakings and have the effect of distorting competition without falling within the ambit of article 90. The fact that the Commission cannot suppress such measures by using its power under article 90 para 3 does not mean that there exists no state responsibility under the Treaty for such measures. The general duty of Member States to abstain from any measures which could jeopardise the Treaty objectives, including that of undistorted competition, is independent of article 90 para 3. A breach of this duty amounts to an infringement of the Treaty with all the consequences that this entails. (6)

In this chapter we shall be concerned with the particular obligation of Member States to ensure the proper functioning of competition and to abstain from any measure which has the effect of distorting it. The responsibility of the States for those of their measures that contravene the other Treaty principles comprised in article 3 of the Treaty (free circulation or goods, services, persons and capital) shall not be the subject of our discussion as those measures are already prohibited by the particular provisions of the Treaty contained in Part II thereof. Contrary to the latter rules, those giving effect to the principle of undistorted competition of article 3(f), with the exception of article 90 and articles 92-94, are addressed only to undertakings; Member States are not, therefore, directly subject to them. (7)

This does not mean that Member States are not obliged to respect the principle of free competition. The Spaak report made it clear that the imposition of the rules of competition on Member States was a necessary supplement of those imposed on undertakings if one of the basic objectives of the Treaty, the establishment of normal conditions of competition, was to be achieved. (8) The drafters of the Treaty considered the absence of monopoly as necessary for the creation of the Common Market and were aware of the distortions which were likely to be caused by the intervention of the States in the economy. (9)

At the same time, the Spaak report did recognize the need to distinguish certain issues of general economic policy, which remain within the discretion of the States and, thus, outside the realm of the Treaty, from those connected with the functioning of the Common Market. (10) Predicting that state intervention is most likely to manifest itself in the protection of local production and state undertakings (11), the drafters of the Treaty included specific provisions therein prohibiting such state intervention outright. However, they left it open to interpretation whether general state measures, which have the effect of distorting competition without at the same time hindering the free movement of goods within the Common Market, are prohibited by the Treaty or whether they fall within the discretion of the Member States. The compatibility of these state measures with the Treaty rules and principles must in each particular case be ascertained in the light of the Treaty objectives and its general spirit, taking into consideration all the relevant factors and the degree of integration and coordination actually achieved.

The liability of Member States for measures which have the effect of distorting competition may be based on the combined effects of article 5 para 2 with articles 3(f), 85 and 86. Article 5 para 2 enshrines and specifies the general duty that the Member States assumed by signing the Treaty to abstain from any measures which could jeopardise the attainment of its objectives. (12) This article, therefore, makes Member States addressees both of the general tasks of the Community contained in Part I of the Treaty and of the particular rules contained in the subsequent chapters, as well as of any new obligations created by the Community institutions, irrespective of who is the specific addressee thereof. Thus, in addition to anticipating the particular obligations of the Member States under the rules contained in Part I or created by secondary law, article 5 para 2 also makes clear that the Member States must abstain from any measures likely to jeopardise the objectives of the competition rules which are contained in Title I, Chapter I of Part II and are addressed to undertakings.

It is necessary to examine which are the state measures which, without contravening a particular Treaty provision contained in Part II of the Treaty and addressed to Member States, may, nevertheless, be held to be contrary to the Treaty under the combined effects of articles 5 para 2, 3(f), 85 and 86.

Three types of state measures may fall under the combined effects of the above articles:

1. Those enabling or facilitating violations of the competition rules.
2. Those equivalent in their effects to a violation of the competition rules.
3. Those imposing a behaviour contrary to the competition rules.

A fourth possible category that could be considered to fall under article 5 para 2 is inaction or passive attitude by the State when the rules of competition are being contravened by undertakings. Such inaction could not, however, be considered as giving rise to responsibility under article 5 para 2 as it does in connection with public undertakings under article 90 para 1. The State has a power of influence and control over the latter which gives rise to a positive duty to act, such possibility of influence not existing in the case of private undertakings. (13) At the same time, Member States do have a positive duty to cooperate under article 5 para 1, which imposes an obligation upon them to take all appropriate measures in order to ensure fulfilment of the obligations arising out of the Treaty or resulting from action taken by the institutions of the Community.

1. STATE MEASURES ENABLING OR FACILITATING VIOLATIONS OF THE COMPETITION RULES

First, with respect to state measures which enable or facilitate agreements and concerted practices or the abuse of dominant position contrary to articles 85 and 86: it now seems to have been clearly established by the ECJ in INNO, despite the important restrictions on its wording brought about by the Van de Haar ruling (14), that 'Member States may not enact measures enabling private undertakings to escape the constraints imposed by articles 85 to 94'. (15) In INNO the Court stated that 'while it is true that article 86 is directed at undertakings it is also true that the Treaty imposes a duty on Member States not to adopt or maintain in force any measure which could deprive that provision of its effectiveness. (16) Similarly, Advocate General Reischl, while noting that 'articles 85 and 86 do not give rise directly to obligations of Member States', concluded that 'combination of the above with article 5 para 2 might mean that state measures are subject to certain restrictions' and that, therefore, 'Member States are obliged to put undertakings outside article 86 and not to create by State measures positions which undertakings are prohibited from creating under article 86'. (17)

The same principle may be considered to have underlain the earlier decision of the ECJ in Deutsche Grammophon. That case concerned a provision of German law relevant to copyright, allowing a sound manufacturer to prohibit, through the use of his right, the reimportation of the products sold by its subsidiary in other Member States. Looking at the same problem from a different angle the Court held that an undertaking should not exercise its rights under national laws if such rights are contrary to the provisions prescribing the free movement of products and the maintenance of a system of undistorted competition. (18)

The issue of state responsibility did not arise in that case since the Court drew a distinction between the existence of a right, which may be justified under article 36, and its exercise which may fall within the prohibition of the Treaty. (19) Nevertheless, Advocate General Roemer did further state that 'in view of the principle contained in the second paragraph of article 5 it must be assumed that national legislation did not intend to disregard the principles of the Treaty in this field and that the meaning of the provisions enacted by it must be interpreted accordingly' (20). That statement must be taken to imply that if an interpretation of the national provisions in a manner consistent with the Treaty is not possible and those provisions are contrary to the principles of the Treaty, including that contained in article 3(f), those national provisions cannot stand and must be abrogated.

A similar approach was followed in the Van Ameyde case where the Court, without ruling on state responsibility under the combined effects of articles 5 para 2 and 85 and 86, nevertheless held that 'directives, recommendations and decisions cannot be regarded as authorizing national provisions or agreements between national bureaux or practices or any conduct by them incompatible with the provisions of the Treaty relating to competition, the right of establishment and freedom to provide services'. (21)

The Van de Haar case concerned Dutch fiscal legislation similar to the Belgian one involved in INNO, which had the effect of imposing as the compulsory retail selling price of tobacco products the price chosen by the manufacturer or importer. In that case a chamber of the Court attempted to limit the potentially wide effects of the statement made in INNO concerning state responsibility. Thus, the ECJ stated that 'whilst it is true that Member States may not enact measures enabling private undertakings to escape the constraints imposed by article 85, the provisions of that article belong to the rules on competition 'applying to undertakings' and are thus intended to govern the conduct of private undertakings in the Common Market. They are therefore not relevant to the question whether legislation such as that involved in the cases before the national court is compatible with Community law'. (22) A similar approach was adopted by Advocate General Reischl, who also happened to be the Advocate General in INNO, who stated that 'it is not possible to accept that in a case such as this state measures must be judged by direct reference to article 85'. He considered that 'apart from the statements in the decision in INNO this view is borne by the fact that the caselaw on national price rules under examination with reference to article 30, would otherwise lose its meaning'. (23)

Despite the wording used by the Advocate General and the Court, which expressly limits the potential effects of the general statements of the Court in INNO regarding the liability of the State, Van de Haar could be distinguished on the basis of the actual facts and the particular formulation of the relevant questions by the referring court. Although the two cases concerned similar legislation in Belgium and in the Netherlands the questions of the national courts did not involve the same provisions of the Treaty. The Belgian court had asked whether the particular legislation was contrary to the combined effects of articles 5 para 2 and 86

(24) in that it enabled manufacturers and importers to abuse their position, since they were free to choose whichever price they liked. On the other hand, the question in Van de Haar was whether the law which forbade wholesalers and retailers from selling below the price indicated by the manufacturer or importer on the tag, was contrary to the combined effects of article 5 para 2 and 85, (25) in that such law had an effect equivalent to price fixing prohibited by the competition laws. In this latter case the conditions of article 85 were not separately met since there was no actual agreement or concerted practice between undertakings.

Leaving aside the actual content of the Van de Haar ruling, which shall be analysed below, it may, therefore, be concluded that this ruling did not overrule the Court's judgment in INNO to the extent that the latter held incompatible with the Treaty those national measures which enable or facilitate agreements or concerted practices or the abuse of dominant position. It only had the effect of restricting its potential application by preventing it from being interpreted any further than that. This may be derived from the actual wording of the Van de Haar judgment. There the Court, starting with the expression 'Whilst it is true', cited the principle established in INNO apparently with approval, before subsequently proceeding to restrict its application.

A similar position, which shall be criticized below, was adopted by Advocate General Warner in his opinion in the Hans Buys case where he attempted to limit the effects of the decision in INNO. Thus, after stating that 'no doubt a Member State would be in breach of article 5 if it enacted legislation calculated to bring about or encourage agreements contrary to 85', he continued that he 'did not think that, in relation to 85, article 5 could be interpreted any further than that (since) to hold that it did would be to render article 90 virtually nugatory' (26). Notwithstanding the objections which will be raised in conjunction with the second type of measures below (27), the above statement seems to uphold the view that the first type of national measure referred to herein falls under the prohibition of article 5 para 2 combined with 85 and 86.

To restrict the application of the combined effects of articles 5 para 2 and 85 and 86 only to those state measures which enable or facilitate violations of the competition rules is consistent with a narrow interpretation of article 90 according to which article 90 is a simple renvoi rule and, as far as the infringement is concerned, subsidiary in character. (28) According to this view article 90 only forbids state instructions which prescribe or lead to the conclusion of an agreement or concerted practice, the reference in article 90 para 1 to other provisions showing that the conditions set in those other provisions must be separately met. Considering that article 90 is only a particular application of article 5 para 2, the criticism of this narrow interpretation of state responsibility which shall follow also applies to state measures falling under article 90.

2. STATE MEASURES PRODUCING EFFECTS EQUIVALENT TO A VIOLATION OF THE COMPETITION RULES

The second category of measures comprises those measures which produce effects equivalent to a violation of the competition rules. Such measures may be taken by the State in the context of its general economic policy and planning or in an attempt to save failing sectors of the economy by means of an extensive and profound restructuring. Particular examples of state measures reducing the degree of competition are price regulation laws, compulsory cartel laws, partitioning of the market, control of investments etc.

The most important issue arising with respect to this type of measure concerns the criteria by virtue of which state measures producing anticompetitive effects may give rise to state liability under the Treaty. Considering that, with the exception of article 90 (which is limited to public undertakings and those to which the State grants special or exclusive rights) and articles 92-94 (which are restricted to state aids), the competition rules of the Treaty and in particular articles 85 and 86 are applicable only to undertakings, the essential questions are the following: whether such state liability may be established under those articles when combined with article 5 para 2 and, if so, which of the conditions contained in those articles and concerning the behaviour of undertakings must be fulfilled before the State is held liable.

In the extreme case, when despite the absence of any behaviour on the part of undertakings state measures have the effect of distorting competition, state liability under the Treaty could be established if one accepted the autonomous application of the general principle of undistorted competition contained in article 3(f).(29) Whether the principles contained in article 3 of the Treaty can by themselves give rise to liability is a matter of considerable dispute, just as it is also disputed whether articles 85 and 86 can provide the basis for state liability under the Treaty in the absence of actual agreement or concerted practice by undertakings or the abuse of dominant position by an undertaking.

It, therefore, becomes necessary to examine: first, whether article 3(f) as such is autonomously and directly applicable, in which case no further discussion of articles 85 and 86 is necessary, and second, if article 3(f) is not so directly applicable, to what extent the conditions of articles 85 and 86 must be fulfilled before state liability may be established, if at all, under those articles when combined with article 5 para 2.

In this respect it must also be examined whether a State may be held responsible for contravening the combined effects of articles 5, 3(f), 85 and 86 in circumstances in which its measures have been held to be consistent with the Treaty under the articles of Part II of the Treaty and in particular article 30. This issue shall be discussed below.

2.1 <u>State liability under article 3(f)</u>

The establishment of state liability solely under article 3(f) cannot easily be upheld, the direct and autonomous application of this article being a matter of considerable doubt. (30) Notwithstanding the general statements made by the ECJ in the Continental Can (31), Deutsche Grammophon (32) and INNO (33) cases which, at first glance, seem to have recognized an autonomous compulsory force and direct applicability to the objectives of article 3 of the Treaty (34) the generally accepted view is that article 3(f) is not directly applicable. (35) As Advocate General Reischl noted with respect to the above mentioned cases, 'one should not be led astray by the observations of the Court in Continental Can where it only stressed the significance of articles 2 and 3 with regard to article 86 which is directly applicable.' (36) Vague support for this view may be found in the statement of the Court in INNO, that the general principle of article 3(f) is made specific in several Treaty provisions including article 86. (37)

Another argument put forward against the autonomous and direct application of article 3(f) (38) is that in such a case it would be hard to explain why the Treaty should contain specific prohibitions, for example on the free circulation of goods. The reasoning behind it is that all these prohibitions would be absorbed in the general prohibition of article 3(f). Although we abide by the general view that article 3(f) cannot by itself provide the basis for holding the State liable for measures which have the effect of distorting competition, nevertheless, the above argument is wrong for the following reasons. First, it ignores that all the principles and Community activities enumerated in article 3 have one common aim, to achieve, through their implementation, the ultimate objectives of article 2, these being the establishment of a Common Market and the progressive approximation of the economic policies of Member States. (39) It is obvious that these principles and activities are not exclusive of each other but that their potential areas of application are, to a certain extent, likely to coincide and converge. Second, the existence of a specific provision does not make a general one invalid since specific provisions always prevail over general ones. Thus, the fact that a state measure has the effect of distorting competition does not preclude the possibility that such measures may also be contrary to a specific provision of the Treaty contained in another section thereof.

Despite the fallacy of the above argument, we must recognize at the present stage of Community development article 3(f) is not yet capable of establishing an independent prohibition under the Treaty. This does not mean, however, that we abide by the extreme and restrictive view that article 3(f) merely anticipates the competition rules. (40) Indeed, article 3(f) by making clear that the maintenance of a system of undistorted competition is one of the basic principles of the Treaty by which Member States must abide performs an essential function: it indicates that the competition rules may apply to Member States despite the absence of a specific Treaty provision providing so and directly addressed to them.

As the drafters of the Treaty noted in the Spaak report, it was not possible to determine in detail in the Treaty all the particular mechanisms and obligations (41) to be provided for, those having been left to be developed in the future in the light of the spirit of the Treaty and its general principles and aims. In this respect, therefore, the general principle contained in article 3(f) contributes to the interpretation of the competition rules and assists in finding that they may be applicable to Member States. It thus prevents the objectives of the Treaty from being frustrated by the absence of a specific and express obligation to that effect contained therein. These objectives would risk being jeopardised if one of the fundamental principles of the Common Market, the maintenance of a system of undistorted competition, did not apply to Member States and could, as a consequence, be circumvented by them.

In the light of the above we shall now examine which conditions must be fulfilled in order to establish state liability for measures having anticompetitive effects under articles 5 para 2, 3(f), 85 and 86 combined. In doing so regard must also be given to the fact that the drafters did not intend all state activity to fall within the realm of the Treaty but, instead, did recognize a certain degree of state discretion in the formulation of general economic policy.

Even if the INNO ruling makes clear that the prohibitions of articles 85 and 86 cannot be circumvented by the adoption of state measures it does not, however, permit the conclusion that it prohibits any distortion of competition which may be caused by state intervention in the economic field. Before attempting to establish the criteria for state liability under the combined effects of articles 3(f), 85 and 86 we shall first try to clarify the relationship between article 30 and the competition rules, particularly with respect to their application to price regulations.

2.2 **Relationship between article 30 and the competition rules**

The problem which has arisen is whether price legislation implementing, for example, a price freeze, setting maximum or minimum prices or controlling price margins may be held contrary to the combined effects of articles 5 para 2 and 85.

It has been established by the ECJ that as a general rule such legislation, when applicable without distinction to domestic and imported products, does not in itself constitute a measure having an effect equivalent to a quantitative restriction, but may have such an effect when prices are fixed at such a level that the sale of imported products becomes either impossible or more difficult than that of domestic products. (42) In each case it is for the national court to decide whether those conditions are satisfied.

Most of the cases before the ECJ where the issue arose concerned national price systems in sections covered by a common organization of the market. In all those cases the Court, while reiterating the above doctrine in connection with article 30, refrained from ruling on the compatibility of national measures with the combined effects of articles 5 para 2 and 85. Although questions to that effect were asked by the national courts the ECJ considered the matter exclusively within the context of article 30 and/or of the common organization of the market. It thus held that the assessment of the compatibility with Community law of the freezing of the price of products subject to a common organization of the market does not depend on the provisions of article 85 but, rather, on the provisions governing the said organization. Therefore, measures relating to price formation at the retail and consumption level are consistent with the Treaty on the condition that they do not jeopardise the aims and functioning of the common organization of the market in question. (43)

The assessment of national measures in sectors subject to a common organization of the market exclusively within the context of the rules set by this common organization is consistent with the general principle of interpretation that, in areas covered by specific Community regulations, these must take precedence over the general rules of the Treaty which the particular regulations are, in any way, supposed to implement. Furthermore, article 42 of the Treaty expressly restricts the application of the rules of competition to the production and trade of agricultural products to the extent determined by the Council within the framework of its power to establish common market organizations. Therefore, the relevant caselaw contains no indication as to the application of article 5 para 2, in combination with articles 85 and 86, to national price systems outside the sectors covered by a common organization of the market.

However, Advocate General Warner in the Hans Buys case did not limit himself to assessing the relevant state measures within the context of the common market organization. As already mentioned, he proceeded to answer the national court's question in the negative by holding that articles 5 and 85 do not apply to national legislation which brings about the same result as article 85. He stated that 'a

Member State would be in breach of article 5 if it enacted legislation calculated to bring about or encourage agreements, decisions or concerted practices but that in relation to article 85, article 5 cannot be interpreted any further than that. To hold that it did' he proceeded 'would be to render article 90 virtually nugatory and would also mean that the Treaty had taken away from Member States all power to control prices, which the judgments of the Court in the Galli, Tasca, SADAM, Van Tiggele, Dechmann and Grosoli cases clearly show that it has not'. (44)

Several remarks may be made in connection with the Advocate General's position. First, he seems to draw a clear distinction between articles 5 and 85, the application of which he unduly restricts, and article 90. By holding that to apply articles 5 and 85, despite the absence of an agreement or concerted practices, to national legislation bringing about the same effects as article 85 would render article 90 virtually nugatory, the Advocate General implies that article 90 is in fact applicable to national legislation concerning public undertakings and bringing about similar anticompetitive results. This view, which provides support for a wide interpretation of article 90, draws an undue distinction between state measures adopted in connection with undertakings in general and those adopted with respect to public undertakings. It is true that the Treaty distinguishes between public and private undertakings by the mere fact that it contains a special article for public undertakings, through which it grants special power to the Commission to address directives or decisions to Member States. However, except for that special power and within the limits which have already been explained in previous chapters, state liability for anticompetitive measures is not fundamentally different whether one considers measures affecting public undertakings alone or measures affecting both public and private undertakings. What is material is the end result which is the contravention of one of the fundamental principles of the Common Market.

Leaving aside the statement of the Advocate General with respect to article 90, his conclusion that to extend the application of the competition rules to price regulations would involve taking away from Member States all power to control prices, which the ECJ has stated that they have, finds support in the opinion of Advocate General Reischl and in the judgment of the ECJ in the case of Van de Haar.

There, the Advocate General observed that if the

criteria of article 85 were applicable, the existence of a measure affecting trade could not easily be denied since an agreement between undertakings to fix prices undeniably produces such effects. The assessment of national measures on prices under article 30 would therefore become superfluous, which would be contrary to ECJ caselaw that, in general, such measures do not amount to a hindrance of imports. (45)

The Advocate General made the above observations in reply to the question whether the national court, in its assessment of the compatibility with article 30 of a regulation applicable indistinctly to national and imported products, may take into consideration criteria developed by the Court in connection with the notion of 'effect on trade' contained in article 85, or whether article 30 must be interpreted autonomously. (46) This question was not concerned with the possible establishment of an independent prohibition addressed to Member States under articles 5 para 2 and 85. Nevertheless, the Commission in its submissions in the same case answered it in the affirmative. By invoking the complementary nature of articles 85 and 30, both aiming at assuring the free movement of goods and the unity of the Common Market, the Commission submitted that, in order to check the compatibility of price regulations with article 30, the principles set out in the rules of competition, especially in article 85, should be taken into consideration. (47)

The Commission's view was rightly rejected both by Advocate General Reischl and by the ECJ. The general statement of the ECJ in INNO that a national measure favouring the abuse of dominant position will generally be incompatible with articles 30-34 (48) must not be interpreted to imply such interchangeable use of the criteria of articles 30 and 85 and 86. Although the general aim of articles 3(a) and (f) and of articles 30 and 85 is to prevent the obstruction of trade and the partitioning of the market by national or private means (49), it is erroneous to believe that the field of application of article 30 covers integrally that of articles 85 and 86 and that all restrictions of competition, if they affect trade between Member States, are forbidden. (50) As the Court held in Van de Haar, article 30, which aims at the elimination of national measures capable of restricting trade, pursues a different objective from article 85 which aims at maintaining an efficient competition between undertakings. (51) Therefore, each provision must be interpreted independently in the light of its position in the Treaty and the function which it performs but by also taking into account the general principles and objectives of the Treaty.

One cannot, however, conclude from the above that article 30 and article 5 para 2 in combination with 85 and 86 are exclusive of each other or that their respective fields of application never coincide. The fact that a national price system has been held not to be a measure of equivalent effect to a quantitative restriction because it does not, directly or indirectly, actually or potentially, hinder imports, does not preclude that same national price regulation from being considered contrary to the combined effects of articles 5 para 2 and 85 and 86 if it has the effect of distorting competition and may affect trade between Member States. To say that a measure which does not have an equivalent effect to a restriction of imports cannot be contrary to the rules of competition implies that the Treaty of Rome merely aims at the creation of a customs union, whereas the Treaty aims at the establishment of a real Common Market for the achievement of the objectives set out in articles 2 and 3 thereof. It is exactly, therefore, the fact that article 30 and the competition rules pursue different objectives that makes necessary the application of the latter to state measures which have the effect of distorting competition without at the same time amounting to a hindrance to imports.

Since anticompetitive effects could, for example, be brought about by the fixing of minimum prices, as in the Van Tiggele case, or by the exclusion of competition at the retail level through the fixing of compulsory margins. Also, as Advocate General Warner himself admitted in Galli, although national price control legislation most often applies only to large scale undertakings partly because of the administrative burden and partly because in many trades the behaviour of large undertakings has a major impact on the market, if it were shown in a particular instance that the financial criteria were pitched at a level calculated to affect only certain specific undertakings, the conclusion might be drawn that objectionable discrimination was intended. (52)

Therefore, in view of the above, although the fields of application of articles 30-34 and 85 in conjunction with 5 para 2 will often coincide, this is not necessarily so, different criteria having to be satisfied for their respective application. For example, it results from EMI v CBS that article 30 does not apply to state measures which have the effect of restricting imports from third countries while article 85 may be applicable to agreements having this effect. (53) Similarly, agreements or abuses which had the effect of restricting the manufacture of a certain product in a Member State have been held to fall under the prohibition of the competition rules (54) while the application of article 34 to national measures which had the same effect has been denied (55) except where products for which there existed a Community marketing organization were involved. (56)

On the other hand, an example of parallel application of article 30 with domestic competition rules appeared in the Van Tiggele case. There the ECJ condemned under article 30 national measures imposing minimum prices for distilled drinks after a judicial decision had declared incompatible with national legislation the vertical agreements which had been previously applied by the majority of manufacturers and produced the same effects. (57) Therefore, it may be concluded that although national price regulations applicable indiscriminately to all undertakings will generally be assessed under article 30 for the purpose of deciding whether they hinder imports directly or indirectly, actually or potentially, state measures which have the effect of fixing prices at a level which creates discrimination or which adversely affects competition may be examined under the combined effects of articles 5 para 2 and 85 as well as under article 30. In this respect a distinction may be drawn between the fixing of maximum and minimum prices. Whereas the imposition of minimum prices by the State is almost always likely to distort competition in the same way as a price cartel, maximum prices are most often part of anti-inflationary policy allowing competition below this limit through reduction of costs or other economies. However, this must not be interpreted to mean that maximum prices can never be contrary to the competition rules, maximum prices potentially stifling innovation and the improvement of quality in the long run.

2.3 State liability under the combined effects of articles 5 para 2, 3(f), 85 and 86

Having, thus, explained that the caselaw of the Court establishing that national price systems are not as such incompatible with article 30 does not preclude the parallel application of the competition rules, we must now determine the conditions and criteria for the establishment of state liability under the latter. As it becomes obvious from the examples cited above, the competition rules have not until now been directly applied to state measures unless there has also been an agreement or concerted practice between undertakings which was either the result of the state measure or the cause of it.

Despite the general statements of the ECJ in INNO (58), the view that the Treaty prohibits national measures restricting competition does not find support in subsequent cases. Although the Court had not dealt with the issue directly until the decisions of Van de Haar (59) and Leclerc (60) which shall be discussed below, certain obiter dicta and observations made by the Advocate Generals point towards a restrictive application of the competition rules to state measures.

Thus, in Van Tiggele, (61) although no relevant question was put by the national court, Advocate General Capotorti minimized the effects of the INNO decision. He considered it clear that if article 86 is to be relied upon in connection with the prohibition of measures having an effect equivalent to quantitative restrictions - the necessity of such connection being open to criticism - the measures adopted by the public authorities must promote an infringement of the rules on competition by those to whom such rules apply, namely undertakings. Similarly, in Duphar (62) where the issue was the legality of state measures excluding certain pharmaceuticals from reimbursement by the social security because of the existence of cheaper drugs with the same therapeutic effects, the Court refused to assess the legality of state measures within the framework of the competition rules and decided it solely on the basis of article 30. The Court held that the relevant Dutch legislation was compatible with article 30 if the determination of the excluded medical preparations involved no discrimination regarding the origin of the products and was carried out on the basis of objective and verifiable criteria such as the existence of less expensive products with the same therapeutic effect. However, the Court's ruling that articles 85 and 86 form part of the rules of competition applicable to undertakings and do not, therefore, come into consideration in the assessment of the conformity of Community law with legislation of this type, may be partly explained by the absence of any reference to article 5 para 2 in the question of the national Court.

In the earlier case of Roussel (63) where the referring Court did ask whether articles 3(f) and 5 in conjunction with 85 and 86 have direct effects, the Court did not deal with the issue but decided the case solely on the basis of article 30. However, Advocate General Madame Rozès adopted a restrictive attitude by refusing to consider the compatibility of national legislation with the competition rules in the absence of an agreement, a decision or a concerted practice or an abuse of a dominant position, notwithstanding the deterioration in normal competition brought about by national legislation. Although the A.G. did recognize the need for some Community control of anticompetitive legislation she considered that it is the task of the Commission to adopt general or specific measures for the implementation of article 5 para 2 in combination with the competition rules and to ascertain whether the conduct of undertakings is not to be traced to provisions of national laws and regulations. (64)

It is important to note that in none of the cases mentioned above did the Court deal directly with the issue of the compatibility of national legislation with article 5 para 2 in conjunction with the competition rules. The first case after the INNO judgment where the Court expressly restricted the potentially wide effects of the statement made therein was Van de Haar. The decision in this latter case was, however, a chamber decision as opposed to the one in INNO which was pronounced by the full Court. As has already been mentioned above, the ECJ in Van de Haar, while disapproving of national measures enabling undertakings to avoid the constraints of article 85, refused to hold contrary to article 85 legislation producing effects analogous to a prohibited agreement or concerted practice. The same view had actually been advocated by the Commission which, although referring to the statement of the Court in INNO, remarked that article 85 is applicable only if there is an agreement or concerted practice between undertakings. It thus concluded that the mere fact that the effect of state intervention is equivalent to that resulting from a retail price fixing system imposed by undertakings cannot give rise to applicability of article 85 in the absence of agreements or concerted practices. (65)

The above view which is based on the literal requirement of an agreement or concerted practice between undertakings and results in the use of different criteria for distortion of competition of public and private origin opens the way to potential abuse. (66) Apart from creating a loophole in the Treaty which Member States may take advantage of, thus frustrating the Treaty objectives, it is likely to lead to inequality and discrimination which cannot be justified by the invocation of the general interest which Member States are supposed to serve. In fact, in Europe where the free enterprise system has never been as rigidly adhered to as in the US and state intervention has played an important role and influenced as well as been influenced by the behaviour of private undertakings in the market, the distinction between general and particular interest has never been sufficiently clear cut, the two often being intermingled. This confusion between general and particular interest, caused by the interdependence between the State and private undertakings, has become even greater nowadays. In view of the economic crisis private undertakings expect that government assistance will help them solve their economic and financial problems, while, at the same time, the State, considering the potential repercussions of unemployment, has an interest in the survival of large private undertakings regardless of their possible inefficiency and of the cost.

As a result of the above, recourse to persuasion and concertation is often preferred to direct government intervention, and state measures are not always inspired by the need to serve the long term general interest. Instead, they are often adopted on an ad hoc basis as a result of successful lobbying by the undertakings themselves. Such, for example, was the case in Belgium where the system of compulsory resale price of tobacco, which was the object of the proceedings in the INNO case, had in fact been previously introduced in the form of a cartel by the organizations of producers and wholesalers of tobacco products. In the particular case the relevant legislative provision rendering the system of resale price compulsory was proposed during the discussion of the draft VAT Code in Parliament by the Secretary of the Tobacco Wholesalers Association himself, who also happened to be a Member of Parliament. (67) In cases where heavy fines may be imposed on private undertakings which form a cartel, the refusal by the Commission and the Court to hold the state measures rendering such a cartel compulsory incompatible with the competition rules creates obvious injustice and leads to unjustifiable discriminations between undertakings. It makes them depend on their political connections and their ability to obtain the necessary legislative cover in order to be dispensed from having to rely on 'agreements' or 'concerted practices'.

Furthermore, the state measures that a Member State purports to take in the public interest do not necessarily serve the Community interest which must always prevail. If Member States were allowed to distort competition in pursuance of their economic policy then one of the basic principles of the Treaty would be frustrated.

Despite the restrictive view adopted by the ECJ in Van de Haar the judgments of the Court in the two subsequent cases of Leclerc (68) indicate a return to a wider interpretation. Thus, although the Commission adopted a conservative approach by suggesting that the application of article 5 para 2 in conjunction with the competition rules should be limited to three exceptional cases in which Member States (a) impose or facilitate the conclusion of prohibited agreements or concerted practices, (b) reinforce their effects by extending them to third parties, or (c) pursue the specific objective of allowing undertakings to circumvent the rules of competition, the ECJ did not limit itself in that manner. Instead, the ECJ made the same, rather sibylline, general statement in both cases, which was however subsequently curtailed and adapted to the facts of each case, that 'it is true that the rules on competition are concerned with the conduct of undertakings and not with the national legislation of Member States. However, Member States are nonetheless obliged under the second paragraph of Article 5 of the Treaty not to detract, by means of national legislation, from the full and uniform application of Community law or from the effectiveness of its implementing measures; nor may they introduce or maintain in force measures, even of a legislative nature, which may render ineffective the rules of competition applicable to undertakings' (69). The ECJ thus envisaged for the first time the possibility that a state measure which makes agreements and concerted practices superfluous could be contrary to article 5 para 2 in combination with 85 and 86.

In the first Leclerc case the Court examined whether the French legislation which imposed upon the retailers the obligation to sell books at a price fixed by the publisher or the importer and which, therefore, rendered the conclusion of an agreement between publishers and retailers superfluous eliminates the effectiveness of 85 and is, as a result, contrary to article 5 para 2 in conjunction with it. However, the Court refrained from ruling on the anticompetitive effect of such legislation in a general sense. Instead and in the absence of a Community policy of competition in the book sector which Member States should respect within the framework of article 5 para 2, the Court concluded that at the present stage of Community law the obligations of Member States flowing from article 5 para 2, in combination with 3(f) and 85, are not sufficiently determined in order to prohibit such legislation provided the other Treaty provisions and in particular those concerning the free circulation of goods are respected. (70) This decision (which once again denies the application of the competition rules to the state measures under discussion) was justified by the great divergence which existed between the national policies with respect to the fixing of the prices of books and by the fact that the Commission had not yet proceeded to the study of those policies which it had declared to be necessary. The Court's reasoning, however, is open to criticism because it leads to the odd result that the States have reserved their competence in those fields in which the Commission has not yet effectively applied articles 85 and 86. Such a situation, in addition to contravening the basic principle of the primacy of Community law, is also contrary to the direct applicability of articles 85 and 86. On the other hand, Advocate General Darmon, while, in principle, in favour of the application of articles 5 para 2 and 85 and 86 to legislation of this type, considered them inapplicable in this particular case in view of the cultural element of the national policies on books. The A.G.'s position is to be preferred and is also consistent with the analysis which shall follow in this chapter. (71)

In the second Leclerc case, where the issue was the legality of state measures fixing a minimum compulsory retail price for petrol, the Court held that such regulation assigning to the government the task of fixing a minimum price by taking into account several factors including the average price fixed by domestic suppliers, did not eliminate the effectiveness of the competition rules. (72)

The difference between the two Leclerc decisions seems to lie in the fact that whereas in Leclerc 2 it was the State that fixed the price of petrol by taking into account several factors among which was the price fixed by the suppliers, in Leclerc I the State let the undertakings decide on the prices. In the latter case the legislator only rendered obligatory a certain minimum price fixed by the importer or the publisher. The Leclerc decisions, therefore, open the way to a new form of application of the competition rules to state measures, where the relevant question is neither whether state measures have in themselves produced effects similar to an agreement or concerted practice under article 85 nor the actual existence of such an agreement or concerted practice. Nevertheless, it appears that the Court still considered the role of the undertakings in the formulation of the prices finally fixed by the State as a necessary element for the establishment of state liability under the competition rules. In this way the State is somehow penalized as an accomplice for substituting the undertakings in producing the anticompetitive effects which the latter might have wished.

We do not believe that the liability of the States under the competition rules should be so limited. Price regulations may have the effect of distorting competition even when imposed by the State purportedly in the public interest and without taking into consideration even the suggestions of the private undertakings concerned. The Leclerc decisions, therefore, although a step forward from the previous decisions of the Court with respect to state liability under the competition rules, do not sufficiently make clear the degree thereof nor provide a satisfactory test for the future.

While, however, it becomes apparent that the adoption of different criteria for assessing distortions of competition of public and private origin may have the effect of frustrating the Treaty objectives by allowing Member States to circumvent the application of the competition rules, it must also be recognized that not all distortions of competition by the State are prohibited. Even if the maintenance of undistorted competition is one of the fundamental principles of the free market economy on which the Community is based (73), the drafters of the Treaty foresaw - and experience has confirmed - that for the purpose of achieving the Community objectives a certain coordination and economic regulation by public authorities is necessary.

As the Commission stated in its reply to a written question of Glinne, M.E.P., the EEC Treaty is inspired, on the one hand, by the need to establish within the Common Market a free market based on the notion of free competition and, on the other, by the assignment to the Community authorities of real powers to develop and implement economic policies. The Treaty framework allows a certain flexibility in the degree of liberalism or regulation that must be observed and enables the Community organs to give the proper directions. (74) Thus, although the EEC Treaty contains no specific mandate for tackling industrial policy, the need for it was spotlighted by the Commission as early as 1970 in its report on the Community Industrial Policy. Particularly in today's crisis where there are many ailing companies and a need to invest in high technology requiring huge investments, some degree of common action is necessary.

In the same vein, the Commission, while reaffirming in its 12th Report on Competition Policy its belief that it is vital to safeguard the operation of fair and workable competition, also realized that during a recession the degree of workable competition cannot be the same as when the market functions smoothly. (75) In the light of this and in order to face the increased competition from outside the Community, the Commission stressed the need to proceed to the necessary industrial adaptation by encouraging restructuring and industrial redeployment provided this is in line with the Community interest and has the least harmful effect on competition. (76)

An illustration of a policy which reduces the degree of competition in order to facilitate an extensive and profound industrial reconstruction is the Community policy with respect to the steel industry. (77) Although this reconstruction is undertaken within a Community framework, the same need for regulation and coordination with potential anticompetitive effects most often appears on a national level in areas where the Community has not yet taken or does not have the means to take action. In such circumstances Member States may themselves take the appropriate measures although such may have potentially anticompetitive effects; however, the Member States may do so only so long as such measures are compatible with the Community objectives.

Although at the present stage of Community integration Member States have considerable discretion in the formulation of their economic policy, nonetheless, the maintenance of undistorted competition is a fundamental principle of the Community, divergence from which may be allowed only if it serves the Community interest. As the

Commission stated in its 11th Report on Competition Policy, while it cannot admit measures which invoke public or private protectionism in order to preserve the national market from competitive pressure from outside, there exist certain measures which whilst having, strictly speaking, a certain anticompetitive effect are nevertheless compatible with the Treaty objectives. (78) Examples of such measures are those promoting the cooperation between small and medium-sized firms, benefiting key sectors of the future, or providing for concerted reduction of production capacity in industries struck by crises or undergoing adaptation. (79)

In the light of the above it becomes apparent that the subjection of state measures to the competition rules cannot depend on the existence or absence of an agreement or concerted practice between undertakings. A pragmatic approach must, therefore, be adopted without too much confidence in the laissez faire policy of the market or in a draconian public intervention. Bearing in mind that active competition policy can play a useful role in solving the persisting economic problems (80), assessment of the compatibility of state measures with the competition rules should take into account not only the restrictive effect but also the purpose and content of the national policy. (81) State measures showing a real effort for restructuring by promoting a final structure which will be compatible with the Community interest and be viable and competitive in the long run shall, therefore, pass the test provided there exist sufficient guarantees against the abuse of market power and probable combines. Under the same conditions there is room for concentration in article 86 but the discretionary margins are more limited than in article 85, the structures resulting from concentrations being irreversible and permanent in time. (82)

It is important to note, however, that on an economic level such restructuring shall be allowed only if the following conditions are satisfied: first, it must be established that the normal functioning of the market is not capable of redressing the situation because ill-adapted undertakings belonging to large groups are maintained alive artificially to the detriment of sound ones. Second, the means used must not restrict the behaviour of undertakings in the market more than necessary by adopting tools such as the fixing of prices, production or sales quotas, the granting of aids etc. (83) Moreover, the need for a Community policy in those areas is paramount and individual state measures must always be looked on by taking into consideration the possible existence of such policy. Competition policy goes hand in hand with industrial policy and is one of the components of the Community's economic policy. Disturbance of the operation of the Common Market should not be tolerated unless this is accompanied by radical restructuring measures. (84)

On a juridicial level the above theory points towards the adoption of a rule of reason equivalent to the one existing in American Antitrust Law. In EEC law this rule may be developed by drawing analogies from articles 85 para 3 (85) or 36. Article 85 para 3, according to its terms, applies to undertakings and has the effect of exempting from the rules of competition agreements or concerted practices which contribute to improving the production or distribution of goods or to promoting technical or economic progress. Nonetheless, its specific criteria when placed in a general context may contribute to the assessment of national measures under the competition rules. Similarly, the exceptions provided for by article 36, although strictly allowed only within the context of articles 30 to 34, could be invoked in order to justify state measures which have the effect of distorting competition.

Although the maintenance of a system of free competition is an essential objective of the Treaty, it must be combined with the other objectives. In assessing, therefore, whether state measures have the effect of distorting competition, articles 5 para 2 in combination with 85 and 86 must be interpreted and applied in the light of the general objectives of the Treaty, not only those contained in the initial provisions but also those deriving from the general spirit thereof. In this respect an analogy may also be drawn from the rule of reason developed within the framework of article 30 where account has been taken of factors such as the general principle of proportionality between ends to be achieved and means used, the existence or absence of a Community policy and the fundamental principle of non discrimination. (86) Thus, in the case of Cassis de Dijon (87) the Court has declared that the obstacles to intra-Community trade resulting from disparities in national legislations relating to the marketing of the products in question must be accepted in so far as those provisions may be recognized as being necessary in order to satisfy mandatory requirements relating in particular to the effectiveness of fiscal supervision, the protection of public health, the fairness of commercial transactions and the defence of the consumer. In its decision in the case of Van Binsbergen (88) concerning the application of article 59, the Court developed a similar rule of reason within the context of the provisions on the free supply of services. It held that professional rules justified by the general interest, such as rules of organization, qualifications, professional ethics, supervision and liability, could be applied to all persons established in the country where service is provided. (89)

Despite the above, however, the adoption of a rule of reason must not be interpreted to mean that the principle of free competition may always be set aside for the benefit of some other potential objective. A temporary loss of competition through regulation and coordination will be tolerated only if this is outweighed by the long run benefit of enhancing the competitive structure of the economy.

2.4 Means to enforce article 5 para 2 in conjunction with the competition rules

At a Community level, an infringement by a Member State of the competition rules may give rise to an action by the Commission or another Member State under articles 169 or 171, respectively. The decisions of the Court in such case have purely declaratory effect but could constitute basis for an action for damages before the national courts. Regulation 17 which enables the Commission to put an end to infringements of competition committed by undertakings and, in addition, impose fines on them cannot be used against Member States. (90)

The various restrictions to the applicability of the competition rules to general state measures which were discussed above cast serious doubt on the possibility of enforcing those rules on a national level. National courts would have to control whether a given national measure, although restrictive of competition, nevertheless promotes some objective which is compatible with the Treaty and, in doing so, does not impose any restrictions that are not necessary to that effect. This requires a pretty sophisticated political and economic evaluation which national courts are not well equipped to make.

3. STATE MEASURES IMPOSING A BEHAVIOUR CONTRARY TO THE COMPETITION RULES

The analysis made with respect to the above two types of measures may also be made with respect to measures imposing upon undertakings behaviour contrary to the competition rules. In the case in which these state measures oblige the undertakings to enter into an agreement or engage in a concerted practice or force them to abuse a dominant position, they must be held to be incompatible with the Treaty for the same reasons as measures that enable or facilitate similar violations. The fact that in such cases the behaviour of the undertakings is not voluntary should not make any difference with respect to the liability of the State even though it may have the effect of absolving the undertakings themselves from liability under articles 85 and 86.

However, it is unlikely that Member States will promulgate laws obliging undertakings to conclude agreements or engage in concerted practices which are prohibited by article 85 or to abuse their dominant position contrary to article 86. It is more probable that they will adopt measures that, while forcing upon the undertakings a behaviour similar to that prohibited under articles 85 and 86, do not bring about agreements or concerted practices. Examples of such measures are compulsory cartels and measures allowing undertakings to fix the resale prices of their products such as were in issue in the INNO, Van de Haar and first Leclerc cases. Even if these measures make undertakings behave in a way very similar to that resulting from an agreement or concerted practice one cannot invoke the existence of an agreement or concerted practice for the purpose of establishing state liability under the competition rules.

The correct view in such cases is to consider that these state measures fall under the category of those producing effects equivalent to a violation of the competition rules and assess them in the light of the conclusions drawn above with respect to this type of measure. Otherwise, considering that it may be justified and necessary to exonerate undertakings from liability under the competition rules, their anticompetitive behaviour having been imposed upon them by the State, a parallel exoneration of the State would create a big loophole in the Treaty and frustrate the Treaty objectives.

NOTES

1. See Waelbroeck, 'La Constitution Européenne et les interventions des Etats-membres en matière economique', In Orde (1982) at p. 331.
2. INNO v ATAB, (1977) ECR at p. 2146, cited supra.
3. See Chapter Three, Section 3.
4. See Chapter Three, Sections 1.3 and 1.4
5. See Waelbroeck, In Orde, op. cit. at p. 336-8.
6. See Chapter Two.
7. Waelbroeck, In Orde, op. cit. at p. 333. See also Joined Cases 40-48, 50, 54-56, 111, 113-4/73, Suiker Unie, (1975) ECR 1663, 1923-4 and Case 5/79, Hans Buys, (1979) ECR 3203, 3231.
8. Spaak Report at p. 15.
9. Ibid at p. 13 et seq.
10. Spaak Report at p. 24.
11. Ibid at p. 16-17.
12. See also Chapter Two.
13. See also Chapter Three, Section 1.5.
14. Joined Cases 177-8/82, Officier Van Justitie v Jan Van de Haar, (1984), ECR 1797.
15. INNO v ATAB, (1977) ECR at p. 2145, cited supra.
16. Ibid at p. 2144.
17. Ibid at p. 2166-7.
18. Deutsche Grammophon, (1971) ECR at p. 499-500, cited supra.
19. Ibid at p. 499-500.
20. Ibid at p. 506.
21. Van Ameyde, (1977) ECR at p. 1123, cited supra.
22. Van de Haar, (1984) ECR at p. 1815-6, cited supra.
23. Van de Haar, (1984) ECR at p. 1826, cited supra.
24. INNO v ATAB, (1977) ECR at p. 2118, cited supra.
25. Van de Haar, (1984) ECR 1797, cited supra.
26. (1979) ECR at p. 3245, cited supra.
27. Section 2.2. of this chapter.
28. E.g. Nicolaysen, Bruges, (1968), op. cit. at p. 346. Also Marenco, op. cit. at p. 513.
29. See Vandencasteele, op. cit. at p. 549.
30. See for example Advocate General Reischl in Sacchi, (1974) ECR at p. 435-6 and Advocate General Warner in Galli, (1975) ECR at p. 72, cited supra.
31. Case 6/72, Continental Can, (1973) ECR 215, 244-5.

32. (1971) ECR at p. 499-500, cited supra.
33. (1977) ECR at p. 2144, cited supra.
34. See also Waelbroeck, In Orde, op. cit. at p. 333-4, where it is stated that the report delivered by Judge Pescatore at the Congress of FIDE in Berlin, in September 1970, under the title 'Das Zusammenwirken der Gemeinschaftsordnungen', and published in Europarecht (1970), p. 322-3, reinforced that view.
35. See for example Commission's submissions in Sacchi, (1974) at p. 414 and Galli, (1975) ECR at p. 51, cited supra. Also Advocate General in Sacchi, (1974) ECR at p. 435-6, and Advocate General in Galli, (1975) ECR at p. 72.
36. Sacchi, (1974) ECR at p. 435.
37. (1977), ECR at p. 2144.
38. See also Advocate General Trabucchi in Geddo, (1973) ECR at p. 883.
39. See Advocate General in Deutsche Grammophon, (1971) ECR at p. 506.
40. This restrictive view has also been adopted by Marenco in a commentary on the ECJ judgment of Van de Haar, where he states that article 3(f) simply anticipates the competition rules of 85-94 which in so far as Member States are concerned only provide for the incompatibility of certain aids, in Revue Trimestrielle de Droit Européen No 3, Juillet Septembre 1984, p. 521-36, at p. 534.
41. Spaak Report at p. 23.
42. See for example Case 31/74, Galli, (1975) ECR 47, Case 65/75, Tasca, (1976) ECR 291, Joined Cases 88-90/75 SADAM, (1976) ECR 323, Case 82/77, Van Tiggele (1978) ECR 25, Case 5/79, Hans Buys, (1979) ECR 3203.
43. Hans Buys, (1979) ECR at p. 3230-1, 3226.
44. (1979) ECR at p. 3245.
45. Van de Haar, (1984) ECR at p. 1822, cited supra.
46. Ibid at p. 1800.
47. Van de Haar, (1984) ECR at p. 1804-5, cited supra.
48. (1977) ECR at p. 2145.
49. See opinion of the Advocate General Roemer in Deutsche Grammophon, (1971) ECR at p. 506.
50. Waelbroeck, In Orde, op. cit. at p. 335.
51. Van de Haar, (1984) ECR 1812, cited supra.
52. (1975) ECR at p. 72-3.
53. Joined Cases 51, 86, 96/75, EMI/CBS, (1976) ECR 811 and 871, 845, 848, 904, 906.
54. See Joined Cases 6, 7/73, Commercial Solvents

Corporation, (1974) ECR 223, 250-3, Suiker Unie, (1975) ECR at p. 2018-19. See also Waelbroeck, In Orde, op. cit. at p. 335-6.

55.   Case 15/79, Groenveld (1979) ECR 3409, 3415. Confirmed in Case 155/80, Oebel, (1981) ECR 1993, 2009 and Joined Cases 141-143/81, Holdijk, (1982) ECR 1299, 1313.

56.   Case 190/73, Van Haaster (1974) ECR 1123, 1134.

57.   (1978) ECR 25, cited supra.

58.   (1977) ECR at p. 2144, 2145.

59.   Van de Haar, (1984) ECR 1797, cited supra.

60.   (1) Case 229/83, Association des Centres Distributeurs Edouard Leclerc v 'Au Blé Vert', (1985) ECR 17. (2) Case 231/83, Henri Cullet v Centre Leclerc à Toulouse, (1985) ECR 315.

61.   (1976) ECR at p. 47-9.

62.   Case 238/82, Duphar v The Netherlands, (1984) ECR 523.

63.   Case 181/82, Roussel v The Netherlands, (1983) ECR 3849.

64.   Ibid at p. 3875.

65.   See also Marenco, Commentaire de l'arrêt 177-78/82 (Van de Haar) in Revue Trimestrielle de Droit Européen (1984), op. cit.

66.   See Waelbroeck, In Orde, op. cit. at p. 336-8.

67.   Waelbroeck, 'The extent to which government interference can constitute justification under article 85 or 86 of the Treaty of Rome', International Business Lawyer (1980) Vol. 8 (IV) p. 113-14.

68.   Cited supra.

69.   Leclerc 1 and 2, cited supra.

70.   Case 229/83, Edouard Leclerc v 'Au Blé Vert', (1985) ECR 17.

71.   Paulis, Emil, 'Les Etats peuvent-ils enfreindre les articles 85 et 86 du Traité CEE?' Journal des Tribunaux, Bruxelles, No 5332, 30.3.85, p. 209-21.

72.   Case 231/83, Cullet v Centre Leclerc, (1985) ECR 315.

73.   12th Commission Report on Competition Policy (1982) at p. 9.

74.   J.O. No C 132/5 of 15.10.69.

75.   12th Commission Report on Competition Policy at p. 9-15.

76.   12th Commission Report on Competition Policy at p. 11. See also EC publication 'An industrial strategy in

Europe', 11/84, June - July 1984.

77.   See Van der Esch, 'Les articles 85 et 86 du Traité CEE et actions nationales de reduction de concurrence', Colloque organisé par des Revues de Droit Européen et l'Institut d'Etudes Européennes de l'ULB, Bruxelles 19-20 mai 1983.

78.   11th Commission Report on Competition Policy (1981) at p. 13.

79.   12th Commission Report on Competition Policy (1982) at p. 11, 13-14.

80.   12th Commission Report on Competition Policy at p. 9.

81.   See Küyper, op. cit. at p. 214, Küyper invoked in support cases such as Suiker Unie, (1975) ECR 1663, cited supra, and Joined Cases 209-215, 218/78, (1980) ECR 3125, where the Court examined the state restrictions but refrained from passing a judgment on state responsibility and came to the conclusion that the reason was that the restriction of competition brought about by the relevant regulations and policies was merely incidental to the policy pursued.

82.   See Van der Esch, Colloque de Bruxelles, op. cit. Also Küyper, op. cit. at p. 226.

83.   Van der Esch, Colloque de Bruxelles, op. cit. at p. 16-17.

84.   See Antitrust and Trade Regulation Report of the Annual Conference of the International Bar Association held in Vienna in September 1984, Vol. 48, p. 219.

85.   Van der Esch, op. cit. at p. 17-21.

86.   See also Daniele, Luigi, Réflexions d'ensemble sur la notion de mesures ayant un effet equivalant à des restrictions quantitatives', (1984) R.M.C., p. 477.

87.   Case 120/78, Cassis de Dijon, (1979) ECR 649, 662.

88.   Case 33/74, Van Binsbergen, (1974) ECR 1299, 1309.

89.   See also Steindorff, Ernst, 'Article 85 and the rule of reason', (1984) 21 C.M.L. Rev. 639.

90.   Council Regulation No 17, J.O. (1962) 204, (1959-1962) Spec. Ed. 87.

Chapter Five

STATE INTERVENTION: SEPARATE RESPONSIBILITY OF UNDERTAKINGS

In addition to the responsibility of the Member States under article 90 para 1, public undertakings are also themselves obliged to obey the competition rules by being directly subject to articles 85 and 86. (1) Therefore, the equality between public and private undertakings, although implicit in article 90 (2), is primarily guaranteed by articles 55 and 56 which apply to all undertakings independently of their legal form and ownership. (3) Article 90 para 1 is, nevertheless, a necessary supplement to articles 85 and 86 when it is the Member States themselves that distort competition by acting through the medium of undertakings which they influence or control. (4) As will be shown below, the liability of the Member States may either be concurrent with that of the public undertakings or exclusive if there is no agreement or concerted practice between undertakings or if anticompetitive behaviour has been imposed by the State without leaving room for alternative action by the undertakings.

The subjection of both public and private undertakings to the competition rules is thus automatic and carries with it the application of all the regulations and directives promulgated within the framework of article 87. (5) The opposite argument, that article 90 para 1 is a lex specialis applicable to public undertakings and that, therefore, those undertakings are not subject to any other Treaty provision, must be rejected (6) for the following reasons: first, articles 85 and 86 do not distinguish between private and public undertakings. (7) In fact, article 66 para 7 of the ECSC Treaty is the only provision of the Communities Treaties which refers to both public and private undertakings dealing with both in the same way, the drafters of the said Treaty having made it specifically clear that nationalized undertakings are naturally subject to the provisions of articles 65 and 66 thereof. (8) The same rationale must be adopted with respect to the EEC Treaty since to hold otherwise would make public undertakings immune from liability when acting on their own initiative and would thus cause inequality. In addition to the fact that any differentiation could bring about discrimination on the grounds of nationality resulting from differences in the internal structures of Member States (9) it would also create injustice since the distinction between private and public undertakings is far from clear. Their respective relations with the State are no longer as transparent as they used to be, the traditional frontier between public and private undertakings fading away (10), and cannot provide a justifiable basis for such distinction.

Second, the subjection of both public and private undertakings to articles 85 and 86 may be explained by the existence of article 90 para 2 which provides an exception from the rules of competition with respect to a particular type of undertaking which is mostly public. Article 90 para 2 would not have been necessary if public undertakings did not fall under articles 85 and 86. (11)

Third, additional support for the above also derives from the exceptional provisions of regulation 141 of the EEC on the application of the competition rules to inland transport (including railways). (12) This regulation would not have been necessary either, railways being in most Member States run by the State itself or state-controlled companies. (13)

In any case, despite the academic arguments and discussions that have at times taken place, it is now firmly established by the practice of the Commission and the judgments of the European Court of Justice that articles 85 and 86 as well as secondary legislation adopted for the enforcement of those rules apply both to public and private undertakings. The Commission made its view clear in its answers to parliamentary questions (14) as well as in its decisions against BNIA (15), BNIC (16), British Telecom (17) and ANSEAU-NAVEWA. (18) The ECJ implicitly adopted the same view in Sacchi which concerned the grant of an exclusive right to a public television company. The Court held that the undertaking itself would be subject to the prohibition of article 86 if it exploited the dominant position which had thus been created. (19) The statement made by the ECJ in the case of the Pigs Marketing Board, that the classification of the Board as an undertaking having special or exclusive rights within the meaning of article 90 would not exempt its activities from Community law, (20) although an obiter dictum, is also indicative of the Court's approach, the Board being a public body. In the most recent cases of ANSEAU-NAVEWA (21) and British Telecom (22) the ECJ clearly applied articles 85 and 86 to public undertakings.

Public undertakings are subject to articles 85 and 86 only when they act in an entrepreneurial as distinct from a sovereign capacity. (23) Whether the activity of a public body is entrepreneurial or regulatory in nature does not depend on the title conferred upon it by the State but on an examination of the facts. (24) As the Commission stated in its 5th Report on Competition Policy, 'if public undertakings become active in the market as suppliers or consumers of goods and services they may be in competition with other undertakings and by their behaviour affect trade between Member States' (25). Thus, any state activity in the production, distribution and sale of goods and services is included independently of the organizational structure of the relevant body, of the manner in which it handles its activity or of the legal instruments used. (26) It is, therefore, the nature of the activity that matters, an activity which is the expression of the exercise of public power being also capable of having a commercial character. (27)

The above view was adopted by the Commission in its decisions in the BNIA and BNIC cases which concerned agreements made within the framework of the French interprofessional organizations of armagnac and cognac respectively. The members of those organizations, who were representatives of the growers and dealers named by the minister from a list of nominees, were grouped in two families which decided, among other matters, on prices. These agreements made within BNIA and BNIC were extended by a ministerial order to non-members and never became binding for their members until the extension was adopted. The Commission rejected the argument that the fact that BNIA and BNIC were entrusted with their functions by decree prevented them from being considered as undertakings. It, therefore, held that, since the specific measures under review were taken within the framework of the commercial sales policy of the undertakings represented in these bodies, they exceeded the measures necessary for the performance of their functions and were, thus, subject to article 85. (28)

The same approach was followed by the ECJ in its decision in BNIC v Clair (29) where, in a reference for preliminary ruling, the Court held that a decision taken within the framework of BNIC amounted to an agreement between associations of undertakings and would thus be contrary to article 85 if its object or effect was to distort competition. The juridicial context in which those agreements were reached could not affect the application of article 85 nor did the fact that the decision of BNIC was extended to third parties by an order of public authority exonerate the association from liability under this article. It was also immaterial that the agreement was not binding on its members until the adoption of the extension decree, as long as its object was to distort competition.

Similarly, in its decision in the British Telecom case which was upheld by the ECJ (30), the Commission took for granted that British Telecom, which was a public corporation and therefore an economic entity carrying out activities of an economic nature, was an undertaking within the meaning of article 86 of the EEC Treaty. (31) The ECJ rejected the contention of the Italian government that the 'Schemes' through which British Telecom abused its dominant position, did not constitute entrepreneurial activity but rather measures laying down rules which were adopted in the exercise of legislative power. (32) Instead, the Court, after observing that the regulatory functions of British Telecom under its statute were confined to the fixing of prices and certain other conditions, concluded that the relevant 'schemes', which were freely fixed by British Telecom, formed part of the economic activity of the undertaking and could, therefore, be assessed under the competition rules. As the Commission submitted before the Court, the legal nature of the schemes was immaterial since, from an economic point of view, they performed the same function as contractual terms determining the commercial conditions on which the services were offered to the users. Even if the U.K. were also liable this could have the effect of attenuating the responsibility of British Telecom with respect to the level of fines but would not exclude the application of the competition rules.

In support of its argument the Italian government invoked the ECJ decision in IGAV. There the Court, when asked about the compatibility with articles 85 and 86 of a complex behaviour emanating from private undertakings, a public body and several laws, distinguished, for the first time, the rules of competition applicable to undertakings (including articles 85 and 86) and those applicable to violations caused by state action. The Court concluded that 'the activities of an institution of a public nature, even if autonomous, fall under the provisions referred to (i.e. articles 90, 92-94, 101, 102, 37 which are applicable to state actions) and not under articles 85 and 86 if the intervention takes place in the public interest and is devoid of commercial character'. (33)

The IGAV decision, however, is not necessarily inconsistent with the position of the ECJ in the British Telecom case. In IGAV the body concerned did not offer a product or a service in the market but performed the functions of an intervention agency. The Court did not hold that the activities of a public body can never fall under articles 85 and 86. It only concluded that the rules of competition are inapplicable to the activities of a public body when they take place in the public interest and are devoid of commercial character. (34) The autonomy of a public body is not sufficient to bring the body under the rules of competition although such autonomy confers upon the body certain of the characteristics of an undertaking. The IGAV decision may thus be interpreted as having confirmed, a contrario, that the commercial activities of public undertakings do fall under the provisions of articles 85 and 86. (35)

In the light of the above it must also be concluded that for the purpose of subjecting the activities of a public undertaking to the competition rules it is prima facie immaterial whether the public undertaking is acting within or outside the tasks conferred upon it by the public authority, this being a factor purportedly taken into consideration by the Commission in its decision in the BNIA and BNIC cases. As we explained above, public undertakings are subject to articles 85 and 86 with respect to all their commercial activities even if such activities can be considered as necessary for the performance of their functions. As Advocate General Darmon observed in his submissions in the British Telecom case, to hold otherwise would mean that every time an undertaking acted by virtue of a state prerogative the application of the rules guaranteeing the principle of free competition would be avoided, thus depriving article 85 of its effectiveness.

Nonetheless, as we shall explain below, an infringement may not be established under those articles and public undertakings may not be held liable if the functions conferred upon them by the State are justified in the circumstances. This is so when those functions promote the Community interest and the effects of the behaviour of undertakings do not exceed those attached to the performance thereof. (36) In addition, while it is clear that the commercial activities of public undertakings do prima facie fall under the competition rules, there may be cases where the undertakings, even private ones, may be exonerated from liability because their anticompetitive behaviour is enabled, encouraged or imposed by the State.

1. LIABILITY OF UNDERTAKINGS WHEN THEIR BEHAVIOUR IS THE RESULT OF THE EXERCISE OF INFORMAL INFLUENCE AND PRESSURE BY THE STATE

We shall first examine the situation where anticompetitive behaviour is adopted by the undertakings as a result of informal influence or pressure by the state authorities, without being enabled, encouraged or imposed by legislative or regulatory provisions. Although article 90 para 1 is only a particular application of the general obligation of article 5 para 2, the responsibility of undertakings, when they act under state pressure exercised through informal means, is not necessarily the same as their responsibility when they act pursuant to a legislative or regulatory provision. Moreover, despite the fact that the traditional frontier between public and private undertakings is fading away and private undertakings are no longer as independent and immune from state pressure as they used to be, such informal state pressures are generally exercised on public undertakings and those to which the State grants special or exclusive rights. It is because of the particularly close relations between the States and those undertakings that article 90 para 1 also imposes an obligation upon the Member States to take positive measures in order to put an end to the anticompetitive behaviour of an undertaking under their influence or control. (37)

However, independently of the liability of the States, the liability of the undertakings themselves, when acting under state pressure, is the same irrespective of whether they are public or private. The fact that the State is responsible for the behaviour of its public undertakings does not mean that those undertakings have no responsibility of their own when operating in the market. Despite the fact that the State may have the final word, if it so wishes, through its control over the majority of the capital or over the board, in so far as the day to day management is concerned and often also for the formulation of a long term policy, public undertakings possess a considerable degree of independence which cannot be altogether ignored. It is also often the case that the State has no reason or time to intervene. In circumstances, therefore, where public undertakings pursue anticompetitive activities on their own it is primarily the public undertakings themselves that are responsible for contravening articles 85 and 86 and it is they that must be held liable. This is so in spite of the potential concurrent liability of the State under article 90, which only exists as a guarantee.

Furthermore, even actual proof of the exercise of state pressure cannot bring public undertakings automatically outside the ambit of articles 85 and 86. The fact that the public undertakings may be engaging in concerted practices or abusing their dominant position pursuant to state recommendations or pressure might make the concurrent liability of the State obvious but cannot exonerate the undertakings themselves from liability, the supremacy of Community law, particularly as against mere informal orders, being paramount. To hold otherwise would make the direct applicability of articles 85 and 86 to public undertakings futile in all cases in which the invocation of some state influence was possible. Therefore, both the national court before which the issue may arise and the Commission under Regulation 17 must examine whether articles 85 and 86 are being violated and, if so, order the undertakings to put an end to the infringement being committed irrespective of whether the undertakings acted under the instigation of the State. In this respect it is important to note that while the Commission will be able to make an examination of facts and take all considerations into account before deciding whether to proceed against the State or the undertakings or even both, the national judge does not have such an option. The latter is under an obligation to decide on the precise issue brought before it. To allow, therefore, the invocation of state control as a defence when an action is brought against public undertakings contravening articles 85 and 86 would greatly hinder the enforcement of those provisions at a national level. A fortiori, it goes without saying that the exercise of state pressure can never be a defence for private undertakings either.

In those cases where the State induces an anticompetitive behaviour through informal means, the invocation of state influence or pressure should not be accepted even as a mitigating factor in the imposition of a fine or damages. In those cases no legal obligation is imposed upon public undertakings to pursue anticompetitive conduct. Therefore, the dilemma with which an undertaking might be faced when forced to adopt anticompetitive conduct by a legislative or regulatory provision and which shall be examined later, does not arise. Public undertakings being part of the apparatus of the State bear a great deal of the responsibility themselves. To the degree that the State interferes with their activities and thus makes them part of the state machine, the State itself is indirectly penalized by the imposition of a fine upon them. Considering that a fine cannot be imposed upon a Member State, to hold otherwise as regards public undertakings would enable Member States to order public undertakings to disobey the competition rules without running the risk of being fined or paying damages under national law.

In fact, the Commission, probably following the same approach but also because of its reluctance to turn against the States, in examining the cases of BNIA, BNIC and British Telecom did not even consider whether such indirect pressure had been exercised upon the undertakings concerned. It simply proceeded to hold the undertakings liable and also imposed upon BNIC a fine. In those cases the exercise of state influence was obvious. This was particularly so in the case of BNIA and BNIC whose members were appointed by the government and their decisions had to be approved by a state representative, but also, potentially, in the case of British Telecom which is a public corporation. However, the Commission must be criticized for exhausting all its resources and severity in penalizing public undertakings while refusing even to consider the respective responsibility of the Member States.

2. LIABILITY OF UNDERTAKINGS WHEN THEIR BEHAVIOUR IS ENABLED OR ENCOURAGED BY STATE LEGISLATION

Having thus established that the exercise of influence or pressure by the State does not exonerate public undertakings from liability despite the fact that the Member States themselves may also be held liable, the next issue to discuss is that of the liability of undertakings under articles 85 and 86 when their behaviour is adopted by virtue of a legislative or regulatory provision and enabled or encouraged by such provision. In those cases public and private undertakings shall be considered together, their eventual responsibility depending on the same factors.

Although it is true that the liability of undertakings cannot be the same when the state measures merely enable or encourage the undertakings to adopt an anticompetitive conduct as when such behaviour is imposed upon them, the frontier between the above situations is not normally sufficiently obvious. As a result, the issue often culminates in a consideration of the relevant facts. The gray areas are mainly those which are so heavily regulated that the question arises whether there is any residual field for effective competition left. (38) In those cases the compatibility of national legislation with the Community rules and the consequent obligation of the undertakings to respect any possibly incompatible national regulations also come into play. In the light of the scarcity of caselaw of the European Court, we shall attempt to trace the general principles which should be applied.

In all cases the primary issue to examine is whether the conditions of articles 85 and 86 are satisfied. Thus, it is necessary to examine whether there has been an agreement or a concerted practice between undertakings or abuse of a dominant position. Once such anticompetitive conduct by the undertakings has been established, the next step is to examine whether it had the effect of appreciably impeding competition or whether the national measures by themselves excluded all competition and left no room for any further restriction of competition by the undertakings.

First, the fact that the undertakings have merely exploited the possibilities offered by national legislation or adopted a restrictive conduct by virtue of a power conferred by the authorities does not exonerate them from liability under articles 85 and 86. As the Advocate General stated in his submissions in the Deutsche Grammophon case, national legislation must not be interpreted as enabling anticompetitive behaviour. (39) Thus, the use of the possibilities offered by national legislation may involve a violation of articles 85 and 86 if this use is the object, the means or the consequence of an agreement or concerted practice or amounts to an abuse of dominant position. (40)

It is no defence that the anticompetitive behaviour has been enabled or encouraged by state legislation. The ECJ specifically held in INNO that, despite any potential liability of the Member States themselves under the Treaty, article 86 prohibits the abuse by one or more undertakings in a dominant position even if such abuse is encouraged by national legislation. (41) That principle was confirmed several times by the ECJ in connection with both articles 85 and 86. Thus, in the cases of Sacchi (42), G.M. Continental (43) and Van Ameyde (44), where the effect of national legislation was to put the undertakings concerned in a dominant position, the Court held that when an undertaking enjoys a monopoly - even if delegated by the State - the undertaking itself may be liable under article 86 if it abuses that position. That would, for example, be the case in G.M. Continental if G.M. imposed unfair prices or trading conditions (45), or in Van Ameyde if the conduct of the national bureau, whose members were exclusively insurers, had as its object or effect the exclusion of undertakings whose business consisted solely in the settlement of accident claims. In the latter case such conduct might fall under article 85 if there existed an agreement or concerted practice, or under article 86 if the national bureau held a dominant position. (46)

The above decisions, therefore, lead to the conclusion that if the state measures merely enable or encourage a certain anticompetitive conduct, or, by looking at it from a different angle, only regulate a particular aspect of the activity of certain undertakings without affecting their behaviour otherwise, such independent anticompetitive behaviour of the undertakings, over and above the obligations imposed upon them by the legislator, will be contrary to the rules of competition. (47) This principle applies with respect to both articles 85 and 86 despite the doubts raised by Advocate General Reischl in FEDETAB about the applicability within the framework of article 85 of the statements made by the Court in the INNO case in regard of article 86. (48) According to Advocate General

Reischl where there is a dominant position competition is already practically impossible and, therefore, the problem of the appreciability of the effect on competition does not arise to the same extent as in the case of article 85. The above explanation offered by the Advocate General is very unsatisfactory since the existence of a dominant position and the granting of an exclusive right are not as such contrary to the Treaty. However, no great weight needs to be given to this statement as it was not immediately relevant to the state measures under consideration. As is explained in the following section, the relevant legislation did not merely encourage anticompetitive behaviour but also created itself a serious distortion of competition.

In considering the effect of the use of the possibilities offered by national legislation in adopting an anticompetitive behaviour, an analogy may be drawn from the cases involving industrial and intellectual property rights. In those cases the Court drew a distinction between the existence and the exercise of a right. Even if the existence of a right is allowed under the Treaty its exercise may fall under the prohibition of the Treaty relevant to competition if it appears to be the object, means or consequence of an agreement or concerted practice. (49)

As the Court held in EMI v CBS, the behaviour of the undertakings must amount to a concertation and produce results similar to an agreement. However, this is not the case if the effects do not exceed those flowing from the mere exercise of the national right of industrial property. (50) The Court thus developed the notion of the specific subject matter of a right (such as a patent) in the light of which protection may be justified.

This notion may, however, be used only when the existence of a particular right is allowed by the Treaty, in which case it will be a question of fact whether the effects of the exercise of such right exceed those attached to it. In such case and provided the conditions of article 85 and 86 are satisfied the undertakings will be held liable. In the case in which the legislation enabling the anticompetitive behaviour is contrary to the Treaty, no exercise whatsoever of such right will be justified.

The above notion of the specific subject matter of a right allowed under the Treaty, which is actually an aspect of the general principle of proportionality, could be used also in the case where an undertaking performs certain activities which are necessary for the carrying out of the functions conferred upon it by legislation. As we already mentioned above, such activities, even if necessary for the performance of the undertakings' functions, fall within the scope of articles 85 and 86 if they are of a commercial nature and imply the existence of concertation and coordination or if they amount to abuse of dominant position. Nonetheless, to the extent that such undertaking performs a useful function and in the long run promotes the Treaty objectives, the activities of that undertaking shall not be held contrary to articles 85 and 86 if their effects do not exceed those necessary for the performance of its functions. In that case whether the legislation establishing the relevant undertaking and assigning it with commercial activities promotes the Treaty objectives shall be judged in the light of the criteria developed in Chapter Four. (51)

3. LIABILITY OF UNDERTAKINGS WHEN THEIR BEHAVIOUR IS IMPOSED OR MADE INEVITABLE BY STATE LEGISLATION

The next step is to discuss the liability of undertakings when their anticompetitive behaviour is either directly imposed by the State or made inevitable by the relevant state legislation. This will normally be the case in heavily regulated sectors of the economy, particularly when the state measures and regulations have a broad and general scope so that they modify fundamentally the position of the undertakings concerned. (52) Although it is most often difficult, if not impossible, to decide at which point state legislation has the effect of eliminating competition in a certain area to the point that there is no room left for any further restriction thereof by the undertakings involved, we shall try to develop certain general guidelines by reviewing the relevant decisions of the Court.

Independently of the liability of the Member States themselves under articles 90 or 5 para 2, in examining the effect of state legislation upon the behaviour of undertakings and the liability of the latter under articles 85 and 86, three different issues must be considered: first, whether the state legislation leaves any residual scope for competition and, if so, whether this has been distorted by the independent behaviour of undertakings. Second, in the case in which competition has been virtually eliminated by the state measures, the legality of the national measures themselves must be examined, as well as the question whether the undertakings concerned are obliged to obey such measures when those contravene Community law; and third, in the case in which despite the restriction of competition, resulting from state legislation certain undertakings are held liable for contravening articles 85 and 86, we must still consider whether the effect of the state measures is to reduce the degree of responsibility of the undertakings with respect to fines and damages.

In the light of the above we shall try to extrapolate the principles laid down by the ECJ.

In Suiker Unie (53) the applicant undertakings requested the annulment of a decision of the Commission (54) holding them liable under articles 85 and 86 and imposing fines upon them, on the ground that the particular conduct for which they were blamed and which they did not dispute, did not fall within the prohibitions laid down in articles 85 and 86. They maintained that, on the one hand, Community rules together with the measures taken by the Italian authorities left no opportunity for any competition in the Italian sugar market which was capable of being prevented, restricted or distorted and that, on the other, the practices complained of were the inevitable consequence of the said measures. The Commission rejected the above submissions by simply saying that the Italian system did not make the behaviour of the applicants necessary. It did not, however, consider whether such behaviour, although not 'necessary' in a legal sense, could perhaps be necessary economically. (55)

The Court criticized the Commission for failing to take seriously into account the effects of the Italian regulatory system on the behaviour of the parties. (56) After making clear that if the relevant system leaves in practice a residual field for competition, that field comes within the provisions of the rules on competition, the Court proceeded to an examination of the relevant legislation. It thus came to the conclusion that the aims of the legislation in question and the way in which it was implemented were to limit imports to the minimum to match local demand, to harmonize the cost of foreign sugar with that of national sugar and to keep prices in Italy at a uniform and relatively low level. The effect of the above was to bring about the concentration of demand in Italy into the hands of the large producers and to lead to the formation of groups of producers-importers and also of suppliers-exporters. (57) The ECJ observed that the only effect which competition could have had within that framework would have been to increase a not inconsiderable component of the cost price for the purchasers, this being contrary to the objectives of the competition rules. (58)

In the light of the above it became apparent that the regulations in question had a decisive effect on the conduct of the applicants so that the behaviour of the undertakings would either have taken a different form or would not have taken place at all in the absence of the legislation. (59) Therefore, the residual field which remained for the operation of the rules of competition was so fundamentally restricted by the special Italian regulations that the conduct complained of could not be said to have appreciably impeded competition. (60)

In Suiker Unie the Court, without dealing directly with the compatibility of the Italian system with the Community rules, appears to have assumed its legality in view of the special conditions that prevailed in the sugar market. (61) Its approval of the system may also be derived from its conclusion that the common organization of the market of sugar contained elements which promoted the development of trade between Member States and consequently effective competition, or, at least, were likely to moderate the opposite effects arising from the preexisting systems. (62)

Advocate General Mayras, however, examined the issue of the legality of the Italian system in greater detail. While accepting that the Court may not, when dealing with a case brought before it under article 173 of the Treaty, deliver a judgment on the legality of state measures - and thus extend its jurisdiction so as to include the procedures specially provided by articles 169 and 92 of the Treaty - he nonetheless criticized the Commission for not considering seriously whether the Italian regulations were not in fact incompatible with the Community rules before taking the decision on the concerted practices in question. He furthermore proceeded to review the relevant Italian regulations and concluded that many of them contravened article 95 of the Treaty and regulation No 1009/67 establishing the common organization of the market for sugar. (63)

However, although the Advocate General did stress that it was the duty of the Commission to carry out a careful examination of the relevant state measures in order to decide whether to proceed under article 169 and despite his own findings that those measures were to a great extent inconsistent with Community law, he came to the same conclusion as the Court: he thought that the applicant undertakings could not be held liable for contravening articles 85 and 86 since the Italian system left no residual field for competition between them. (64)

In the same vein the Commission, in its decision in SSI (65), which was affirmed by the ECJ, once again made clear that the Member States' sovereignty to enact legislation in pursuance of their fiscal, counter inflationary and general social and economic policy extends only to the point of not conflicting with Community law. It also confirmed that the undertakings have the duty to observe Community law which overrides national law. Nevertheless, the Commission also proceeded to draw a distinction between government regulations, which undertakings were clearly bound to observe, and government recommendations and consultations which were not binding on undertakings and could not therefore exonerate them from liability. Although the above distinction was actually an obiter dictum, the relevant agreements and concerted practices of the SSI having been found to restrict the residual field of competition, it is still unjustifiable in the circumstances. It must be admitted that the obligation of the undertakings to observe government regulations irrespective of their compatibility with Community law is somehow at odds with the primacy of Community law which the Commission itself pronounced. The Court in SSI, while upholding the decision of the Commission that the undertakings concerned restricted the residual field of competition left, did not discuss the issue of the compatibility of the national legislation with EEC law. While assuming the legality of the relevant state measures, in examining the effect of the exercise of state pressure upon the undertakings concerned the ECJ restricted itself to stating that it had not been proven that the public authorities had indicated that their objectives should have been realized through the adoption of agreements restricting competition. (66)

In practice the conclusion of the Advocate General in Suiker Unie and of the Commission's statements in SSI may be explained by the fact that the undertakings which operate within a regulated sector of the economy cannot be expected to examine each time whether the relevant laws and regulations are compatible with Community law. Apart from any complaint which they may raise, it is logical that the undertakings will try to adapt themselves to the circumstances and possibly cooperate and coordinate their activities if this becomes necessary. Whether they are found liable under article 85 or 86 is a different matter which depends on whether their behaviour was the inevitable result of the state regulation or whether it had the effect of restraining any residual competition which might have remained notwithstanding the existence of the state regulation. However, irrespective of the actual liability of the undertakings themselves for having complied with measures contravening Community law, the possibility remains that a certain anticompetitive behaviour which cannot be imputed to undertakings but, nevertheless, frustrates the Treaty objectives continues undisturbed.

When the issue arises before the Commission, there should be no danger that a distortion of competition continues undisturbed, since the Commission is able to examine the relevant legislation before deciding whether to proceed against the State under article 169 or against the undertakings under articles 85 and 86 or both. In the case in which the Commission considers that, despite the restriction of competition brought about by the state measures, the undertakings themselves were responsible for distorting it even further, it may order the undertakings concerned to put an end to the infringement. This is independent of the liability of the Member States, the effect of the state measures being possibly an attenuating factor in the calculation of the fine against the undertakings. (67)

On the other hand, in the situation where the undertakings cannot be blamed for contravening articles 85 or 86, the state measures having virtually eliminated any effective competition, the option is open to the Commission to initiate the procedure of article 169 against the State. With respect to measures regarding public undertakings the Commission may also address a decision to the Member States concerned under article 90 para 3.

The issue becomes more complicated if the problem is raised before a national judge. Although the latter is in a position to assess the legality of state measures for the purpose of deciding on the liability of undertakings under articles 85 and 86, he cannot order that they should be repealed. If the relevant state measures leave no residual field for competition the national judge shall be faced with the dilemma of letting an infringement of competition go undisturbed or establishing a violation under articles 85 and 86 notwithstanding the fact that the behaviour of the undertakings was made inevitable by state legislation. A good illustration of the dilemma facing the national judge and the unavoidable inconsistencies which are likely to result from the decisions of the national courts is the case where a penal action is brought against one or more undertakings for contravening national regulations which are incompatible with Community law. It is therefore possible that national regulations which have the effect of distorting competition and are inconsistent with Community law are observed by some undertakings while disobeyed by others without the national courts condemning either.

In such circumstances we must distinguish between those cases where the undertakings disobey national laws which are incompatible with Community law and those where the undertakings comply with such national laws and adopt a behaviour which is either imposed upon them or made inevitable by the said regulations. In the former case it is obvious that the national court must apply the relevant directly applicable Community provisions which prevail over the national ones, the latter being void to the extent that they are inconsistent with the former. Otherwise undertakings would be penalized for obeying Community law.

In the latter case, however, we must separate two issues, that of the prohibition of the national regulation and that of the liability of the undertakings. To the extent that the undertakings cannot be held liable for further restraining competition they cannot be subjected to fines or damages; however, it would frustrate the Treaty objectives to let them continue with their anticompetitive behaviour only because they obey state regulations. In such cases the national judge should consider the legality of the state measures for the purpose of deciding whether the behaviour of the undertakings in combination with the relevant state regulation amounts to a violation of the competition rules which must be stopped. It goes without saying that in those cases the national court must also take into consideration whether the relevant state measures may in the long run promote the Community objectives in which case they may be justified under the Treaty. In this respect the criteria developed in Chapter Four shall apply.

The ECJ decision in the Suiker Unie was invoked by the applicants in the FEDETAB case (68) against a decision of the Commission (69) whereby certain agreements between producers and importers of tobacco and certain decisions of

FEDETAB, the association of such producers and importers, concerning the organization of the distribution and sale of tobacco products in Belgium were held to constitute an infringement of article 85. The applicants in FEDETAB, like in Suiker Unie, argued that, in view of the fiscal regulations for tobacco in existence, there was no room left for any further restriction of competition. The Commission rejected that argument by invoking the decision of the Court in INNO and by maintaining that if the national legislation had the effect of restricting competition the added effects of private arrangements could only be the more significant.

The Court in FEDETAB upheld the decision of the Commission. While reiterating that serious consideration must be given to the effect of the national legislation upon the behaviour of the undertakings, it interpreted the relevant legislation more restrictively than in Suiker Unie. It thus concluded that although the effect of the fiscal legislation was to restrict competition, nonetheless there remained some field of competition which had been restrained by the behaviour of the undertakings concerned.

The same approach was adopted by the Commission in its decision in the SSI case (70) which concerned an application for negative clearance under article 2 of Regulation No 17 of certain agreements and concerted practices between the members of the SSI, the association of cigarette manufacturers and importers trading in the Netherlands. The Commission held that although the Netherlands' legal framework which was to a great extent similar to the Belgian one which was the object of the decision in FEDETAB, admittedly limited to some extent the scope of competition, it is exactly in those cases where the scope of competition is so limited that the firms should make no agreements nor engage in practices restricting it still further.

As already mentioned, the Court in SSI affirmed the decision of the Commission by holding that although Dutch legislation made more difficult an action by the producers of manufactured tobacco regarding price competition, nevertheless it gave the producers the possibility to create a price differential between their products and those of their competitors either by lowering their prices or by maintaining the same prices when the others increased theirs.

The decisions of the ECJ in Suiker Unie, FEDETAB and SSI, although different in their results, make clear that the fact that a sector is so heavily regulated that there is virtually no room for effective competition left does not exonerate the undertakings from their obligation to obey articles 85 and 86. Nonetheless, the state regulations must be seriously examined for the purpose of determining whether they leave any residual field of competition or whether their effect upon the behaviour of the parties was such that the latter could not restrain competition any further. (71) The possible application of articles 85 and 86 in heavily regulated areas is, therefore, a question of fact depending on the relevant weight to be given to the effect of the legislation on the behaviour of the undertakings, the independent responsibility of the latter and the actual repercussion of their practices on competition and interstate trade.

Even when the effect of the state measures upon the behaviour of the undertakings is not sufficient to exonerate the latter from liability under articles 85 and 86 it must, nevertheless, be taken into consideration in assessing the good faith of the undertakings and may be a mitigating factor in the calculation of the fine or damages. (72) Such was, for example, the position adopted by the Commission in its decisions in ABG where British Petroleum was found to have abused its position. However, no fine was imposed upon it in view of the confusion that had been created by the state measures adopted in the Netherlands during the petrol crisis and the difficulty of assessing the extent and the importance of the effect that those measures had upon the behaviour of the undertakings. (73)

In assessing the conformity of the behaviour of undertakings with the rules of competition in circumstances in which state legislation leaves no residual field of competition, the compatibility of such legislation with Community law should also come into play. However, the ECJ has refrained from dealing with this issue, thus leaving a gap in the enforcement of the competition rules and leaving the door open to potential abuse. Nevertheless some guidance may be derived from the Leclerc cases (74) where the national courts, in dealing with contravention of national provisions allegedly contrary to the competition rules, referred to the ECJ the issue of the compatibility of national legislation with the principle of undistorted competition. The ECJ held that Member States are under an obligation not to adopt legislation which, without going so far as to impose the conclusion of an agreement or concerted practice, reduces the effectiveness of the competition rules by making such behaviour unnecessary. The above decision may be interpreted to mean that the legality of state measures comes automatically into play when the distortion of competition cannot be imputed to undertakings.

NOTES

1. The commentators are unanimous. See for example Colliard, Les Novelles, op. cit. at p. 856, Catalano, op. cit. at p. 133, Pappalardo, Bruges (1968), op. cit. at p. 79, Franck, op. cit. at pp. 66-7, Deringer, R.M.C., op. cit. (1966) at p. 661, Schindler, op. cit. at p. 58, Van Hecke, op. cit. at p. 452, Waelbroeck, Le Droit de la CEE, Vol. 4, op. cit. at p. 82.

2. Colliard, Les Novelles, op. cit. at p. 853-4, Catalano, op. cit. at p. 133, Waelbroeck, Le Droit de la CEE, Vol. 4, op. cit. at p. 82, Van Gerven, FIDE, Equal Treatment, op. cit. at p. 2.2., Mathijsen, FIDE, Equal Treatment, op. cit. at p. 11.01, Vandencasteele, op. cit. at p. 552.

3. Deringer, R.M.C., op. cit. (1966) at p. 661, Marenco, op. cit. at p. 496-9.

4. Colliard, Les Novelles, op. cit. at p. 856.

5. Catalano, op. cit. at p. 134.

6. See Marenco, op. cit. at p. 498, where the author criticises the view that article 90 is a lex specialis.

7. Colliard, Les Novelles, op. cit. at p. 856, Catalano, op. cit. at p. 139, Deringer, R.M.C., op. cit. (1966) at p. 661, Marenco, op. cit. at p. 497.

8. See Report of the French delegation on the Treaty establishing the ECSC, Ministère des Affaires Etrangéres, Paris (1951), p. 100, where it is stated that 'the nationalized undertakings are naturally subject to the provisions of articles 65 and 66 equally if they are themselves parties to an agreement as if they acquire participation in other undertakings'. Marenco, op. cit. at p. 497-8, comments that since the French negotiators were hardly antagonistic towards the public sector this would appear strong evidence that, at least in ECSC, public and private undertakings are equal (cf. Reuter, la CECA, Paris, 1957).

9. Catalano, op. cit. at p. 139.

10.   See Pappalardo, Bruges (1977), op. cit. at p. 541-2, and 'Tendances actuelles de l'initiative industrielle publique en France, au Royaume-Uni et en Italie', op. cit. at p. 327. Also Waelbroeck, 'La Constitution Européenne et les interventions des Etas-Membres en matière économique', op. cit. at p. 336-8.

11.   Deringer, R.M.C., op. cit. (1966) at p. 661-2, Colliard, Les Novelles, op. cit. at p. 856, Catalano, op. cit. at p. 139, Schindler, op. cit. at p. 68, Marenco, op. cit. at p. 498.

12.   Council Regulation No 141, J.O. 1962, p. 2751.

13.   Deringer, R.M.C., op. cit. (1966) at p. 662, Colliard, Les Novelles, op. cit. at p. 856.

14.   See Reply to Parliamentary Question No 48 of Burgbacher, M.E.P. of 27.6.63, J.O. 1963, p. 2235, and more recent replies to Written Questions No 413/82 and 1152/80 of Puvot and Bonde, M.E.P., O.J. C339/5-6 and 15 of 27.12.82.

15.   Commission Decision 76/684, O.J. No L 231/24 of 21.8.76.

16.   Commission Decision 82/896, O.J. No L 379/1 of 31.12.82.

17.   Commission Decision 82/861, O.J. No L 360/36 of 21.12.82.

18.   Commission Decision 82/371, O.J. No L 167/39 of 15.6.82.

19.   Case 127/73, Sacchi, (1974) ECR 409, 430.

20.   Case 83/78, Pigs Marketing Board v Redmond, (1978) ECR 2347, 2369.

21.   Joined Cases 96 to 102, 104, 105, 108 and 110/82, ANSEAU-NAVEWA, (1983) ECR 3369.

22.   Case 41/83, Italy v Commission, (1985) ECR 881.

23.   See Deringer, FIDE, Equal Treatment, op. cit. at p. 1.6. See also Chapter Three, Section 1.3.

24.   See submissions of the Commission in case 41/83, Italy v Commission, cited supra.

25.   5th Commission Report on Competition Policy (1976) para 173.

26.   Deringer, FIDE, Equal Treatment at p. 1.6-1.7.

27.   Huth, op. cit. at p. 323, 325 and Ipsen, 'Offentliche Unternehmen in Gemeinsamen Markt' (1964) 17 N.J.W., op. cit. at p. 2338, maintain that economic activity under articles 85 and 86 means activity under private law. The same was maintained by the Italian government in its action against the decision of the Commission on British

Telecom. The Commission made no such distinction, its view having been upheld by the Court in Italy v Commission, cited supra. See also Commission's reply to Parliamentary Question No. 149/68 of Deringer, M.E.P., J.O. 1968 of 23.10.68, No C 109/5.

28.   BNIA, O.J. No L 231/24 of 21.8.76 at p. 27 and BNIC, O.J. No L 379/9 of 31.12.82 at p.11.

29.   Case 123/83, BNIC v Clair, (1985) ECR 402.

30.   Case 41/83, Italy v Commission, cited supra.

31.   British Telecom, O.J. No L. 360/36 of 21.12.82 at p. 39.

32.   See also action brought by Italy against the Commission, O.J. No C99/4 of 13.4.83.

33.   Case 94/74, IGAV v ENCC, (1974) ECR 699, 713.

34.   See also Pappalardo, Bruges (1977), op. cit. at p. 546-7.

35.   The same interpretation could be given to the statement of Advocate General Reischl in Case 52/76, Benedetti v Munari, (1977) ECR 163, 191, that 'it is doubtful whether a public body acting on state instructions with social objectives can be regarded as a public undertaking. Such an organization does not take part in economic life and economic competition as an undertaking does ... Basically the State itself acts in a sovereign capacity ... The question is therefore quite simply one of the responsibility of the State in assessing which reference to the provisions on competition in the Treaty appears artificial'. The Court did not deal with the issue but decided the case exclusively within the framework of the common organization of the market.

36.   See Chapter Four.

37.   See Chapter Three.

38.   See Vandencasteele, op. cit. at p. 552 et seq.

39.   Case 78/70, Deutsche Grammophon v METRO, (1971) ECR 487, 506, where Advocate General Roemer stated that 'in view of the principle contained in the second paragraph of article 5 it must be assumed that national legislation did not intend to disregard the principles of the Treaty in this field and that the meaning of the provisions enacted by it must be interpreted accordingly'.

40.   See Joined Cases 56, 58/64, Consten and Grundig, (1966) ECR 299, 345-6, Joined Cases 40/70, Sirena, (1971) ECR 69, 81-83, Case 51/75, EMI v CBS U.K., (1976) ECR 811, 848.

41.   (1977) ECR at p. 2145, cited supra.

42.   (1974) ECR 409, cited supra.
43.   Case 26/75, G.M. Continental v Commission, (1975) ECR 1367.
44.   (1977) ECR 1091, cited supra.
45.   (1975) ECR at p. 1378-80, cited supra.
46.   (1977) ECR at p. 1126, cited supra.
47.   See Vandencasteele, op. cit. at p. 559-62.
48.   Joined Cases 209-215, 218/78, Van Landewyck v Commission (herein referred to as FEDETAB), (1980) ECR 3125, 3325.
49.   See Consten and Grundig, (1966) ECR at p. 345-6, cited supra, Case 24/67, Parke, Davis, (1968) ECR 55; 71-72, Sirena, (1971) ECR 69, 81-83 and EMI-CBS U.K., (1976) ECR 811, 848, cited supra.
50.   Ibid at p. 849.
51.   The statements made by the Commission in its decisions in BNIA and BNIC, that the specific measures taken by those two bodies did fall under the prohibitions of article 85 because, among others, they exceeded the scope of measures necessary for the performance of their function, should also be looked at from that angle.
52.   See also Vandencasteele, op. cit. at p. 562-9.
53.   Suiker Unie, (1975) ECR 1663, cited supra.
54.   Commission Decision No 73/109 of 2.1.73 in European Sugar Industry, O.J. No L 140/17 of 26.5.73.
55.   Vandencasteele, op. cit. at p. 563.
56.   Suiker Unie, (1975) ECR at p. 1923, cited supra.
57.   Suiker Unie, (1975) ECR at p. 1921-2, cited supra.
58.   Ibid at p. 1924. The only effective competition which the Italian regulations, at least ostensibly, allowed to remain was competition as to the amounts of the 'sovraprezzo' to be tendered by potential importers, this being a levy imposed on domestic and imported sugar equivalent to the difference between the price applied in Italy and the Community intervention price. With respect to foreign sugar this levy was reduced in order to offset the costs of foreign sugar in excess of those of national sugar and thus facilitate imports. Since the intention of the Italian administration was to obtain the highest amount of 'sovraprezzo' and award import quotas according to the quantity and amount of the 'sovraprezzo' offered by the tenderers, those were induced to come to an agreement on the amount of the 'sovraprezzo' to be offered in order to avoid being excluded because the amount offered was too low. In the absence of such an agreement there would be

competition as to the amount of 'sovraprezzo' offered which would have the effect of increasing the final price of sugar.

59. Suiker Unie, (1975) ECR at p. 1923, cited supra.
60. Suiker Unie, ibid at p. 1924.
61. Ibid at p. 1914-5.
62. Ibid at p. 1915.
63. (1975) ECR at p. 2073-6. This view was subsequently confirmed by the Court in Case 77/76, Cucchi v Avez, (1977) ECR 987, Interzuccheri, Case 105/76, (1977) ECR 1029 and Case 73/79, Commission v Italy, (1980) ECR 1533.
64. Suiker Unie, (1975) ECR at p. 2076, cited supra.
65. Commission Decision No 82/506 of 15.7.82 in SSI, O.J. No L 232/1 of 6.8.82
66. Joined Cases 240-42, 261, 262, 268, 269/82, SSI v Commission, Decision of 10.12.82, still unpublished.
67. Suiker Unie, (1975) ECR at p. 2022-3, cited supra.
68. Van Landewyck v Commission, (1980) ECR 3125, cited supra.
69. Commission Decision No 78/670 of 20.7.78 in FEDETAB, O.J. No L 224/29 of 15.8.78.
70. Cited supra in footnote 65.
71. See also Commission Decision No 77/327 of 19.4.77 in ABG, O.J. No L 117/1 of 9.5.77 and Case 77/77, BP v Commission, (1978) ECR 1513.
72. Suiker Unie, (1975) ECR at p. 2022-3, cited supra.
73. Commission Decision in ABG, cited supra.
74. Case 229/83, Association des Centres Distributeurs Edouard Leclerc v 'Au Blé Vert', (1985) ECR 17, and Case 231/83, Henri Cullet v Leclerc à Toulouse, (1985) ECR 315.

Chapter Six

CONCLUSION

As becomes apparent from the preceding analysis, the extent to which Member States are subject to the rules of competition has not been clearly defined as yet. Although the institution of a system ensuring that competition is not distorted is one of the basic Community objectives, nevertheless, both because of its ideological and political content and because of the lack of a specific provision addressed to Member States, its application remains unclear.

It is arguable that the drafters of the Treaty wanted the operation of the principle of free competition to be flexible and adaptable to changing circumstances. It is noteworthy that while the specific provisions implementing the free circulation of goods, persons, services and capital are included in the Treaty under the title 'Foundations of the Community' and impose a clear and specific obligation upon Member States to eliminate any restrictions thereto, the rules relating to competition form part of a different section of the Treaty titled 'Policy of the Community'. They only cover distortions of competition by undertakings and specific forms of distortion of competition by the States.

This does not mean that the application of the rules relating to the foundations of the Common Market has been or continues to be free of any political and ideological conflict. Indeed, certain commentators and governments still argue that free circulation operates to the disadvantage of the poorer countries which are doomed to eternal dependence upon the richer ones. The proposal put forward by certain countries in the context of the negotiations for a new Treaty that the convergence of the economies of the

Member States must precede the final materialization of a Common Market, is indicative of this approach. Nevertheless, independently of the results of the negotiations for a new Treaty the clarity and specificity of the existing provisions relating to the foundations of the Community, by contributing to their direct enforcement in Member States, show that the elimination of all obstacles to the free circulation of goods, persons, services and capital was considered by the signatories the very essence of the Community. They were convinced that the long term benefit would supersede any short term cost or imbalance which might occur in the economies of the Member States as a result of the direct and unconditional applicability of the relevant provisions.

On the other hand, the lack of a specific, unconditional and directly applicable provision addressed to Member States and prohibiting any state measure which may have the effect of distorting competition shows that the drafters of the Treaty considered that the obligations of the State flowing from the competition rules should be left to be defined at a later stage, in the light of the prevailing socio-economic and political circumstances. Furthermore, since every state economic measure is likely, somehow, to affect the market mechanism and since the formulation of economic policy is now generally considered to be an essential function of the State, it shall always be necessary to distinguish between those economic measures which remain within the State's discretion and those which should be prohibited as incompatible with the proper functioning of the Common Market.

It must be observed that although the Treaty of Rome aims not only at creating a simple customs union but at establishing a Common Market where goods, persons, services and capital circulate freely and all economic operators compete on equal terms, it does not regulate matters of domestic policy which do not have any effect on intracommunity relations and trade. State intervention, whatever its anticompetitive effect, will not, therefore, be incompatible with the Treaty if it does not also have an effect on interstate trade. At the same time, however, the drafters did predict that state intervention was likely to manifest itself in the protection of local production and of state undertakings and that this intervention would normally produce effects beyond the frontiers of any Member State. They, therefore, took special precaution by including specific provisions in the Treaty prohibiting such distortions of competition by the States outright.

Thus, article 90 makes clear that from the moment a State decides to intervene in the market as entrepreneur, through the medium of undertakings which it controls, whichever form its intervention takes it is subject to the competition rules in the same way as a private undertaking. In such case Member States are also subject to the Commission's jurisdiction under article 90 para 3.

Certain commentators have argued that state influence and control is not necessarily a function of the State's public ownership of the undertaking but rather of the undertaking's size. Indeed, the collapse of a big industry may have adverse effects upon the economy as a whole. These commentators, therefore, consider that if article 90 is to be fully effective, it should be extended to include such undertakings. We believe that big private industry is not covered by article 90 para 1 by the simple fact of its size and the potential of state influence. In each case, an examination of the facts must be made in order to ascertain whether the private undertaking actually formulates its policy on its own, subject of course to general laws applicable indiscriminately to all, or whether the State has a grip on it. The latter may possibly be the result of the undertaking's bad financial conditions, potential state intervention through capitalization of state loans or other assistance etc. Such analysis may be relevant irrespective of the size of the undertaking.

In addition to article 90, the rules on competition comprise articles 92-94 which are also addressed to Member States and prohibit state aids which have the effect of distorting competition. State subsidies are often granted to make local production more competitive in the international market, which clearly is contrary to the objectives of the Common Market.

However, apart from clear cases of distortion of competition by the State prohibited by articles 90 and 92-94, it is possible that general state measures adopted within the framework of domestic policy may have the effect of distorting competition in a way that affects intracommunity trade without necessarily falling under the above mentioned articles. Examples of such are price regulating laws, compulsory cartel laws, partitioning of the market, control of investments etc. To let such state measures go undisturbed because of the absence of a specific provision addressed to Member States would frustrate a basic objective of the Treaty, that of free competition. Furthermore, these measures would amount to a violation of the obligation which Member States assumed by virtue of article 5 para 2.

The principle of free competition, whatever its ideological connotation, in addition to being part of the Treaty objectives in a literal sense, is also a necessary prerequisite for the good functioning of the Common Market as envisaged by the Treaty. Without a comparable environment and similar market conditions and rules in all Member States, the free circulation of goods, persons, services and capital would be an illusion. The EEC with its common institutions and rules was intended to be more than an international agreement to abolish tariffs and quotas. It aims further at creating the conditions for fair and equal competition between economic operators functioning in a free market environment, an objective which cannot be achieved if all the Member States do not abide by the principles of a market-oriented economy.

This does not mean that the State cannot take social, monetary or fiscal measures in the public interest for the achievement of its long term economic objectives. A free market economy can accommodate different ideologies advocating a higher or lower degree of state intervention and social welfare within the boundaries of the free market system. Moreover, the present day crisis has shown that the free market mechanism cannot always, by itself, correct certain imbalances. Very often coordinated action is necessary to set the general guidelines and avoid that conflicting state measures frustrate the Treaty objectives.

Agreement as to the industrial priorities of Europe and coordination of the industrial policies of the Member States are, therefore, necessary in order to enhance EEC competitiveness vis-à-vis the outside world. As explained in Chapter Four, the European economies are in need of reconstruction and redeployment which can only be achieved through coordinated Community action. In addition to the fact that due to internal constraints inherent in each Member State, the market mechanism does not by itself operate efficiently enough to enable the private initiative to carry, alone, the burden of recovery, absolute market freedom could also lead to unacceptable results from a social point of view.

As a result of state regulation and coordination of

industrial policies, it is unavoidable that the degree of competition cannot be the same as when the market functions smoothly. This should not be taken to mean, however, that the principle of undistorted competition can be put aside to the benefit of a state controlled economy. The maintenance of undistorted competition is a fundamental objective of the Common Market which must accompany any industrial policy and divergence from which may be allowed only in order to create the conditions of healthier competition in the long run.

In the light of the above and until the formulation of a Community policy or the adoption of common guidelines, Member States are allowed to take measures interfering in the competition process only when acting in furtherance of a national industrial policy which is not inconsistent with the Community objectives and distorts competition to the minimum.

It is, therefore, that kind of flexibility which the Treaty wanted to allow by specifically restricting only clearly unacceptable distortions of competition by the State while allowing other forms of distortion of competition to be judged under article 5 para 2 in combination with the general principle of competition and articles 85 and 86.

From a legal viewpoint the decisions of the ECJ in the Leclerc cases contributed to the clarification of state liability under the competition rules. By holding that even if articles 85 and 86 refer to behaviour of undertakings, Member States may not enact measures capable of eliminating the effectiveness of the competition rules applicable to undertakings, the ECJ showed that the freedom of states' action is limited by the operation of articles 85 and 86. In a free market economy it is normal that the competition rules are addressed to the undertakings which are the economic operators therein. State liability may come into play only to the extent that the State participates in the market as entrepreneur or regulates the market to such an extent that it can no more function as a free market. As a result of state regulation articles 85 and 86 become inoperative as against private undertakings. It is, therefore, logical that the obligations arising thereunder be transferred, by virtue of article 5 para 2, to Member States.

While agreeing with the above mentioned general principle stated by the ECJ in the Leclerc cases we do not believe that the Court went far enough in applying that principle to the facts of the cases. As we already noted, it appears that what the Court considered material for holding that the fixing of prices by the state infringed the competition rules was the origin of the prices finally rendered compulsory through state measures. Thus, in Leclerc 1 the Court seems to have been unduly influenced by the fact that the State had not determined the price of books itself but only imposed upon the retailers the obligation to sell at a certain minimum price freely fixed by the importer or the publisher. Although, in view of the absence of a Community policy on books, the Court finally upheld the state measures, it may be derived from its reasoning that the Court considered that the state measures under discussion were capable of eliminating the effectiveness of the competition rules on the ground that they rendered unnecessary the conclusion of a price fixing agreement between private operators.

On the other hand, in Leclerc 2 the Court refused to hold that the State infringed the competition rules when it fixed a minimum retail price for petrol after taking into account several factors, including the average price fixed by the suppliers. As the Court stated, the mere fact that the price fixed by suppliers was one of the elements taken into consideration in order to determine the minimum price of petrol, did not deprive a regulation of its state character and did not, thus, eliminate the effectiveness of the competition rules. It is obvious that the Court was not really concerned with the effect of the state measures on the consumers. Although the state measures under discussion had the effect of precluding any competition vis-à-vis the consumers with respect to prices the Court considered that they were not capable of eliminating the effectiveness of competition rules since private operators had played no role in the formulation of the price.

We do not agree that the origin of the state measures should play any role in holding the State liable under the competition rules. State measures, including price regulations, are subject to the competition rules independently of whether they have been adopted pursuant to or against the wishes of private undertakings. It is the effect of the state measures on the economy which should count. As we already explained in Chapter Four, the application of the competition rules to state measures may only be put aside on the basis of a rule of reason. Such rule involves balancing the objectives pursued by the national measures as against the degree of distortion of competition which they create. What is important is whether national measures are promoting a national industrial policy which is consistent with the Community objectives and whether they keep the distortion of competition at a minimum.

It might be argued that the ECJ decisions in the Leclerc cases could also be explained on the basis of the rule of reason. Thus, in Leclerc 1 the cultural element of books could arguably be invoked as a basis for setting aside the competition rules, the lack of Community policy being, in our opinion, a wrong ground for the decision. Similarly, in Leclerc 2 the plurality of factors taken into consideration by the State in fixing a minimum price for petrol may have had the effect of reducing the distortion of competition to the minimum. However, the above is a rather theoretical construction since the Court actually found that the 'plurality of factors' did not prevent the regulation fixing a minimum price for petrol from infringing article 30.

It is hoped that the ECJ will make use of a rule of reason more openly in the future. In doing so it may also develop certain rules regarding the application of the competition rules to Member States, which shall be sufficiently clear and unequivocal as to enable their direct enforcement by national courts. At the present stage of Community development, however, the decision whether a national measure, although restrictive of competition, promotes some other objective of the Treaty, involves a sophisticated political and economic evaluation which national courts are not equipped to make. The main burden lies with the Council and the Commission to set the guidelines for coordinated action in order to avoid that national policies lead to conflicting results which may jeopardise the Common Market objectives.

LIST OF CASES

Case 19/61, Mannesmann AG v High Authority, (1962) ECR 357.
Case 26/62, NV Algemene Transport - en Expeditie Onderneming Van Gend en Loos v Netherlands Inland Revenue Administration, (1963) ECR 1.
Case 6/64, Costa v ENEL, (1964) ECR 585.
Case 56, 58/64, Consten S.R.L. and Grundig GmbH v Commission, (1966) ECR 299.
Case 57/65, Lütticke GmbH v Hauptzollamt Saarlouis, (1966) ECR 205.
Case 24/67, Parke, Davis & Co v Probel, (1968) ECR 55.
Case 9/70, Grad v Finanzamt Traunstein, (1970) ECR 825.
Case 40/70, Sirena S.R.L. v Eda S.R.L., (1971) ECR 69.
Case 78/70, Deutsche Grammophon GmbH v Metro GmbH, (1971) ECR 487.
Case 10/71, Ministère Public of Luxemburg v Madeleine Hein (Port of Mertert), (1971) ECR 723.
Case 22/71, Beguelin Import Co v S.A.G.L. Import-Export, (1971) ECR 949.
Case 82/71, Publico Ministero Italiano v SAIL, (1972) ECR 119.
Case 6/72, Europemballage Corporation and Continental Can Co. Inc. v Commission, (1973) ECR 215.
Case 2/73, Geddo v Ente Nazionali Risi, (1973) ECR 865.
Case 4/73, Nold v Commission, (1974) ECR 491.
Cases 6, 7/73, ICI and Commercial Solvents Corporation v Commission, (1974) ECR 223.
Case 9/73, Firma Schlüter v Hauptzollamt Lörrach, (1973) ECR 1135.
Joined Cases 40-48, 50, 54-56, 111, 113-4/73, Suiker Unie v Commission, (1975) ECR 1663.

Case 127/73, BRT v SV SABAM and NV FONIOR, (1974) ECR 313.

Case 155/73, Italian State v Sacchi, (1974) ECR 409.

Case 190/73, Van Haaster, (1974) ECR 1123.

Case 192/73, Van Zuylen Frères v Hag, (1974) ECR 731.

Case 15/74, Centrafarm BV v Sterling Drug Inc, (1974) ECR 1147.

Case 16/74, Centrafarm BV v Winthrop BV, (1974) ECR 1183.

Case 31/74, Galli, (1975) ECR 47

Case 33/74, Van Binsbergen v Bestuur, (1974) ECR 1299.

Case 94/74, IGAV v ENCC, (1975) ECR 699.

Case 26/75, GM Continental v Commission, (1975) ECR 1367.

Case 26/75, General Motors Continental NV v Commission, (1975) ECR 1367.

Case 45/75, Rewe-Zentrale v Hauptzollamt Landau, (1976) ECR 181.

Case 51/75, EMI Records v CBS U.K., (1976) ECR 811.

Case 86/75, EMI v CBS Grammofon A/S, (1976) ECR 871.

Case 96/75, EMI v CBS Schallplatten GmbH, (1976) ECR 913.

Case 59/75, Pubblico Ministero v Manghera, (1976) ECR 91.

Case 65/75, Ricardo v Tasca, (1976) ECR 291.

Case 88-90/75, SADAM v Comitato Interministeriale dei prezzi, (1976) ECR 323.

Case 91/75, Hauptzollamt Göttingen v Miritz, (1976) ECR 217.

Case 59/76, Benedetti v Munari, (1977) ECR 163.

Case 77/76, Cucchi v Avez, (1977) ECR 987.

Case 78/76, Firma Steinike und Weinlig v Germany, (1977) ECR 595.

Case 90/76, Van Ameyde v UCI, (1977) ECR 1091.

Case 105/76, Interzuccheri, (1977) ECR 1029.

Case 13/77, GB-INNO-BM v ATAB, (1977) ECR 2115.

Case 77/77, BP v Commission, (1978) ECR 1513.

Case 82/77, Openbaar Ministerie v Van Tiggele, (1978) ECR 25.

Case 154/77, Dechmann, (1978) ECR 1573.

Case 13/78, Eggers Sohn & Co v Frei Hansenstadt Bremen, (1978) ECR 1935.

Case 83/78, Pigs Marketing Board v Raymond Redmond, (1978) ECR 2347.

Case 120/78, Rewe v Bundesmonopolverwaltung für Branntwein (Cassis de Dijon), (1979) ECR 649.

Case 130/78, Salumificio di Cornuda v Financial Administration of the State, (1979) ECR 867.

Case 168/78, Commission v France, (1980) ECR 347.

Case 169/78, Commission v Italy, (1980) ECR 385.

Case 171/78, Commission v Denmark, (1980) ECR 447.

Joined Cases 209-215, 218/78, Van Landewyck v Commission (FEDETAB), (1980) ECR 3125.

Case 5/79, Procureur General v Hans Buys, (1979) ECR 3203.

Case 15/79, Groenveld v Produktschap voor Vee en Vlees, (1979) ECR 3409.

Case 44/79, Hauer v Land Rheinland-Pfalz, (1979) ECR 3727.

Case 68/79, Hans Just v Danish Ministry of Tax, (1980) ECR 501.

Case 73/79, Commission v Italy, (1980) ECR 1533.

Case 91/79, Commission v Italy, (1980) ECR 1099.

Case 61/80, Stremsel, (1981) ECR 871.

Case 130/80, Commission v Belgium, (1981) ECR 2393.

Case 144/81, Keurkoop BV v Nancy Kean Gifts BV, (1981) ECR 2853.

Case 155/80, Sergius v Oebel, (1981) ECR 1993.

Case 172/80, Züchner v Bayerische Vereinsbank AG, (1981) ECR 2021.

Joined Cases 188-90/80, France, Italy and U.K. v Commission (Transparency Directive Case), (1982) ECR 2545.

Joined Cases 141-143/81, Holdijk, (1982) ECR 1299.

Case 249/81, Commission v Ireland, (1982) ECR 4005.

Case 271/81, Amelioration de l'élevage v Mialocq, (Artificial Insemination), (1983) ECR 2057.

Case 78/82, Commission v Italy, (1983) ECR 1955.

Joined Cases 96-102, 104, 105, 108, 110/82, ANSEAU-NAVEWA, (1983) ECR 3369.

Case 172/82, Syndicat National des Fabricants Raffineurs d'Huile de Graissage v Groupement d'Intérêt Economique 'Inter-Huiles', (1983) ECR 555.

Joined Cases 177-8/82, Officier Van Justitie v Jan Van de Haar and Kaveka de Meern BV, (1984) ECR 1797.

Case 181/82, Roussel v The Netherlands, (1983) ECR 3849.

Case 238/82, Duphar v The Netherlands, (1984) ECR 523.

Joined Cases 240-42, 261, 262, 268, 269/82, SSI v Commission, Decision of 10.12.85, still unpublished.

Case 41/83, Italy v Commission, (1985) ECR 881.

Case 72/83, Campus Oil Ltd v The Ministry of Industry and

LIST OF COMMISSION DECISIONS

Decision No 69/195/EEC in Christiani and Nielsen, J.O. No L 165/12 of 5.7.69.
Decision No 70/332/EEC in Kodak, J.O. No L 147/24 of 7.7.70.
Decision No 71/224/EEC in GEMA, J.O. No L 134/15 of 20.6.71.
Decision No 73/109/EEC in European Sugar Industry, O.J. No L 140/17 of 26.5.73.
Decision No 76/29/EEC in A.O.I.P.-Beyrard, O.J. No L 6/8 of 13.1.76.
Decision No 76/634/EEC in Franco-Japanese Ballbearings, O.J. No L 343/19 of 21.12.74.
Decision No 76/684/EEC in Pabst and Richarz/BNIA, O.J. No L 231/24 of 21.8.76.
Decision No 77/327/EEC in ABG, O.J. No L 117/1 of 9.5.77.
Decision No 78/670/EEC in FEDETAB, O.J. No L 224/29 of 15.8.78.
Decision No 81/1030/EEC in GVL, O.J. No L 370/49 of 28.12.81.
Decision No 82/371/EEC in NAVEWA-ANSEAU, O.J. No L 167/39 of 15.6.82.
Decision No 82/506/EEC in SSI, O.J. No L 232/1 of 6.8.82.
Decision No 82/861/EEC in British Telecom, O.J. No L 360/36 of 21.12.82.
Decision No 82/896/EEC in AROW/BNIC, O.J. No L 379/1 of 31.12.82.
Decision No 83/671/EEC in International Energy Agency, O.J. No L 376/30 of 31.12.82.
Decision No 85/276/EEC concerning the insurance in Greece of public property and loans granted by state-owned banks,

O.J. No L 152/25 of 11.6.85.

BIBLIOGRAPHY

Andriessen, F. 'The Role of Anti-Trust in the Face of
Economic Recession: State Aids in the EEC', (1983)
ECLR 286

Balog, N. 'L'organisation administrative des Entreprises
publiques', Rapport général, 23eme Congrès des
sciences administratives (Paris, 20-23 Julliet 1965),
Institut International des Sciences Administratives,
Bruxelles (1966)

Barents, R. 'New developments in measures having
equivalent effect', (1981) 18 C.M.L. Rev. 271.
'Instruments Juridiques des politiques économiques
nationales et leur compatibilité avec le droit
Communautaire: Pays Bas', Discipline Communautaire
et politiques économiques nationales: Community order
and national economic policies, Colloque organisé par
des Revues de Droit Européen et l'Institut d'Etudes
Européenes de l'ULB, 19-20 Mai 1983, Kluwer, Deventer
etc. (1984)

Baron Snoy et d'Oppuers, 'La notion de l'intérèt de la
Communauté a l'article 90 du Traité de Rome sur le
Marché Commun' Colloque de Bruxelles organise par la
Ligue Internationale contre la Concurrence Deloyale,
(1963) Riv. Dir. Ind. 247

Barounos, D., Hall, D.F., James, J.R. 'EEC Anti-Trust Law.
Principles and Practice' Butterworth, London (1975)

Beraud, R.-C. and Ventura, S. 'Les aspects juridiques de la
Politique Industrielle de la Communauté', (1971) R.M.C.
371

Berlin, D. 'L'adaptation du régime juridique des entreprises
publiques aux normes internationales et européennes',

Revue Trimestrielle de Droit Européen, Année 19, No 3, Juillet-Septembre, 1983, p. 393

Bourke, P. 'Semi-State Bodies', Business and Finance, Oct. 1979, p. 56

Bouysou, F. 'Les garanties supralegislatives du droit de propriété', Receuil Dalloz, Paris, No 39, 22.11.84, p. 231

Brothwood, M. 'Equal Treatment of Public and Private Enterprises. United Kingdom Report', Rapport du 8me Congrès de FIDE, Copenhague 22-24 Juin 1978, Vol. 2, FIDE, Bruxelles (1978) p. 10.1.

'The Commission Directive on Transparency of Financial Relations between Member States and Public Undertakings', (1981) C.M.L. Rev. 207.

'The Court of Justice on Article 90 of the EEC Treaty', (1983) C.M.L. Rev. 335

Buttgenbach, A. 'Manuel de Droit Administratif', Larcier, Bruxelles (1959).

'La notion d'Entreprise Publique', Colloque de Bruxelles, (1963) Riv. Dir. Ind. 227

Catalano, N. 'Application de dispositions du Traité CEE (et notamment des règles de concurrence) aux entreprises publiques', in Festschrift für Otto Riese Aus Antass Seines Siebzigsten Geburtstages, Muller, Kalsruhe, (1964), p. 133.

'Manuel de Droit de CEE', Dalloz and Sirey, Paris (1965)

Chiplin, B. and Wright, M. 'Competition policy and State Enterprises in the U.K.', The Antitrust Bulletin, Vol. 27, No 4 Winter 1982, p. 921

Colliard, C.-A., 'L'entreprise publique et l'evolution du Marché Commun', (1965) Revue Trimestrielle de Droit Europeen, p. 1.

'Le Régime des Entreprises Publiques', Les Novelles, Droit de CEE, Bruxelles (1969) p. 853

Comité de Politique Economique (Budget) CEE: Seminaire sur les Relations Financières entre l'Etat et les entreprises publiques, Londres, 12 et 13 Oct. 1978

Constantini, J. 'Concurrence et Entreprises Publiques Communautaires', Revue Suisse du Droit International de la Concurrence, (1980) No 9, p. 1

Cooke, J. 'Equal Treatment of Public and Private Enterprises. National Report for Ireland', Rapport du 8me Congrès de FIDE, Copenhague 22-24 Juin 1978, Vol. 2, FIDE, Bruxelles (1978) p. 6.1

Costa, A. 'Public Undertakings and Article 90 of the EEC

Treaty (after the European Commission's Decision in the ANSEAU-NAVEWA Case), Mezzogiorno d'Europa, April-June 1984, p. 263

Daniele, L. 'Reflexions d'ensemble sur la notion de mesures ayant un effet equivalant a des restrictions quantitatives', (1984) R.M.C. 477

Dashwood, A. and Sharpe, T. 'The Industry Acts 1972 and 75 and European Community law' (1978) 15 C.M.L. Rev. 9

Delion, A. 'Entreprises Publiques et CEE', (1966) R.M.C. 67. 'France - La place des Entreprises Publiques dans l'Economie', 'Problèmes Economiques' (1983) No 1824, p. 2.
'La notion d'entreprise publique', L'Actualité Juridique - Droit Administratif, Paris (1979) No 4, p.3

Deringer, A. 'The interpretation of article 90 of the EEC Treaty', (1964-65) 2 C.M.L. Rev. 'Les règles de la Concurrence au Sein de la CEE, (Analyse et Commentaires des articles 85 à 94 du Traité)', (1966-7) R.M.C. 'Les articles 90 et 37 dans leur relations avec un régime de concurrence non falsifiée'. L'entreprise publique et la concurrence. Les articles 90 et 37 de Traité CEE et leur relations avec la concurrence, College d'Europe, De Tempel, Bruges (1969) p. 387. 'Equal Treatment of Public and Private Enterprises. General Report', Rapport du 8me Congrès de FIDE, Copenhague 22-24 Juin 1978, Vol. 2, FIDE, Bruxelles (1978) p.1.1

Devellenes, Y. Commentaire de l'arrêt 229/83 (Leclerc), La Semaine Juridique, Paris, No 18, 1985, Jurisprudence 20395

Dubouis, L. 'La France face a l'Europe du livre et de l'essence', Revue Francaise de Droit Administratif, Paris, Mars-Avril, 1985, p. 289

Emmerich, V. 'Das Wirtschaftsrecht der öffentlichen Unternehmen' Gehlen, Bad Homburg, Berlin, Zurich (1969)

Escarmelle, J.-M. and Melis, P. 'Essai de definition du concept d'entreprise publique', Revue Internationale des Sciences Administratives, Bruxelles (1981) No 4, p. 365

Evans, A.-C. 'Public Enterprise and EEC Law: The case of the British National Oil Corp.' (1982) ECLR, Vol. 3, No 1, p. 86

Fausto, D. 'The Finance of Italian Public Enterprises', Annales de l'Economie Publique, Sociale et Cooperative, Liege (1982) p. 3

Ferrari-Bravo, L. 'Les articles 90 et 37 dans leur relations avec un régime de concurrence non falsifiée', L'entreprise publique et la concurrence. Les articles 90 et 37 du Traité CEE et leur relation avec la concurrence. College d'Europe, De Tempel, Bruges (1969)

Focsaneanu, L. and Elsen, P. 'Le droit de la Concurrence face à la crise', (1985) R.M.C. 271

Focsaneanu, L. 'Le contrôle français des prix sous controle communautaire. Observations sur les arrêts de la Cour de Justice des CEE des 10.1.85 (prix du livre) et 29.1.85 (prix des carburants)', La Semaine Juridique, Cahiers de Droit de l'Entreprise, Paris No 23, 6.6.85, p. 329.
'Pour un droit conjoncturel de la concurrence. Essai de rapprochement des articles 85 et 103', (1985) Revue Trimestrielle de Droit Européen, No 2, p. 343

Franceschelli, R. 'La notion de Service d'Intérèt Economique General' Colloque de Bruxelles (1963) Riv. Dir. Ind. 238

Franck, P. Annuaire du Congrès de Dusseldorf de la Ligue Internationale contre la Concurrence Deloyage (1962). 'Les entreprises visées aux articles 90 et 37 du Traité CEE'. L'entreprise publique et la concurrence. Les articles 90 et 37 du Traité CEE et leur relation avec la concurrence. College d'Europe, De Tempel, Bruges (1969) p.21

Gide, Loyrette et Nouel, 'Le droit de la Concurrence de la CEE' Juridictionnaires Joly, Paris (1982)

Gleiss, A. Hirsch, M. EWG Kartellrecht, Kommentar zu den Art. 85 und 86 des EWG - Vertrages und den EWG-Verordnungen Nr 17, Nr 27 und Nr 26. Verlagsgesellsch. 'Recht und Wirtschaft', Heidelberg (1962)

Groupe de Banque Mondiale, 'Le role des societés nationales de financement du développement dans le développement industriel', Industrialization et Productivité, Bulletin 14, Nations Unies, N.Y. (1969)

Heymann, P. and Rossollin, F. 'Le poids du secteur public', 30 Jours d'Europe, p. 9

Hochbaum, I. Article 90. Extract from 'Les ententes et les positions dominantes dans le droit de la CEE' by Thiesing, Schröter and Hochbaum, Paris (1977) p.270

Horn, J. 'Le gouvernement de l'Entreprise Publique', Reflets et Perspectives de la Vie Economique, Formes d'Entreprises en France (1970) p. 121

Houssiaux, J. 'Régime de l'Article 90 du Traité CEE: Les aspects économique', L'entreprise publique et la concurrence. Les articles 90 et 37 du Traité CEE et leur relation avec la concurrence. College d'Europe, De Tempel, Bruges (1968) p. 105

Huth, K.D. 'Die Sonderstellung der öffentlichen Hand in den Europäischen Gemeinschaften'. Eine rechtstatsacchliche und rechtsdogmatische Untersuchung unter Einbeziehung Grossbritanniens' Gerber, Hamburg (1965)

International Bar Association, Antitrust and Trade Regulation Report, Vol. 48, 24.1.85 of the Vienna IBA Annual Conference

Ipsen, H.-P. 'Offentliche Unternehmen in Gemeinsamen Markt', (1964) 17 N.J.W. 2336.
'Europäisches Gemeinschaftsrecht', Mohr, Tubingen (1972)

Jacobsen, C.-B. 'Equal Treatment of public and private enterprises in Denmark', Rapport du 8me Congrès de FIDE, Copenhague 22-24 Juin, 1978, Vol. 2, FIDE, Bruxelles (1978) p. 3.1

Jeantet, F.-C. 'Un progrès dans la notion d'unité de Marché de la CEE', (1984) Cahiers de Droit Européen, No 5-6, p. 521

Joliet, R. 'Contribution a l'étude du régime des entreprises publiques dans la CEE', (1965) Annales de la Faculté de Droit de Liege, p. 23

Kavanagh, L. 'Ireland's semi state sector', (1981) Business and Finance, Vol. 17, No 49, p. 23

Korah, V. 'An Introductory Guide to EEC Competition Law and Practice', ESC Publishing Limited, Oxford (1981)

Küyper, P.-J. 'Airline Fare Fixing and Competition: An English Lord, Commission Proposals and US parallels', (1983) 20 C.M.L. Rev. 203

Lanzarone, G. 'La nationalization de l'industrie electrique en Italie', (1971) Revue de la Société d'Etudes et d'Expansion, No 244, p. 58

Laveissiere, J. 'Instruments Juridiques des politiques économiques nationales et leur compatibilité avec le droit Communautaire: France', Discipline Communautaire et politiques économiques nationales: Community order and national economic policies, Colloque organisé par des revues de Droit Européen et l'Institut d'Etudes Européennes de l'ULB, 19-20 Mai 1983, Kluwer, Deventer etc. (1984)

Lecourt, R. 'L'Entreprise, Actions des Etats', Extract from book 'L'Europe des Juges' Bruylant, Bruxelles (1976)

Lipstein, K. 'The law of the European Economic

Community', Butterworth, London (1974)

Marenco, G. 'Public Sector and Community Law', (1983) 20 C.M.L. Rev. 495.

Commentaire de l'arrêt 177-178/82 (Van de Haar), Revue Trimestrielle de Droit Europeen No 3, Juillet-Septembre 1984, p. 521-36

Mathijsen, P. 'Egalité de Traitement des Entreprises dans le Droit des CEE', Rapport du 8me Congrès de FIDE, Copenhague, 22-24 Juin 1978, Vol. 2, FIDE, Bruxelles (1978) p. 11.1.
'State Aids, State Monopolies, and Public Enterprises in the Common Market' Law and Contemporary Problems, Spring 1972, p. 376

Mazzolini, R. 'Government Controlled Enterprises: What's the Difference'? Columbia Journal of World Business N.Y., Summer 1980, p. 28.
'Government Policies and Government Controlled Enterprises', Columbia Journal of World Business N.Y., Fall 1980, p. 47

Menzies, H. 'U.S. companies in unequal combat' (1979) Fortune, Vol. 99, No 77, p. 102

Mestmäcker, E.J. 'Offene Märkte im System unverfalschten Wettbewerbs in der E.W.G.' in Wirtschaftsordnung und Rechtsordnung Festschrift zum 70 Geburtstag von Franz Bohm am 16 Feb. 1967, Muller, Karlruhe (1965). 'Europäisches Wettbewerbsrecht', Beck, München (1974).

Monaco, R. 'Community controls over public undertakings', (1981) Mezzogiorno d'Europa, p. 31

Moschel, W. 'Le contrôle des prix d'après le droit Allemand et Européen sur les restrictions de la Concurrence', (1977) R.M.C. 262

Musso, D. et Distel, M. 'Les entreprises publiques françaises et le droit Communautaire', Rapport du 8me Colloque de FIDE, Copenhague 22-24 Juin 1978, Vol. 2, FIDE, Bruxelles (1978) p. 5.1

Neri, S. Sperl, H. 'Traité Instituant la CEE, Travaux Preparatoires. Declarations interpretatives de Six Gouvernements. Documents parlementaires', Cour de Justice, Luxemburg (1960)

Nicolaysen, G. 'Le secteur public dans le cadre d'un plan national'. L'entreprise publique et la concurrence. Les articles 90 et 37 du Traité CEE et leur relations avec la concurrence. College d'Europe, De Tempel, Bruges (1969) p. 325.

'Instruments Juridiques des politiques économiques nationales et leur compatibilité avec le droit Communautaire: Allemagne', Discipline Communautaire et politiques économiques nationales: Community order and national economic policies. Colloque organisé par des Revues de Droit Européen et l'Institut d'Etudes Européennes de l'ULB, 19-20 Mai 1983, Kluwer, Deventer etc. (1984)

Nielsen, R. 'Competitive Advantages of State Owned and Controlled Business', Management International Review, Wiesbaden (1981) Vol. 21, No 3, p. 56

Nora, 'Le rapport Nora sur les entreprises publiques', Perspectives, Paris, 30 Nov. 1968

Oliver, P. 'Measures of Equivalent Effect: A Reappraisal', (1982) 19 C.M.L. Rev. 217.
'A review of the case law of the Court of Justice on articles 30 to 36 EEC in 1983', (1984) 21 C.M.L. Rev. 221

Page, A. 'Member States, Public Undertakings and Article 90' (1982) E.L. Rev. 19.
'The new Directive on Transparency of Financial Relations between Member States and Public Undertakings', (1982) E.L. Rev. 492. 'Instruments Juridiques des politiques économiques nationales et leur compatibilité avec le droit communautaire: Royaume-Uni' Discipline Communautaire et politiques économiques nationales: Community order and national economic policies. Colloque organisé par des Revues de Droit Européen et l'Institut d'Etudes Européennes de l'ULB, 19-20 Mai 1983, Kluwer, Deventer etc. (1984)

Pappalardo, A. 'Régime de l'Article 90 du Traité CEE: Les aspects juridiques'. L'entreprise publique et la concurrence. Les articles 90 et 37 du Traité CEE et leur relations avec la concurrence. College d'Europe, De Tempel, Bruges (1969).
'Position des Monopoles publics par rapport aux monopoles privés', Regulating the Behaviour of Monopolies and Dominant Undertakings in Community Law, Semaine de Bruges (1977) Ed. Van Damme, De Tempel, Bruges (1977) p. 538.
'Tendances actuelles de l'initiative industrielle publique en France, au R.U. et en Italie', Reflets et Perspectives de la Vie Economique, Bruxelles, (1978) Tome 17, No 5, p. 317

Paulis, E. 'Les Etats peuvent-ils enfreindre les articles 85 et

86 du Traité CEE?', Journal des Tribunaux, Bruxelles, No 5332, 30.3.85

Praet, P. and Vanden Abbele, M. 'Les contraintes de la politique Economique dans la CEE', Discipline Communautaire et politiques économiques nationales: Community order and national economic policies. Colloque organisé par des Revues de Droit Européen et l'Institut d'Etudes Européenes de l'ULB, 19-20 Mai 1983, Kluwer, Deventer etc. (1984)

Redwood, 'Public Enterprises in Crisis. The future of Nationalized Industries', Blackwell, Oxford (1980)

Reuter, P. 'La Communauté du Charbon et de l'Acier', Librairie Générale de droit de la jurisprudence, Paris (1953)

Salzman, A. 'IATA, Airline Rate-fixing and the EEC Competition Rules', (1977) E.L. Rev. 409

Schindler, P. 'Public Enterprises and the EEC Treaty' (1970) C.M.L. Rev. 57

Schlogel, M. 'Stade ou Hopital' (Interview), Entreprise, No 804, Fev. 1971

Schumacher, H. 'Le système du droit de la concurrence', (1971) Revue Trimestrielle de Droit Européen, p. 40

Selvaggi, C. 'Equal Treatment of Public and Private Enterprises in Italy', Rapport de 8me Congrès de FIDE, Copenhague 22-24 Juin 1978, Vol. 2, FIDE, Bruxelles (1978) p. 7.1

Snow, M. 'Telecommunications Deregulation in the F.R.G.' The Columbia Journal of World Business, Spring 1983, p. 53

Spaak: Rapport des Chefs de Delegation aux Ministres des Affaires Etrangères. Comité intergouvernementale crée par la Conference de Messine. Bruxelles, Secretariat - Comité Intergouvernementale (1956)

Steenbergen, J. 'Instruments Juridiques des politiques économiques nationales et leur compatibilité avec le Droit Communautaire: Belgique', Discipline Communautaire et politiques économiques nationales: Community order and national economic policies. Colloque organisé par des Revues de Droit Européen et l'Institut d'Etudes Européennes de l'ULB, 19-20 Mai 1983, Kluwer, Deventer etc. (1984)

Steindorff, E. 'Article 85 and the rule of reason', (1984) 21 C.M.L. Rev. 639

Sundberg-Weitman, B. 'Discrimination on Grounds of Nationality' (1977)

UNICE: 'Distortion of Competition between public and private enterprises', Competition law in the European Communities, London, March 1979, Vol. 2, Issue No 3, p. 21

Vandencasteele, A. 'Libre concurrence et intervention des Etats dans la vie économique', (1979) Cahiers de Droit Européen, p. 540

Van der Esch, B. 'French Oil Legislation and the EEC Treaty', (1970) C.M.L. Rev. 36.
'Les articles 85 and 86 du Traité CEE et actions nationales de reduction de concurrence', Discipline Communautaire et politiques économiques nationales: Community order and national economic policies. Colloque organisé par des Revues de Droit Européen et l'Institut d'Etudes Européennes de l'ULB, 19-20 Mai 1983, Kluwer, Deventer etc. (1984)

Van Gerven, W. 'Egalite d'entreprises privées et publiques devant la loi belge', (1977) Journal des Tribunaux, No 5078, p. 241.
'The recent case law of the Court of Justice concerning articles 30 and 36 of the Treaty', (1977) C.M.L. Rev. 5.
'Traitement Egal d'entreprises privees et publiques en droit Belge', Rapports du 8me Congrès de FIDE, Copenhague 22-24 Juin 1978, Vol. 2, FIDE, Bruxelles (1978) p. 2.1

Van Hecke, G. 'Government Enterprises and National Monopolies under the EEC Treaty', (1970) C.M.L. Rev. 450

Van Reepinghen, Ch. 'Procedure à suivre pour les litiges portes devant la Commission Européene et devant la Court de Justice', Colloque de Bruxelles, (1963) Riv. Dir. Ind. 211

Veloren Van Themaat, P. 'A case involving article 90 of the EEC Treaty', European Competition Policy (1973), Essays of the Leiden Working Group on Cartel Problems, Ed. by the European Institute of the University of Leiden with a foreword by H.H. Maas, Sijthoff, London (1973) p. 240.
La Libre circulation des marchandises après l'arrêt 'Cassis de Dijon', (1982) Cahiers de Droit Européen, 123

Vygen, K. 'Offentliche Unternehmen im Wettbewerbsrecht der EWG, Ihre Stellung nach Art 90 EWGV in Vergleich zu Privaten Unternehmen', Heymanns, Köln-Berlin-Bonn-München (1967)

Waelbroeck, M. 'Le droit de la Communauté Economique

Européene, Commentaire, Vol. 4, Concurrence, Bruxelles (1972).

'The Extent to which Government Interference can constitute Justification under Article 85 or 86 of the Treaty of Rome', (1980) International Business Lawyer, Vol. 8 (IV).

'La Constitution Européene et les interventions des Etats-Membres en matière économique', In Orde Liber Amicorum P Verloren Van Thermaat, Kluwer, Deventer (1982), p. 331

Walters, K. and Monsen, J. 'Des concurrents dangereux: Les entreprises publiques', (1979) Harvard-L'Expansion, Paris No 14, p. 31

Winter, J. 'Application du Traité CEE en temps de crise: Aides d'Etat (art. 92 et 93)', Discipline Communautaire et politiques économiques nationales, Community order and national economic policies. Colloque organisé par des Revues de Droit Européen et l'Institut d'Etudes Européennes de l'ULB, 19-20 Mai 1983, Kluwer, Deventer etc. (1984)

Wyatt, D. and Dashwood, A. 'The Substantive law of the EEC', Sweet and Maxwell, London (1980)